2

D0909057

COLLABORATIVE LIBRARY SYSTEMS DEVELOPMENT

COLLABORATIVE
LIBRARY SYSTEMS DEVELOPMENT

Edited by
Paul J. Fasana and Allen Veaner

The M.I.T. Press
Cambridge, Massachusetts, and London, England

ISBN 0 262 06046 9 (hardcover)

Library of Congress catalog card number: 71-165076

This book was prepared under a grant from the National Science Foundation.

First published in October, 1971.

PUBLISHER'S FOREWORD

The aim of this format is to close the time gap between the preparation of a monographic work and its publication in book form. A large number of significant though specialized manuscripts make the transition to formal publication either after a considerable delay or not at all. The time and expense of detailed text editing and composition in print may act to prevent publication or so to delay it that currency of content is affected.

The text of this book has been photographed directly from the typescript. It is edited to a satisfactory level of completeness and comprehensibility though not necessarily to the standard of consistency of minor editorial detail present in typeset books issued under our imprint.

The MIT Press

PREFACE

In 1968 the National Science Foundation awarded a grant (NSF GN 724) of approximately $60,000 to support a project called "Collaborative Library Systems Development (CLSD)." Participants in the project were the libraries of The University of Chicago, Columbia University, and Stanford University. Two of the more important objectives of the CLSD Project were: 1) to test certain technical assumptions such as the feasibility of developing a mechanism to facilitate cooperative work, and the possibility of developing compatible and transferable automated library systems; and 2) to communicate the findings and experience of the project group to the general library community.

Two invitational conferences were organized to report on the CLSD effort, the first at Stanford in 1968, and the second in New York in 1970.* Approximately 100 people from large research libraries involved in automation attended these conferences. At each, the program was divided between papers describing CLSD project efforts and invited papers on topics of general interest. The reaction to both conferences was favorable.

This volume contains all of the major papers presented at the New York Conference (Section I), a selection of the papers presented at the Stanford conference (Section II), and a paper describing and summarizing CLSD experience from 1968 through 1970.

This volume has been assembled, edited, and published in the hope that it will be of use to other libraries currently engaged in or contemplating undertaking an automation effort.

P. J. F.

---

*The transcript of the Stanford Conference was published by The Stanford University Library in 1969.

CONTENTS

CONTENTS (continued)

SECTION I

The New York Collaborative Library Systems Development Conference: Papers

The following section contains an edited version of all papers presented at the New York CLSD Conference, together with a selection from the discussions that followed. The full transcript of the Conference, containing a verbatim recording of all papers as presented and the discussions that ensued, is on deposit in the Oral History Collection, Columbia University Library.

1

Three Approaches to the Design, Development, and Implementation of an Integrated Technical Services System: The Chicago, Columbia, and Stanford Experiences

Introduction

A casual review of the automated systems under development at Chicago, Columbia, and Stanford would seem to indicate that each had developed independently, without cognizance of each other. Nothing, in fact, would be farther from the truth. For the past three years, senior technical personnel responsible for systems development in each institution have worked together closely with the objective of testing the feasibility of designing and implementing a common or compatible system. This effort was funded by the National Science Foundation (GN-724) and was called the Collaborative Library Systems Development Project (CLSD). Quite early in the effort it was established that this objective was unrealistic for a variety of technical and logistic reasons, and it was decided that a more realistic and achievable objective would be to attempt to work on a more general design level. Even on this level it was apparent that significant differences existed in terms of philosophy, approach, and scope which could not and, in the opinion of the participants, probably should not be resolved at this stage of library automation development. After lengthy review and discussion it was decided that the most valuable contribution that these three institutions could make would be to develop individual systems that would reflect different yet technically valid approaches to the solution of a common problem. What exists today in each of these libraries are systems that do precisely this. Grossly stated, Stanford's approach is to make the fullest and most innovative use of the on-line, interactive potential of computer technology. At the opposite extreme, Columbia's approach emphasizes using the technology conservatively stressing off-line, batch-oriented operations. Chicago's approach falls between these two extremes stressing the use of batched, on-line operations against fully integrated files.

The purpose of this session was to describe and contrast the existing systems in these three institutions. Given the scale and complexity of these efforts, this was a formidable and challenging undertaking. The method chosen for presentation was to develop a general outline and have each institution describe its experience on each of the topics included. Emphasis was placed on informality and breadth. Three major topics were defined; they were:

1. Origin and history of project including scope, approach, staffing, and budgeting.

2. Major systems design features, including file design, hardware, software, integration of MARC data, and products.

3. Phasing and scheduling of project efforts.

The program was divided into three parts corresponding to these topics and each institution was allowed 20 minutes to make a statement on each topic. A question and answer period followed each part. The transcript of the session was sprawling and disjointed. Therefore, for the sake of clarity and continuity each institution's presentation has been edited separately and is presented here as a unit.

The Chicago Experience

Charles T. Payne

I. General Background

The developmental project for a bibliographic data processing system at the University of Chicago Library has been underway since 1966. The scope and approach to development of this project originated in a series of systems studies conducted at the University of Chicago during the years 1964-1966. The program that was developed then was one of the first of the long-range, comprehensive library systems development plans. It was never "total system" in scope; rather, it was a plan for the development of an integrated-file, bibliographic data processing system and was so described.

Our original proposal for development was prepared in 1966. It proposed these major developmental tasks: 1) develop a computerized bibliographic data processing system; 2) implement this system into library operations; 3) develop improved library character set capability; 4) cooperate in MARC development; 5) develop a circulation system; 6) conduct processing operations studies; 7) study serial system design; and 8) study large file organization and access.

We did not propose during this phase of development to replace card catalogs. In scope, the system was intended during this phase to provide support for the Library's technical processing operations and to provide machine-readable records for the start of a machine-readable data base.

The central importance of bibliographic data handling to library automation was recognized and a large part of our early efforts went into data element definitions and establishment of conventions for handling bibliographic and other library processing data. The approach to development has been to build production level systems and implement them and to adjust, modify, and update them through time until useful systems were in operation.

The developmental project at the University of Chicago Library was funded by the National Science Foundations for a period of four years and four months and has just come to an end. I want to add that we really haven't stopped working; we have plenty of tidying up to do and there are reports to write. We will also continue to completion some of the ongoing developmental work now under way. We have been working at the transition of operations from developmental status to library production status for quite a long while. Even so, an important phase of our development has ended.

Project staffing levels have ranged from thinly staffed to badly understaffed for the level of work being attempted. We have had variously from two to three full-time equivalents on the library systems staff. We have tried to maintain from three to five full-time equivalents on the computer systems and programming staff, although during the period of the NSF budget stretch-out we fell below two F.T.E. programmers for an extended period because of existing high fixed costs and commitments.

The programming and computer system staff have largely been provided by the custom programming service of the University Computation Center. These people are administratively under the control of the Computation Center but work for and under the direction of the Library project staff in terms of actual effort. This arrangement has both good and bad aspects. One good aspect is that it has allowed flexibility in adjustment of staff up or down depending upon needs and money. Probably the best aspect of this arrangement is that it has provided a basis for close cooperation between the Computation Center and the Library in planning for equipment and operating system changes, in planning future computer system capacities, in establishing priorities for getting production work done, etc.

Housing of the staff has been split between the Library and the Computation Center, and both have been cramped for space. The Library, however, has recently moved into the new Joseph Regenstein Library and we are planning to house most of the staff in the Library in the future.

National Science Foundation support of this project has been in the amount of six hundred and two thousand dollars for a period of four years and four months, an average of one hundred and forty thousand dollars a year. The University of Chicago has also contributed substantially to the project. It has provided major system staff personnel and support, clerical input and data processing staff, and large investments of time by various members of the professional staffs of the Library and the Computation Center.

Obviously, the University of Chicago also has a longer range commitment and not only to ongoing production costs but to system maintenance and to expanded development. Among the many things that we have learned is that system maintenance costs are certain, if unpredictable. These costs can be high, particularly through periods of computer equipment or operating system changes. We have also learned that every change in MARC data format, for example, requires programming changes and testing. Also, within our library there are changing requirements and conditions which frequently require programming changes. In addition to these maintenance costs there are sure to be continuing pressures to add new or supplemental capabilities to the system, requiring further developmental work and further staff to do the work.

II. Major Systems Design Features

A report, *The University of Chicago Library Bibliographic Data Processing System; Documentation and Report as of October 31, 1969,* has just been issued. It gives a greater amount of detail on systems design and systems features than is possible here.

This report has been in preparation for a long time. Its final form resulted from several successive efforts to document a very detailed and complex system. The table of contents is several pages long, but to summarize: section one gives a system overview; the second section, Data, gives definitions and detailed specifications for system files, records, data fields, character sets, and the formats for their machine representation and storage; the third section, Processing, describes the processing of data in the system—input, machine processing, and output. Computer programs are described briefly and detailed formatting specifications for output products are given.

The basic design concept is for an integrated file system in which a single machine-held record is created and maintained for each bibliographic item. Item records are variously processed for output products, which include acquisitions purchase orders, fiscal reports, catalog cards, charge cards, and book pocket labels. The system is built around an on-line Master In-Process File to which records and data can be variously entered as needed at the time of ordering, order record update, cataloging, or any other time during processing.

In operation, the Master File always contains records in many stages of completion. The usual file size is around forty thousand records. Altogether more than one hundred thousand complete machine-readable bibliographic records have been created through the system. This large data base is held on magnetic tape and is called the Historical File. Master File records are transferred to the Historical File when their processing phase is completed.

More than one hundred computer programs or routines have been written and are operational. They are written in Basic Assembly Language (BAL). The Library system currently runs on the University Computation Center's IBM 360/65 which operates under OS, MVT, version 18. On-line files are maintained on an IBM 2314 Direct Access Storage Facility. System products are printed on an IBM 1403 high-speed printer with a special Library print train.

We have two methods for data input. One is through the Library Data Processing Unit. The staff keyboards data using IBM 1050 terminals. Large-scale data input is handled by keyboarding to paper tape and the subsequent reading of this paper tape on-line to the computer system. Updates and error corrections are also handled in this way.

MARC tapes are the second source for data input to the system. MARC tapes are processed weekly and data from wanted MARC records are merged with corresponding local data into Master File records. Subsequent machine processing and product formatting and printing are independent of the source of data input.

I would like to refer to our project documentation report to give some detail on our experiences with files. The original concept was of a single, on-line master file into which all data would flow and from which all products would be produced. The system as it now operates, however, uses not a single file, but 78 defined and named temporary permanent files or data sets.

An inventory of these files shows that there are three major bibliographic files: the Master File (on-line), the Historical file (the large data base of records on tape), and the CUMARC file (a file of MARC records converted to the Chicago cataloging format). There are also seven supplement, overflow, and index files. There are four program libraries, three program or programming utility files, four output request tables or stacks, five interim generation files (*e.g.*, temporary files of processed items prior to sorting), seven temporary output files, and 45 backup files or prior generation files used for backup. Up to six levels of backup—called generation data groups—are maintained for some files. Files seem to proliferate faster in a computer system than they do in a library.

III. Phasing and Scheduling

In this section I will discuss: developed systems, systems under development, and project schedules.

At Chicago, we have developed and implemented a bibliographic data processing system. It is in operation as a regular part of the library processing operations. Following are brief descriptions of various aspects of the system operations:

Catalog card production. Catalog cards are printed in arrays specifically ordered for the desired catalogs or other locations receiving cards. These arrays are rough-sorted in various filing orders, whether for main entry catalogs, author-title-subject dictionary catalogs, or shelflist catalogs. Catalog cards are printed in batches, usually daily. Within a printout batch there are a large number of separate arrays each with its own header card giving location information. During fiscal year 1969–70 more than 37,000 bibliographic titles were processed through this system and approximately 413,000 catalog cards were individually formatted and printed out.

Book card and label production. The same bibliographic data used in catalog card production are also processed with a different output format and array directory to produce book cards and pocket labels. Catalog card sets are based on a single item record for each title, but book finishing products are required for each physical volume. The programs handle this by an expansion of a relatively simple holdings statement. It is not unusual for this operation to produce 20 or 30 sets of cards and labels for multiple volume and multiple copy materials. Book card and label production operations also cover a wider range of materials than does catalog card production. Book cards and labels are being produced for virtually all materials, using romanized entries and titles where necessary. This creates machine records within the data base which are acceptable for some uses, if not for catalog card production. During the fiscal year 1969–70, approximately 81,600 sets of book cards and labels were produced through the system.

Purchase order production. Orders are printed in batches, usually daily. Within a printing batch, orders are printed in arrays ordered first by library destination, then by vendor and within vendor, by main entry. During fiscal year 1969–70, more than 57,000 purchase orders were produced through the system.

Other system products. Among the other printed products of this system are: Catalog Card Test Products (used for final proofing), MARC Selector Cards, Fund Commitment Totals List, Daily Vendor List, and various file printouts and statistical production counts.

MARC utilization. The basic steps for utilizing MARC records in Chicago production operations are: 1) convert MARC records and data element formats to those of Chicago, and 2) merge the converted MARC bibliographic data with local processing data in our Master File records. During fiscal year 1969–70, 2,762 MARC records were utilized to provide order data and 8,162 MARC records provided bibliographic data for cataloging.

Our MARC utilization system has been under further development since that time however. The new system has been implemented and during the last several weeks we have used an average of over 250 MARC records per week.

Other systems currently under development include claiming—an overdue-order claiming system. This has been designed and programmed but not thoroughly tested in operational situations. Also under development is a library fiscal system. This is still in the design phase. We are also currently working on a file processing and report generation system. Parts of this for the on-line files are being tested but there is still considerable work to be done.

Work on the fiscal system and the file processing system will extend beyond the end of December, 1970, the target date for our final project report, but the design of these systems should be final enough for inclusion.

Of the tasks in our original proposal enumerated earlier, we did well with the first four: the development and the implementation of computerized bibliographic data processing system, the development of library character set capability, and cooperation with MARC development. In regard to the remaining tasks (circulation system development, operations studies, serials system design, and study of large file organization and access), we have done a lot of study, we have indeed conducted some of the processing operation studies, but we have not built and implemented real systems that satisfy the difficult requirements of these systems. We do have immediate and longer range plans covering these tasks, however, and these will be described in a later paper.[1]

---

[1] See Section IV, *What We Can Discern from Present Activities and Where Are We Going in the Immediate Future* by Charles Payne.

The Columbia Experience

Paul J. Fasana

I. General Background

In 1965, a systematic study was done of all library activities by a team made up of Columbia Librarians and IBM personnel. A recommendation of this study team was that a Systems Office be established; accordingly, in 1966 a staff office reporting directly to the Director of Libraries was created. The initial guidelines for the Systems Office were stated generally as follows:

a. Systems efficiency. The primary objective of the office was to analyze all library operations and to recommend changes in procedures and policy to achieve the most efficient operating system possible within the constraints of budget, instructional priorites, and research aims of the University.

b. Automation. Computers were to be used wherever systems analysis indicated that EDP technology was feasible and promising. All automation efforts, already existing or newly initiated, would by coordinated by this office.

c. Staff eduction. A continuing effort was to be made to train librarians in the use of new technologies, especially systems analysis and computers.

Scope. After preliminary study, five basic assumptions were articulated by the Systems Office which defined more precisely its immediate scope. Briefly these assumptions were:

1. The Libraries should undertake a long range effort to automate its basic, *housekeeping* operations. Long range was defined as extending up to 10 years. Two phases were identified; the first phase, lasting up to 5 years (1966 through 1971), was devoted to developing systems primarily in the technical services area concentrating on translating manual procedures to machine assisted methods. The second phase (1971-1976) would be devoted to developing and experimenting with user oriented services, integrating user services with previously developed technical service systems, and evaluating and refining prototype systems developed during the first phase.

2. To a large degree, the first five years was to be an applications research effort. Systems developed would closely parallel (or simulate) previously existing manual systems. The main objectives of this phase of work would be to gain experience in the application of computers to library activites, to create an hospitable environment for automated systems within the Libraries, and to develop a basic processing capability using computers.

3. Because of the rapidly changing nature of computer hardware and software, automated systems would be designed to make conservative use of computers. In general, this has meant that only off-the-shelf hardware and software has been used. No major commitment to software development has been made.

4. Systems development work should in no way disrupt the existing level of service, the continuity of collections, or the integrity of files with the library.

Approach. Columbia's automation approach during the past five years can be defined as a systematic effort to develop in a series of defined steps (or phases) an integrated bibliographic processing system. Implied in this definition is the idea of identifying major sub-systems, designing and developing relatively autonomous applications programs for these sub-systems, and testing, operating and evaluating the sub-system modules. Gradually these modules are being integrated into a single integrated processing flow beginning with acquisitions and extending through a variety of user services. The major sub-systems identified and the sequence in which they have been worked on is as follows:

1. Circulation
2. Reserves
3. Acquisitions
4. Cataloging
5. Serials
6. Reference

Five factors critically affected the types of systems developed at Columbia to date; they are:

1. Flexibility. In order to insure that a high degree of flexibility is inherent in all systems, higher level programming languages are used, even though this results in an increase of machine processing time. After major experimentation with FORTRAN, COBOL, SNOBOL, and PL/1, a decision was made to use PL/1 for all applications programs.

2. Modularization. Because of the complexity of scheduling, the limitations of budget, and the critical shortage of technical personnel, all systems are highly modular in design.

3. Batch Processing. Because of the limitations imposed by the technology itself and the use of a centralized computing facility, systems are batch-oriented and require a significant amount of printing. On-line processing, though theoretically more desirable, has in general been excluded from design considerations.

4. Generalized Systems. Because of the inherent limitations of batch-processing, especially with respect to enquiry and up-dating of files, all systems are general and simple in design.

5. Production Oriented Systems. Although it was realized that initial systems would be to a large degree experimental in nature, all systems developed are designed and used to relieve as much of the processing load as possible in any application. In effect, this has meant that systems are designed to handle the major processing loads in each area and exclude activities that are exceptional, overly complex, or relatively low in terms of processing volume.

Organization and Staffing. (See Appendix A.) Initially a single office was established and charged with the responsibility of coordinating all aspects of system and automation work within the Libraries. It was realized that at some point, not clearly discernible at the time, that organizational distinctions would eventually be necessary. During the first four years of operation, the Systems Office assumed responsibility for development, implementation, and maintenance of all computer based systems. Organizationally, the office was made up of four components:

1. *Systems Analysts* who were librarians trained in the techniques of systems analysis and responsible for analyzing operations, developing systems specifications, developing systems and procedural documentation, managing implementation efforts, and maintaining production systems.

2. *Programmers* who were trained technicians responsible for developing program documentation, coding applications programs, and maintaining production systems.

3. *Input Personnel* made up of keypunchers and tape typists who were responsible for preparing data for input to automated systems.

4. *Department Librarians* who periodically assisted in the analysis of operations and the evaluation of systems design.

As more production systems were developed and implemented it became apparent that an organizational structure was necessary which would reflect more closely the types of work and responsibility characteristic of each phase of a systems effort. In 1970 it was decided that the Systems Office should be reorganized as two separate components, one responsible primarily for research and development, and the second responsible for data preparation and maintenance of on-going systems. Accordingly, in July 1970 the following two components were established.

1. A Data Control Section was organized and attached to the Technical Services Division. The responsibilities of this section include data preparation for input, program maintenance for production systems, and participation in evaluation and redesign of on-going systems.

2. A newly defined Dystems Office was established. The responsibilities of this Office include development of new systems, implementation of developed

systems, and prime responsibility for the evaluation and redesign of production systems. The Systems Office continues as a staff group reporting directly to the Director.

Since this reorganization has been in effect for less than six months, we do not know yet if it is the optimal solution. It has, though, forced us to analyze critically what is being done and who should have the responsibility for doing it. For example, a major problem before the reorganization was trying to disassociate programmers from programs they had written. No amount of threatening would insure that programmers would not make what seemed to them trivial changes in production programs. These trivial changes almost inevitably caused programs to fail, which in turn meant that output was delayed and the department librarian was left with no updated list. Disruptions of this kind seriously undermine a librarian's confidence in the computer's ability to produce lists on schedule or for computer based systems to operate efficiently. Since the reorganization, all production programs are literally locked up and operating efficiency has increased significantly.

Budgeting. If we've learned nothing else, we now know that library automation is expensive, but just how expensive is yet to be established with any precision. Automation requires not only a significant capital outlay but also what seems to be high fixed operating expenses relative to manual systems. I say seems because it is impossible in many instances to find a valid basis for comparison. Manual systems are not in general thoroughly costed and, in many instances, true costs are not even known. This situation is further complicated by the fact that automated systems currently being developed will probably have relatively short lives. At Columbia we estimate that an applications program probably has a life expectancy of 5 to 7 years and prorate development costs accordingly. This means that the operating cost of a system is extremely high. The rationale used by many systems people is that automated systems will provide more and better services and unlimited growth, even though they may not reduce unit costs; this is undermined by their argument that the large, complex systems that they are attempting to develop are, to an unknown degree, research projects. Therefore, it is unfair to require that they be asked to guarantee that the resulting systems will be efficient or even, in some cases, operable. This is a difficult problem, one that probably cannot be solved at present. I personally am convinced, though, that present efforts are necessary and should be continued. I am depressed, in turn, by the fact that there seems to be no way of effectively coordinating efforts to obviate duplication of efforts. Each large research library, it seems, will be forced for at least another couple of years to reinvent the wheel for itself.

There are a number of pitfalls in budgeting a major in-house automation effort. Two that we have been especially aware of are source of funds and the identification of true costs. Our most recent estimate is that we have spent in excess of 1.1 million dollars during the past 5 years (see Appendix B for a detailed breakdown of this figure). The actual number of dollars spent is significant, but more important in my mind are the sources of the dollars spent. During the 60's it was relatively easy to find Federal funding for library automation projects and, as a consequence, a number of libraries undertook major development commitments without being fiscally responsible. Easy availability of Federal funds creates an artificial fiscal environment which can adversely affect scheduling, staffing, and objectives. Columbia's aim has been to insure that its automation budget must be made up of in-house and Federal funds with the percentage of in-house funds continually increasing. The overall proportion for the past five years of work at columbia has been roughly 60 percent in-house funds and 40 percent Federal funds. Future plans call for phasing out all Federal funding within the next two to three years. Unless an automation budget can be completely integrated or absorbed into the regular Library budget the effort is potentially in serious danger.

II. Systems Design Features

As mentioned above, most of the systems developed at Columbia are batch-oriented. In the main, the reasons for this are economic and technical, but I would hasten to add that we are not as convinced as many that on-line, interactive processing is necessary across-the-board or even, in many activities, clearly desirable or conclusively preferrable. Printed lists have many disadvantages, admittedly, but it is unclear whether, for example, on-line terminals are to be preferred for acquisitions searching or for circulation enquiry. In circulation enquiry, list searching is far more rapid and accurate than searching via a terminal.

In the following paragraphs I intend to talk generally about basic design philosophy as it has affected files, hardware, software, and MARC data utilization. (A complete inventory and brief description of Columbia automation projects is included in Appendix C.)

File Design. Because of the emphasis on modularity, no effort has been made to develop a single processing file to encompass both acquisitions and cataloging. Preliminary studies indicated that given the peculiarities of the Columbis system, it was inadvisable to attempt such an approach since little formal bibliographic data was available during the ordering process. This factor will change, we realize, with the use of MARC tapes, title II cards, and blanket orders in selection and ordering process.

The present system design defines 5 major files for the technical services system. They are:

1. In Process File.
2. Fiscal File.
3. MARC Files.
4. Cataloging Proof Files.
5. Permanent Bibliographic Files.

A brief description of each is given in the following paragraphs.

1. In Process (IP) File. (See Figures 1 and 3 of Appendix C.) The IP File contains a record of all items from the moment ordered until the time the item has finished cataloging and cards are filed in the public catalog. Records in the IP file are updated with status changes only (*i.e.,* item received, sent to cataloging, etc.). No attempt is made to input initially a complete bibliographic record. No attempt is made to augment or update a record with bibliographic information as it is discovered or made available during the processing cycle. Only those data elements necessary for ordering and processing control are used in the system.

2. Fiscal File. (See Figure 2 of Appendix D.) As data are processed for the IP File, selected fund and fiscal data are extracted automatically and passed to the Fiscal Module. These data are accumulated (normally for a week) and then input to the Fiscal System.

3. MARC Files. (See Figure 4 of Appendix D.) Selected search data are identified from the IP input and are searched against the CUMARC files. Successful searches cause a record to be printed and also released to the Cataloging Proof File. Unsuccessful searches are held and automatically re-searched each time the CUMARC File is updated (*i.e.*, the arrival of a new MARC tape).

4. Cataloging Proof File. Records released from the CUMARC file and input for original cataloging are integrated in the Cataloging Proof File for correction and updating purposes. As records complete processing they are released to the Print Program.

5. Permanent Bibliographic File. As records are printed, they are released to the Permanent Bibliographic File. The Permanent Bibiliographic File is made up of a tape file for bibliographic data and a disc for inventory data.

As is apparent from this brief description of files, each program (or processing) module can be operated as a self-contained package or can be integrated with other modules. Emphasis to date has been to operate and test these modules separately. In the next year our emphasis will shift to testing and operating these modules in a more integrated fashion. There are several advantages to the approach implied in this series of files. They are:

1. Flexible scheduling for development work allowing for the efficient use of technical personnel.
2. Low-keyed training of library staff.
3. A gradual build-up of processing capability allowing full testing of programs and procedures.
4. The ability to design and develop relatively simple file structures and procedures.
5. The ability to make greater use of off-the-shelf more reliable hardware and software.
6. Phased, incremental orientation and training of computer technical personnel to complex library operations.

The disadvantages are:

1. The ability of one person to exercise complete control and coordination of simultaneous development efforts.
2. Complexity of designing adequate interface programs.
3. The ability to stabilize designs of several systems at the same or comparable level of complexity.

Hardware. The Columbia Libraries use the centralized University computing facility which currently is an IBM 360 Model 91 coupled with 360/75. The relationship and attitude between the Libraries and the Computer Center have changed continually during the last 5 years, and, I am happy to report, is at present quite positive. This has not always been the case for a variety of reasons. Two that have been most significant are:

1. The mission of a research computing facility. Administrative data processing and research use of computers are at opposite ends of a spectrum. In administrative work, the pole towards which library processing tends, production scheduling is critical; a list must be produced and delivered on time. In batch-oriented library systems, this factor is made more critical because of the frequency of production runs. Research computing, by contrast, tends to be more relaxed. If a run fails, it's resubmitted and no one seems to be greatly inconvenienced if it takes several days to get results.

2. Hardware changes. When the Libraries began using computers in 1965, the University facility was a second generation system. Since then a complete transition to a very complex and powerful third generation system has been completed (or at least I hope it's been completed). This transition was not simple or painless and has required no less than 6 or 7 different steps, each step having in essence a different computer configuration (*i.e.*, from a 7094/7040 coupled, to a 7094 stand alone, to 360/50–360/75 coupled, to a 360/75 stand alone, etc.)

Each change has had significant (usually devastating) consequences on the Libaries' systems. (The moral, if there is one here, is not to attempt to develop and certainly *not* to implement production systems during such a period.)

At present, the hardware configuration is relatively stable which has created an atmosphere of relative harmony and peace (but not complacency; the traumatic experience of the past 5 years has so deeply scarred the confidence of several librarians that it probably will take several years to completely heal).

As an example of the current attitude of cooperation, the Libraries and the Computing Center are jointly studying two basic problems:

1. Relationship and responsibility of the Libraries and the Center. The Library Systems staff has been administratively separate from the Center and probably will continue to work in this way. Greater participation of Library personnel in Center policy and planning is being reviewed and effected. The Libraries currently enjoy a "preferred user status" at the Center and is allocated an operating budget for computing services from central administrative funds.

2. Optimal use of the centralized computing facility. Columbia's computing facility is one of the most powerful in the world. Given the broad spectrum of users and their diverse needs, it is difficult to balance optimization *of use* of the system and optimization *to users* of the system. The Libraries represents a severe drain on the Center's relatively scarce printing resource. The solution to this problem is not immediately apparent. Two alternatives are being explored and experimented with; one involves creating a network of small-scale satellite processors wired to the central computer; the second, using an off-line mini-computer for I/0 activities. The latter approach seems at present to offer greater advantages to the Libraries for the immediate future.

Software. As has already been stated, a basic decision was made not to invest any substantial sum in software development but to use where possible that which was available. This has meant that the Libraries' software development effort has been entirely devoted to writing applications programs. After reviewing and testing virtually all of the more obvious languages, a decision was made to use PL/1 exclusively. This decision may seem obvious today but 3 years ago when it was made it required considerable soul-searching. The advantages (real and potential) of using PL/1 are as follows:

1. Simplification of in-house staffing requirements by using a single programming language.
2. Use of a powerful, generalized language which is amenable to Library processing.
3. Use of a language which is relatively simple to learn, program in, and debug.

4. The development of hardware independent programs that are potentially transferable.
5. The development of programs that are flexible and relatively easy to change.

MARC Usage. The MARC Service is potentially one of the most important developments in libraries since the initiation of LC's card service. I would emphasize "potentially" because to date no one has been able to master fully the MARC format. At Columbia we acknowledge that the MARC Service will be the cornerstone of our automated technical services system. But how does one design and develop an extremely complex processing system around a service about which there is little knowledge and even less experience? The only answer is, cautiously.

For more than a year, Columbia's MARC development effort has focussed on:

1. critically studying and evaluating the MARC format relative to internal needs,
2. exhuastive statistical analysis of records distributed by the MARC service,
3. tentative development of a variety of MARC services and products to be used experimentally for selection and search activities,
4. and the development and testing of utility and processing programs.

Following are a number of conclusions that we have reached:
1. The format should be accepted and used as is. Though complex and initially difficult to work with, the format is logically developed given the restrictions imposed on it by existing bibliographic standards.
2. Input procedures for local cataloging should be developed using the MARC format as a standard.
3. Overall MARC data flow should probably be separate and parallel from acquisitions data flow.
4. An integrated data flow mixing MARC data and original cataloging data is essential.

Major Products and Services. (See Appendix D for examples of Columbia's MARC Products.) The most important products to date using MARC data are designed primarily to assist librarians in selection, searching, and verification. Two general types of products are distinguished; they are:
1. Lists. More than 75 different lists are prepared weekly. Each list reflects a different user profile based on characteristics such as class number, subject headings, geographic codes, etc. The majority of the lists are noncumulating and used either as selection tools or current awareness bulletins. A small number of

lists are cumulated and used as special bibliographies or reference tools. These include, for example, reprint lists, publications from or about Africa, etc.

2. Indices. Indices by main entry, title, and card number are produced and cumulated weekly. These indexes are used both for acquisitions and cataloging search activities.

In addition, programs are being tested to produce a variety of products to be used in cataloging. These include, for example, MARC diagnostic worksheets, proofreading copy, and catalog card sets.

III. Phasing and Scheduling

(See Appendix E.) Phasing and scheduling of a large-scale library automation effort is complex and challenging. Columbia's approach to this problem has been conditioned by the following five factors:

1. The environment is dynamic and rapidly and continually changing. There are a great many unknowns and an even greater number of factors beyond one's control. As a consequence, it is virtually impossible (and probably not desirable) to develop rigid, detailed long-range plans and schedules. At best, one should attempt to define a goal or controlling concept, and define detailed plans and establish schedules as work progresses.

2. Relative to library needs (especially in the area of peripheral devices), computer technology is in a wild state of flux. More input and output devices have been announced, marketed, and discontinued in the past year than probably have existed in the entire history of computer technology prior to 1970. The ability of any one person to familiarize himself with the array of input devices currently produced, let alone attempt to incorporate any such device in a system design, is questionable. The delays that can be caused as a result in a development schedule are formidable.

3. Competent technical personnel, in spite of the current recession, are still scarce, expensive, and unstable. Even when available, a considerable investment is necessary to educate technical personnel to the peculiarities of library processing.

4. By far the most formidable and least appreciated problem in library automation is training of library staff. It is not sufficient to write procedures and brief library personnel. A continuing and aggressive program of monitoring and supervision is necessary.

5. To date, library automation efforts have focussed exclusively on system development and, to a much lesser degree, implementation. Little effort has been given to evaluation of new systems, or to the problem of systematic redesign of systems.

Columbia's approach to scheduling in view of these factors can be characterized as being low keyed, long range, and flexible. Automation efforts at Columbia are scheduled and budgeted by project. Projects are initially defined to reflect management priorities, but once undertaken, they are integrated into the overall schedule controlling all projects and phased in such a way to make the most efficient use of manpower and resources. Within each project, 5 more or less successive phases are distinguished and systematically worked on. (See Appendix E for a description of these phases.) At present, Columbia has 6 major projects in progress, each of which is at a different stage of development. Because of the careful planning, coordination of these projects has not to date been a serious problem.

Conclusion. By way of conclusion I would like to emphasize the following points:

1. Columbia's objective for the past 5 years has been to develop a series of program modules focussing on housekeeping functions mainly in the area of technical services.

2. Emphasis has been placed on the conservative use of computer hardware and software.

3. Experience indicates that detailed planning is essential but flexibility of attitude is possibly of greater importance.

4. Automation is costly but there are still no acceptable measures by which to evaluate costs.

5. The most difficult aspects of an automation effort are not those involved with design and development; implementation, maintenance, and evaluation are emerging as the more difficult and probably the more critical aspects.

COLUMBIA UNIVERSITY LIBRARIES

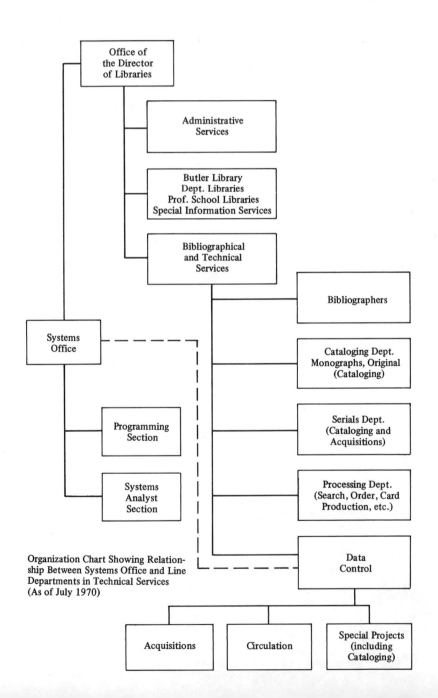

Organization Chart Showing Relationship Between Systems Office and Line Departments in Technical Services (As of July 1970)

Appendix B: Cost of Library Systems Development

The following figures reflect an estimate of the amount of money expended by Columbia Libraries for its primary automation effort during the past five years (1966–1970). Costs for development and maintenance of peripheral projects (such as the Parkinson Information Center and the Upper Mangle Information Center) are *not* included. Reconstructing and compiling these figures was difficult since there was often no single source reflecting true expenditures. For example, personnel costs for Systems Office staff does not include or reflect the amount of time contributed by departments. Records of time contributed were kept for certain aspects of an effort, for example, systems analysis, design, testing, and implementation. No records were kept for certain other aspects of an effort, such as maintenance and evaluation of production systems. Whenever there was a question to include or exclude a figure, the decision was usually to be conservative and exclude it. Figures, though estimates, are probably accurate to within 10 percent of the actual cost, tending to be under rather than over.

1. **Year:** Calendar year.
2. **Budgeted Positions: SO** The number of budgeted clerical and professional positions assigned directly to the Systems Office. Note that not all positions were completely filled during an entire year in some instances; therefore, the number of dollars spent (columns 3 and 4) do not correspond directly to the number of budgeted positions.
3. **Salaries Paid: SO** Reflects the amount spent rather than the amount that may have been budgeted for staffing of the Systems Office. For 1970, this figure includes a portion of Data Control staff.
4. **Salaries Paid: LIB** Reflects the amount (in part, estimated) spent for support activities provided by library departments other than the Systems Office. Support activities include participation in systems analysis design and implementation.
5. **Input Equipment** Reflects the dollar value for input equipment used within the libraries (*i.e.*, keypunches, tape typewriters, etc.). The figure includes maintenance charges where applicable.
6. **Computer Charges** Reflects the dollar value of computer time assigned and used. (Because of CU's inhouse pricing for omputer services this figure is extremely low if compared with similar computer service from commercial sources. Roughly, to calculate a comparable cost one should probable multiply this figure by 2 or 3.)

23

7. **Applied Research: Percent** Reflects an attempt to estimate the percentage of the total automation effort that might be considered essentially research. "Research" is defined to include analysis, design, development and initial test implementation.
8. **Production Systems: Percent** Reflects an attempt to estimate the percentage of the total automation effort that might be considered as maintenance of production systems. This includes preparation of input data, computer time for production runs, and maintenance of production systems.

Year	Budgeted Positions SO		Salaries Paid SO	Salaries Paid LIB	Input Equipment	Computer Time	Percent Research	Production Systems Percent
	Prof.	*Cl.*						
1966	2	1	$ 20K	$ 3K	$ 4K	$ 3K	100	0
1967	3	4	$ 45K	$ 7K	$ 18K	$ 10K	95	5
1968	5	10	$ 98K	$15K	$22–25K	$ 50K	90	10
1969	7	12	$115K	$25K	$ 28K	$ 75K	80	20
1970	$7\frac{1}{2}$	16	$180K	$35K	$ 30K	$100K	70–75	25–30

Total Personnel Cost	$ 545K
Fringe & Overhead (40%)	$ 218K
Grand Total	$ 763K
Total Machine Cost	$ 104K
Total Computer Cost	$ 238K
Total Dollar Amount Spent	$1105K
Total Amount from Federal Sources	$ 463K (42%)
Total Amount from In-House Funds	$ 642K (58%)

Current Projects:

a. 1965-present. Upper Mantle Project (IGY). A project to design and operate an information center to collect, organize, and disseminate on a world-wide basis data of the Upper Mantle Project. Computer used to create book form catalogs. Partially supported by funds from the National Science Foundation.

Status: Production mode for input and proof processing; production mode for book catalog production. Programs are in PL/1 version 5 for the IBM.

b. 1966-present. Circulation. A computer-based circulation system has been designed, programmed, and tested for several environments with varying work loads. Implementation of the system has been scheduled in several phases. Phase I calls for a batch-oriented system, producing master circulation lists daily, and recall and overdue notices several times per week. Phase II provides source data collection procedures which create machine readable records to be converted by an optical scanning device into computer input.

Status: Phase I: fully operational in Central Circulation (file size 80,000 records, daily transaction volume of 3,000) and Burgess Carpenter Library (file size 30,000 records, daily transaction volume of 1,500); partially implemented in Business Library. Programs are written in COBOL F for IBM 360; region size is approximately 220k. Phase II: design specifications developed; reevaluation of proposed procedures and optical scanning devices initiated September 1970.

c. 1966-present. Union List of Serials. A project to create union lists of serials for various different subject areas using the computer primarily for reformatting and listing purposes. Conceived as the first phase of an integrated serials system which eventually will include the functions of ordering, check-in, cataloging, and binding.

Status: Union List of Serials for Engineering, Science and Medicine, 2d edition, completed and contains approximately 10,000 titles. Basic file converted to a MARC compatible format (July 1970). Programs are written in PL/1, Version 5, for IBM 360.

d. 1967-present. Reserve Book Processing. Phase I: a computer-based reserve system has been designed, programmed, and tested. The system is batch oriented for the record creation, file management and book inventory aspects of reserve processing, and on-line for data input. Phase II: on-line circulation activities are being studied for possible integration with the basic processing system. Phase III: integration of the basic system with a master cataloging system being studied.

Status: Phase I: programs have been written and tested. The system is implemented in College Library (file size 17,000 records) and Business Library (file size 7,000 records). Programs are written in COBOL F for IBM 360; region size is approximately 180k. Phases II and III: study and design in progress. No definite implementation schedule established.

e. 1968–present. Columbia University Libraries User Survey. A number of user surveys have been designed to sample utilization of the Libraries in terms of types of users, types of materials used, types of services requested, space utilization, book storage, processing costs, etc.

Status: Final report on first two years of sampling prepared.

f. 1968–present. Collaborative Library Systems Development project. Research in the area of computers and generalized library systems undertaken in cooperation with Stanford and Chicago. Objectives: (1) facilitate prompt exchange of working dats; (2) explore the feasibility of developing general computer-based systems, and (3) establish and maintain liaison with key national agencies. Partially supported by a grant from the National Science Foundation.

Status: Mechanism for collaborative work established; joint specifications for an acquisitions system are being developed; monthly technical meetings held.

g. 1968–present. Acquisitions Project. A systematic analysis of acquisitions activities has been done. Specifications for a total integrated acquisitions system have been developed and documented.

Status: Phase I, which includes control of encoding data, printing orders, preparing and writing checks, creating and maintaining a comprehensive fiscal file covering all library accounts, and preparing input for the University Controller files, has been programmed and fully implemented. Phase II, which includes process control for materials, integration of MARC data, and integration with cataloging activities, is being programmed and is scheduled for implementation during the 4th quarter of 1970. Programs are written in PL/1, Version 5 for IBM 360.

h. 1968–present. Cataloging Project. A systematic analysis of cataloging activities has been accomplished. Specifications for an automated cataloging system have been developed.

Status: Experimental use of MARC data initiated. Utility programs and interface with the acquisitions system have been prepared and implemented. Programs for encoding, proofreading and updating bibliographic records have been written and tested. Specifications for a catalog card production system have been developed and are being programmed. Prototype book catalog specifications have been developed and experimented with. Programs are written in PL/1, Version 5 for IBM 360.

i. 1968–present. Integrated Technical Processing System. A systems study of acquisitions and cataloging has been done. Emphasis is placed on (1) developing a generalized system design which will have applicability to other institutions, and (2) coordinating development and design work with other large research libraries engaged in similar work. (Partially supported by a grant from the National Science Foundation.)

Status: Description and analysis of monograph acquisitions and cataloging procedures completed; total system specifications have been developed. Various selection lists and indexes are being produced using the LC MARC Service as input.

j. 1969–present. Special Collections. Techniques and programs developed to produce bookform catalogs and indices are being experimentally used for several special collections.

Status: Hart Crane Correspondence analyzed and encoded; and experimental sample of the Oral History Collection has been analyzed, encoded and printed in book form.

k. 1970–present. User Survey. Identification and analysis of various library users undertaken. Object of the project is to identify specialized needs of different user groups and to experiment with providing them with innovative services.

Status: Working in conjunction with the Illinois Institute of Technology Research Institute (IITRI), an experimental SDI service has been established for a limited number of scientific users.

Past Projects:

a. 1963. Simulation of Columbia University Library (SCUL). A computer simulation model was developed to research library activities. Partially supported by a grant from the Council on Library Resources.

Status: Preliminary study completed; project discontinued for lack of fund.

b. 1964–1965. Library Systems Study. A study of the Library's total operations was conducted by a team made up of library staff and IBM researchers. A total processing system was designed making extensive use of computers in an on-line environment.

Status: Conceptual design completed.

c. 1961–1966. Columbia-Harvard-Yale Medical Computerization Project. A cooperative effort to develop automated techniques for acquisitions and cataloging. A final system was conceived of as an on-line, wire-linked information network. Partially supported by a grant from the National Science Foundation.

Status: Discontinued.

d. 1964–1970. Parkinson Information Center. A project designed to establish and operate a computer-based information center to collect, organize, and disseminate information in the subject area of Parkinsonism and related disorders. Work done under contract from the National Institute of Neurological Diseases and Blindness.

Status: Center disbanded as of 1 July 1970. Programs and machine readable data bases (30,000 + records) turned over to NINDB.

The following set of flowcharts describes the major program modules of the Columbia Libraries Technical Services System. The flowcharts are drawn to emphasize:

1. Major files used
2. Major products produced
3. Major interface points

Not all aspects of the total system are fully developed at this time. If the current development and implementation schedule is realized, the full system will be operational by the second or third quarter of 1971. Following is a brief description of each module:

1. *Acquisitions System Program Module.* The Acquisitions sub-system is made up of two program modules, ENCODE/IN PROCESS and WEEKLY/MONTHLY PG/CHECKWRITE. The entire system, with the exception of IN PROCESS, is fully implemented and operational. IN PROCESS is at present being programmed and should be implemented during the second quarter of 1971.

2. *Fiscal Module.* The Fiscal Module, consisting of the WEEKLY/MONTHLY and CHECKWRITE programs, was implemented in July 1969 and has been operational since. Its major features are: processing checks to pay for all book and serial orders; maintenance of a magnetic file of fiscal information and transactions; the generation of frequent printed fiscal statements; and creation of machine readable input to the University Controller's fiscal system.

3. *ENCODE/IN PROCESS Module.* The ENCODE program was implemented in June 1970 and has been operational since. IN PROCESS is under development and is scheduled for full implementation before June 1971. The major functions of ENCODE are to print purchase orders and various routing and processing slips to be used for monograph orders; to assemble and pass fiscal data to the Fiscal Module; and to pass bibliographic search information to the MARC Module. The major functions of IN PROCESS will be to print a comprehensive list of requests in process (*i.e.,* on order, received, in cataloging, completed cataloging) which will replace the manual on-order file; to create and maintain a magnetic file of all requests in process; and to review frequently the in-process file to produce claims, cancellations, etc.

4. *Bibliographic Module.* The MARC SEARCH/MARC PROC module has been fully developed and is currently being implemented. Its major features are translating and integrating weekly MARC tapes into the CU system; accepting and doing searches against the CU MARC file; printing a number of indexes and lists to assist in search, verification, and cataloging activities. CAT PROOF has been developed and is currently being implemented. Its major features are accepting records from MARC; accepting catalog records for original cataloging records; and producing copy for proofreading and updating activities. CAT PRINT is under development and should be implemented by the end of the first quarter of 1971. Its major features are printing catalog card sets; producing various different catalog products (*i.e.,* accession lists, spine labels, etc.) and creating a permanent magnetic file of bibliographic records.

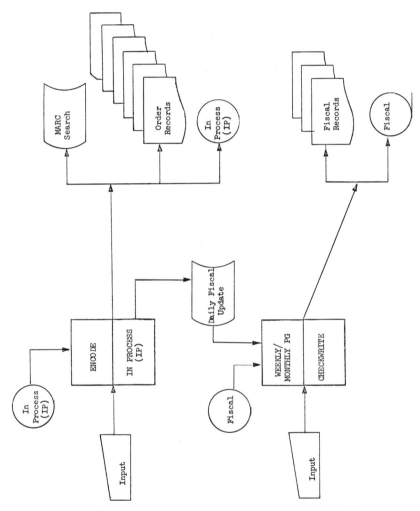

Figure 1: Acquisitions System Program Modules

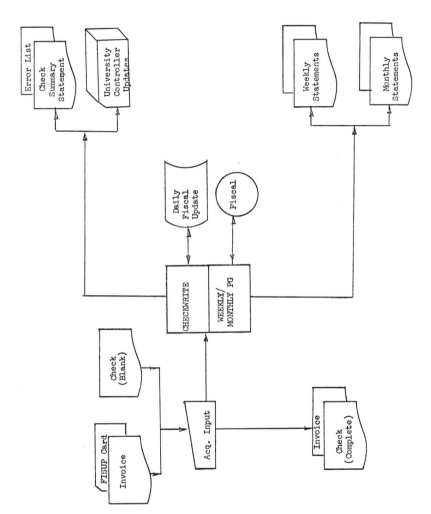

Figure 2: Fiscal Module

Columbia University Libraries
Systems Office

Acquisitions Fiscal Products

COLUMBIA UNIVERSITY LIBRARIES   DROPPED ENCUMBRANCE STATEMENT

	BOOKS AND SERIALS RESERVE	CENTRAL CIRCULATION	
350			
C44146	5.95	E49604	6.60	C49979	3.31
C55407	15.75	E49613	9.50	E49980	21.20
E01338	18.00	E49614	3.25	E49924	1.50
E01340	3.75	E49616	10.00	E50051	7.50

COLUMBIA UNIVERSITY LIBRARIES   EXPENDITURE STATEMENT   FOR PERIOD ENDING AUGUST 31

350   BOOKS AND SERIALS RESERVE   CENTRAL CIRCULATION   56482700005

CHECK	DESCRIPTION	BALANCE	ALLOCATION	INCOME	EXPENDITURE
	ENCUMBERED BALANCE FORWARD	.03*	.00		.00
	BALANCE FROM LAST YEAR				.50
	M. IPYKEN - CARRIAGE			6,535.42CP	
	DOUBLE EXPENDITURE ON CHK L167				
T00966	DOUBLE				
T01035	DOUBLE				
T01100	DOUBLE				
T01109	DOUBLE				
T01100	DOUBLE				
L14547	LIBRARY				
L14560	LIBRARY				
L14557	LIBRARY				
L14574	BYBLOS				
L14626	BERNARD				
L14700	S.S.				
L14702	UNITED				
L14033	DER BUC				
L14894	OTTO HA				
L14896	OTTO HA				
L14959	OTTO HA				

COLUMBIA UNIVERSITY LIBRARIES   MONTHLY ENCUMBRANCE STATEMENT

350   BOOKS AND SERIALS RESERVE   CENTRAL CIRCULATION

E51005	4.80	E52825	35.00	E53304	1.26
E51006	14.16	E52033	9.00	E53305	3.00
E51174	2.52	E52059	6.95	E53031	5.00
E51209	147.20	E52864	3.50	E53276	7.50
E51234	16.03	E52080	4.50	E53034	8.24

COLUMBIA UNIVERSITY LIBRARIES   TRIAL BALANCE   FOR PERIOD ENDING: AUGUST

CENTRAL CIRCULATION

FUND	ACCOUNT NO.	NAME OF ACCOUNT	BALANCE	ALLOCATION	INCOME	EXPENDITURE
110	56482700005	GREEK AND LATIN	1,673.82*	.30	958.13CR	1,450.51
115	56482700005	EN	0.148 846	.00	1.061 255R	9.036 66
128	56482700005	CC				
133	56482700005	FR				
135	56482700005	GE				
140	56482700005	SF				
143	56482700005	SU				
144	56482700005	IT				

COLUMBIA UNIVERSITY LIBRARIES   CHECK SUMMARY STATEMENT   COLUMBIA UNIVERSITY LIBRARIES

CHECK	AMOUNT	DEALER	FUND	UNIV.
L19126	27.20	SAGE PUBLICATIONS, INC.	C260	51382F

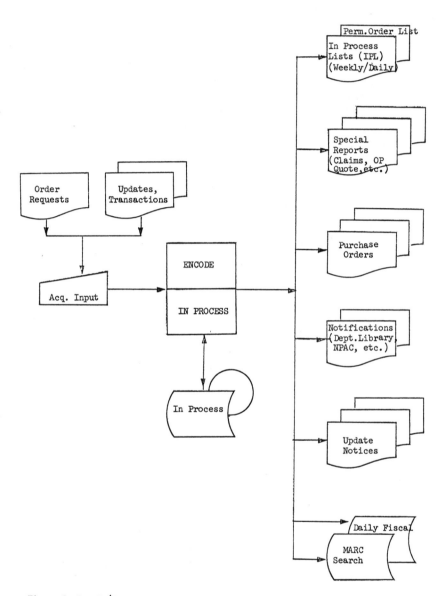

Figure 3: Encode/In Process Module

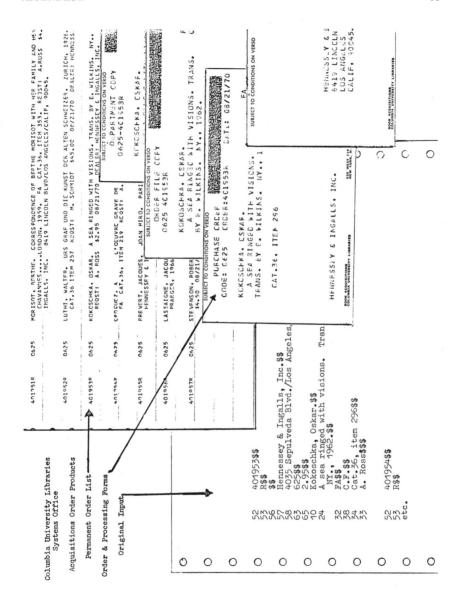

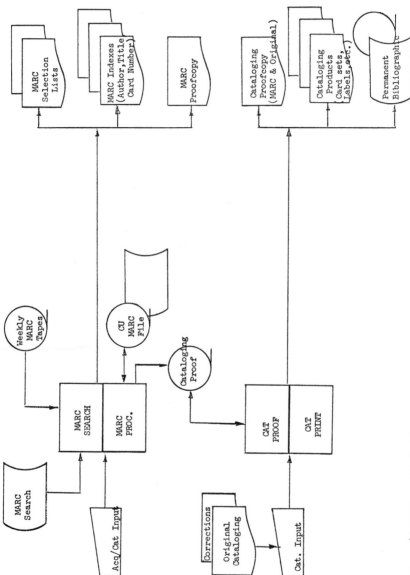

Figure 4: Bibliographic Module

Columbia University Libraries. Systems Office.   1 November 1970

Weekly Selection Lists
From MARC Tapes

By Type of
Material

By LC Class

CLASS REPRINTS

MARC VOL. 2, NO. 27   ROUTE: A. Lib
                                                           PROCESSING DATE
                                      of the 1909 ed. published under title:
Adams, Henry Carter, 1851-1921. Taxation in the United   foreign aras & arbour.)
      States, 1789-1816. New York, B. Franklin [1970]
      79 p. 23 cm. Selected essays in history [1970]
      economics, & social science. 140 Burt Franklin
      research & source works series, 498. Aadric, John. Siam. [1st American ed.] Sout
      U.S.--History.   HJ2369 .14 1970. 78-122836   A. S. Barnes [1970, c1969]. 208 p. il
      68993 REPRINT (Reprint of the 1884 ed.)   cm.   5.95   1. Thailand--Social life

MARC VOL. 2, NO. 19   CLASS B - P

Adams, John Qui
      Case o   Paso, Tex.--Directories
      Press,   Alisky, Marvin. Uruguay, a contemporary survey. New York,   170
      crusad   Praeger [1969] vii, 174 p. illus., map, ports. 22
      [REPRIN   cm. 6.50   1. Uruguay.   P27708 .A62   76-
      title: 75236 500
      Supream   Discovery Women's Institute. S
      the Un   Territories.[24 ed.
      other   Rannie Publications Co.
      by Li   Ash, Sidney R., 1928- Petrified forest; the story behind the   map. 28 cm. 2.00
      and 1:   scenery. Holbrook, Ariz., Petrified Forest Museum   P1100.5.D5 D5 76-465
                       Associat
                       cm. 1   CLASS D (EXCEPT DS)
                       May, D:

Alding, Peter.   MARC VOL. 2, NO. 19
      New Yo   Crvenkovski
      cm.   Bell, David, 1924- Nice old time in Newcastle. Newcastle   th
      ISBN0u4   upon Tyne, Oriel P., 1969.   [30] p. illus. 22 cm.   Pre
                               5/-   1. Newcastle-upon-Tyne--Social life and   Co
                               customs.   I. Patterson, Elwin Frederick, joint   thi
American Anti-   author.   B70-02847   DA690.N6 B4   Inf
      York,   ISBN853620733   76-108957 518   of
      slaver   1.
      United   Bul
      Kossut   Bideford Rural District; the official guide. Carshalton,   Yug
      Lloyd,   Home Publishing, [1969]. 28 p. illus., maps. 19 cm.   Sek
      76-822   --unpriced   1. Bideford Rural District--Description   C75
                       --Guide-books.   DA690.B56 B5   71-
Book of the 150th   479568   208
      [Connersv
      274 p.]   Dalziel, Ra
      Weiser,   Burn, Andrew Robert. Greece and Rome, 750 B.C./A.D. 565,
      1. As   [Glenview, Ill.] Scott, Foresman [1970] 216 p.   Zea
      74-   illus., maps, ports. 24 cm.   Scott, Foresman world
      with a   civilization series, v. 2. 1. Civilization, Greco-
                      Roman.   I. Edwards, J. M., joint author.
Anrias, David,   (Series)   DE59 .D8   72-77544   238
      Weiser,
      1. As
      74-1
      with :
                                                        Durv, Georgi
Ashdown, Charl
      [Tallahas
      [1965]

Columbia University Libraries. Systems Office.

Printed Indices To MARC

1 November 1970

LC Card Number Index

L.C. CARD NO. INDEX - C.U. MARC - VOL. 1, NOS. 1-54   PAGE

67-61502	21493N	67-61788	893N	67-62148	3467.1N	45977N	67-63637
67-61505	39759N	67-61791	353N	67-62150	15677N	33754N	67-63635
67-61506	20045N	67-61793	465.3N	67-62157	2855N	10055N	67-63642
67-61512	338N	67-61795	45975N	67-62168	15674N	23555N	67-63643
67-61528	339A	67-61798	360N	67-62171	18434N	44856N	67-63647
67-61530	340N	67-61800	13431N	67-62172	3PCA	18435A	67-63650
67-61532	341A						
67-61534	228REN						
67A61534	33435N						
67-61550	21494N						
67-61563	34605N						
67-61565	342N						
67-61565	11764N						

Title Index

TITLE INDEX - MARC VOL. 1, NOS. 1-54

COLUMBIA UNIVERSITY LIBRARIES SYSTEMS OFFICE

67-61594	17512A
67-61611	15670CN
67-61612	343N
67-61613	34466N
67-61615	34344N
67-61625	20044N
67-61627	15571N
67-61630	34345N
67-61632	346A
67-61635	347A
67-61645	42867N
67-61646	34467N
67-61673	13489N
67-61680	14342N

U.S.Govt. Print. Off., 1969. (26652)

National minorities; Claude, Inis L. Greenwood Press
[1969, c1955] [JC] (43563)

National Museum, Tokyo. 78-90486
Newsweek [c1968] 68-20029 [N]
(31505)

National Museum, Tokyo. Newsweek [c1968] 68-20029 [N]
(32651)

National Museum, Toky
Newsweek [c19

National nominating c
A. Taft Insti
[JX] (5890)

National oceanographi
Committee on
Oceanogr
Off ...ashin..

National Park Service

Govt. Print.
National school libu
Committee on
Off., 1969.
National Science Fou
[1969]
National Science Fou

Main Entry Index

MAIN ENTRY INDEX

COLUMBIA UNIVERSITY LIBRARIES SYSTEMS OFFICE

67-61704	343N
67-61709	42868A
67-61717	39000N
67-61717	97334N
67-61725	34CN
67-61728	44055A
67-61728	31470N
67-61732	340N
67-61736	37267N
67-61736	351N
67-61741	37264A
67-61741	13490N
67-61746	352A
67-61754	34466N
67-61767	20652A
67-61765	26752N
67-61773	353A
67-61774	34754N
67-61774	18431A
67-61775	354A
67-61730	10652A
67-61730	25950N

Committee on
Subcommittee
Govt. Print.

National policy for t
1913- U.S.
[HC] (6162)

National prejudice an
John Ashley S
[JX] (25293)

National priorities;
[UA] (30303)

National problems, 189
Greenwood Pr

National program of r
evaluation on
Hussein, Al
[DD] (27393)

National register of
of prominent

Mosemann, Ruth Histand, 1907- Family directory of Samuel
Swartz Histand and Susan Overholt Landis; Evangel
Press] 1969. 74-7775 [CS] (29634)

Moser, Charles A. Pisemsky; a provincial realist Harvard
University Press, 1969. 78-78522 [PG] (9434a)

Moser, Mary C., 1906- One-syllable words C. E. Merrill
[1965] [PE] (4419)

Moser, Reta C. Space-age acronyms; 3d ed., rev. and enl.
IFI/Plenum 1969. 69-19416 [TL] (41027)

Moser, Robert H. Diseases of medical progress;
C. Thomas [1969] 68-18298 [RC] (942)

Moser, Roy Radford, 1902- Descendants of Dunham Martin
Moser, 1803-1895. Printed for the family, 1968.
74-8466 [CS] (3549)

Moses, Fred. Dynamic allocation routine. 75-4091Z
[VM] (28757)

Moses, John Anthony, 1930- War aims of imperial Germany:
University of Queensland Press, 196. 70-417378
[DD] (27393)

Moses, Ray Edward, 1941- Scientific proof in criminal cases;
Lakeland Press [1960] 78-7959 [KF] (3C369)

Moses, Robert, 1888- Public works; McGraw-Hill [1970]
77-90021 [HD] (45597)

Moses ben Maimon, 1135-1204. Commentary to Mishnah Khoth
53-27081 [BM] (1572)

Call Number

Destination

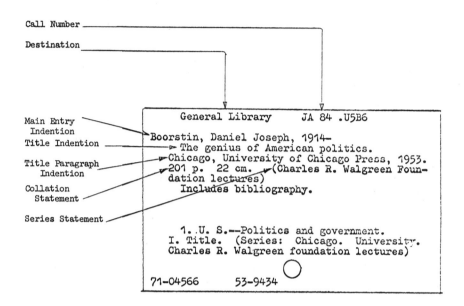

Main Entry
Indention
Title Indention

Title Paragraph
Indention

Collation
Statement

Series Statement

General Library   JA 84 .U5B6

Boorstin, Daniel Joseph, 1914–
    The genius of American politics.
    Chicago, University of Chicago Press, 1953.
    201 p.   22 cm.   (Charles R. Walgreen Foun-
    dation lectures)
        Includes bibliography.

        1. .U. S.--Politics and government.
    I. Title. (Series: Chicago. University.
    Charles R. Walgreen foundation lectures)

    71-04566   53-9434

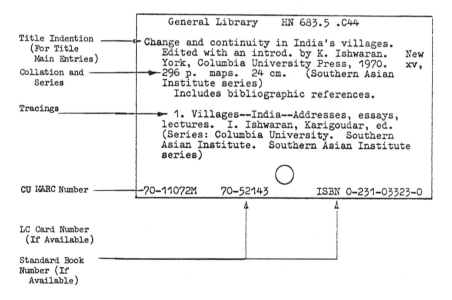

Title Indention
(For Title
Main Entries)

Collation and
Series

Tracings

General Library   HN 683.5 .C44

Change and continuity in India's villages.
    Edited with an introd. by K. Ishwaran.   New
    York, Columbia University Press, 1970.   xv,
    296 p. maps. 24 cm.   (Southern Asian
    Institute series)
        Includes bibliographic references.

    1. Villages--India--Addresses, essays,
    lectures. I. Ishwaran, Karigoudar, ed.
    (Series: Columbia University. Southern
    Asian Institute. Southern Asian Institute
    series)

CU MARC Number

    70-11072M   70-52143   ISBN 0-231-03323-0

LC Card Number
(If Available)

Standard Book
Number (If
Available)

Columbia University Libraries   Proposed Catalog Card Format
    Systems Office

The following chart generally characterizes project scheduling for Columbia's automation effort during the past five years and projects scheduling for the next two years.

Analysis & Design (----------) Includes all system analysis effort required to develop a new design, such as inventorying and analyzing files, forms, and procedures; flowcharting operations; establishing priorities and work schedules, etc.

Development (0000000000) Includes all activities needed to develop, evaluate and program a new system, such as development of alternate conceptual designs, writing preliminary system specifications, programming, prototype testing, etc.

Implementation (///////////) Includes all activities involved with emplementing a new system into a working environment, such as preliminary program documentation, procedural documentation, staff orientation and training, parallel processing and testing, etc.

Production (————————) Includes all activities involved with monitoring and maintaining a production system, such as writing final systems documentation, developing and implementing procedures for production and quality control, maintaining programs for daily use, formalizing feed-back for evaluative purposes, etc.

Evaluation and Redesign (XXXXXXXXXX) Includes all activities involved with making major modifications to a production system, such as redesigning parts of the system for greater manual processing efficiency, recoding parts of production programs for greater machine efficiency, integrating new functions and devices, etc.

Columbia University Libraries
Project Scheduling

1. Circulation

2. Reserves

3. Acquisitions

4. MARC

5. Cataloging

6. User Services

1966 1967 1968 1969 1970 1971 1972

Design ------------
Development OOOOOOOOOOOOOOOO
Implementation ///////////////
Production
Redesign XXXXXXXXXXXXXXXXXXX

The Stanford Experience

Allen Veaner, Hank Epstein, and John Schroeder

I. General Background

My summary of BALLOTS contains three major points. First, I wish to give a background sketch of Project BALLOTS and specifically its relationship to its sister project SPIRES. The second major point covers our experience with our prototype technical processing system, designated BALLOTS I, and the son or daughter of that development, our production system, BALLOTS II. The third point covers our use of MARC files. Parts two and three of the presentation will be given by John Schroeder and Hank Epstein, respectively.

During the past six years at Stanford the work load in technical processing has increased by a factor of approximately three, while productivity has fallen. Productivity per dollar declined owing to inflation and unit productivity for employee was falling because of increasing organizational complexity.

In 1967, one year following Chicago's original grant, we were given the opportunity to apply for some research money from the Title II-B of the Higher Education Act of 1965. We thought it would be worthwhile developing a system that would allow us to take advantage of the most advanced computer techniques then available, namely, third generation equipment with its on-line access to files through visual terminals. Our original intent was to support only file oriented functions, such as technical processing and circulation, and to stay away from reference or information retrieval.

In conducting the project, our staffing reflects a collaborative effort of three organizations on campus: (1) the Stanford Computation Center which installed and managed the IBM 360 model 67 since May of 1967; (2) the Library; and (3) the Institute for Communication Research. The staffing has ranged from some ten to twenty-five persons, including librarians, systems analysts, systems programmers, and applications programmers, as well as a great deal of time contributed by the library administration and many of the regular professional working staff.

Those of you who attended the 1968 Stanford Conference may recall that two Stanford projects, BALLOTS and SPIRES, were merged in 1968 with the goal of creating common software useable for both library automation and information retrieval. We found this combination exceptionally effective. Hank Epstein is Project Director of the combined staff which now numbers something

42

over twenty people. He has four major subsections on his organization: a manager of technical development; a manager of system services; a manager of project documentation; and a technical design staff.

Major policy matters are determined by a project Executive Committee chaired by Stanford's Vice President for Research. Members of the committee include David Weber, Director of University Libraries, Edwin B. Parker, Hank Epstein, Charles Dickens, Director of the Stanford Computation Center, W. F. Miller, Vice President for Research, and myself.

I shall now describe the physical and computer facilities we have. We started out with a staff located in the Library and partly in the Computation Center. Our experience in the development of a large and complex on-line system is that such a geographic separation simply doesn't work. In February, 1970, we consolidated the entire staff under one roof; they now occupy space equal to three 12 X 60 foot trailers adjacent to the Computation Center. This has served to improve intra-project communications.

The IBM 360/67 has been our principle instrument of research and development, but for reasons I will explain in a few moments it cannot be the device that runs a production system for on-line information retrieval and library automation. As far as budget is concerned, the library at this time contributes about fifty thousand dollars per year of its general funds to support automation. We hope to increase this significantly in the near future.

Over a forty-two month period, we have received grants from the Office of Education (OEG-1-7-071145-4428; OEG-0-70-2262) totaling 1.2 million dollars. SPIRES has received from the National Science Foundation (NSF 6N 600, 742, and 830) 1.13 million dollars.

One of the most significant expenditures which doesn't show up in these outside ollars is the amount of in-house time expended. Over the past several months we have had three librarians taken from their regular professional duties who work full time on library automation. This has had a very signficant impact on our ability to keep up with the work load in the manual system. So, I will echo and re-echo the warnings that Paul and Charles have given you: there is no small effort required of your own staff, because library automation is not something that a group of outside experts can do for you. If you don't involve the users of the system in the design of the system, you simply cannot have a successful system.

We decided from the outset that BALLOTS would represent an effective combination of manual and automated procedures and that we would not try to automate those functions which were deviant from the main flow of activities, those functions which did not occur frequently enough to warrant automation.

One of our expectations at the start was that by using IBM's time sharing system, we would be able to operate in a production mode on the 360/67. The time-sharing problem proved much too difficult even for IBM. But there is now a much more realistic hope that we can go in that direction. It was certainly not the case three years ago when we started.

We are also attempting to make our design as generalized as possible by using IBM's Operating System (OS), by using standard programming languages, and by making programs table driven.

To facilitate the development of a unified system we created last year within the library a unified department of technical services. Designated Bibliographic Operations, the new department comprehends acquisition, automation, and cataloging. We are following a formalized system development process which has six overlapping phases which I'm sure are quite familiar to many of you. They are the following: preliminary analysis, detailed analysis, general design, detailed design, implementation, and installation. We have developed some unique project management techniques which concern project control, scheduling, breaking down large systems into specific, exhaustive task assignments. We believe we have developed some useful and unique documentation techniques which can be useful to other projects.

One example is the document which specifies the system requirements for the ordering process and the acquisition function. I think the bulk of it—about 700 pages—will give you some idea of how sizeable an on-line project is.

A document entitled *Data Element Notebook* covers elements—which number approximately 125—plus statistical analyses of MARC tapes and our own in-process file from our prototype system. These analyses were carried out for the purpose of designing screens for visual displays in the production system. (An explanation of how these statistical analyses were used for design of the screens will be given by Mr. Epstein in Part III below.)

The prototype system (BALLOTS I) functioned from February through October 1969. It supported an on-line in-process file, an experimental MARC file, and a number of other files, with terminal query at 2741 typewriter terminals. Outputs produced included purchase orders, claims, cancellations, notifications, and, of course, display at the typewriter terminal of the contents of our in-process file. Approximately thirty persons on the staff were trained to inquire of the file and also to input. During this nine-month period, we built an in-process file which comprehended thirty percent of the acquisition department's throughput. All this was coded, edited, input, and made searchable at terminals.

We had several problems with the 360/67, only two of which I will allude to. One concerned software. File integrity could not be guaranteed because Stanford's 360/67 was not originally set up for that purpose. Stanford's model 67 is geared to maximize throughput at the expense of file integrity. This is appropriate for scientific computing but not for file oriented applications.

A second problem was pricing. The billing algorithm used on the model 67 was intended to encourage people to get off the machine as quickly as possible. All day operations would have resulted in economic penalties which we could not tolerate. This software and billing algorithm are quite defensible and proper for a job mix of up to five thousand jobs per day from researchers and students. Both are intolerable for a system that has to be up all day long.

Another problem which we had continually faced (and my colleagues have alluded to) is system complexity. We don't have any number by which we can gauge our system complexity, but at various times in comparir; our system development work to a batch process like the undergraduate library book catalog at Stanford, we have guessed that the system we are now working on is somewhere between twenty and fifty times as complex as that. And the documentation on the simpler system is about a foot high! That will give you some idea of the size of the system we are working on.

Another problem was distinguishing the enormous difference between a prototype and a production system. Still another is marshalling the intellectual resources to get done specific, assigned tasks, and get them done on schedule. We have found it absolutely essential to bring in a person with extensive experience at implementing successful on-line systems.

In BALLOTS II, our production system, we are designing a system which will have high reliability software with rapid recovery features. We believe these are the most important characteristics for an on-line library system. We can't have operators sitting around half a day while we are reconstructing the file. It has to be characterized also by cost acceptability and it must be oriented toward the users.

It's very time consuming and expensive to design such a system. My colleague, Mr. Epstein, sys, "If the user, the machine or the programmer never make a single mistake, we could implement the whole system for half of what it's costing us."

Let me describe our application of MARC tapes. Since MARC tapes were issued in a code different from that used by IBM computers, we had to write a routine to convert from ASCII to EBCDIC code. We then format the records, *i.e.,* change their format from the communication format to a form searchable by this machine. In the prototype system this was done neither easily nor economically, but we hope will be done much better in a production system. We removed unwanted records by scanning MARC against a table of classification numbers. We organized the file so that we could search it by author, by words in the title, by LC card number, by corporate author, by conference author, and also by imprint date or combination of any of those other search arguments. We conducted intensive statistical analyses of both the MARC records and our own in-process file to design the visual screens. This is a very important consideration because we wanted to have screen designs that would, in effect, give us automatic format recognition as we entered records. Hence, we had to know the distribution of lengths of data elements so that we could solve the overflow problem in an economical way, and I believe that's one notable achievment in this project.

We also wanted to use MARC as an authority file. We wanted the catalogers to have access to it at their terminals and we also wanted to support standing search requests.

II. Major Systems Design Features

The hardware configuration used in the BALLOTS I system has already been described. We expect in the BALLOTS II system to be using an IBM system 370/145 with 512-K storage. Delivery on this machine has been promised on August 20, 1971.

The primary storage medium for our files is the new IBM 3330 direct device. This device offers significantly more storage for less unit cost than the IBM 2314. It is also significantly faster as far as access time is concerned. The terminal network will be composed of twenty to thirty Sanders 720 cathode ray tube terminals which will be located throughout the Main Library and the Meyer Undergraduate Library at Stanford.

Files are the heart of any system, but this is particularly true of an on-line system. We plan to center our system around four basic files. The first of these is the In-Process File and it is the most important of the four files. The In-Process File provides a collection point for information regarding a bibliographic item as it moves through the technical processing pipeline. It is a multiple index file, that is, it is searchable on-line by several different access points. These will be a title word index, a personal name index, combined conference and corporate author name index, and an ID index.

The second file will be a MARC file, also searchable on-line. The indexes for the MARC file will be exactly the same as the In-Process File with one exception: instead of having an ID index, we will have an LC card number index. In a moment I will go into a little more detail about how we intend to use the MARC file.

The third and fourth files are analogous to one another, the third one being a Catalog Data File, to be used primarily in the Main Library. After an item has been catalogued and is ready to be shelved, purchasing information from the In-Process File will be stripped off and the bibliographic data copied into a Catalog Data File. This record will look like an LC card. There will be holding statements as well.

The analog in the Meyer library we are calling a Circulation Inventory File. It will be used in the same way that the Catalog Data File is used in the Main Library, that is, for reference by members of the technical staff and patrons. It will also serve as an inventory file for circulation, that is, charging and discharging will take place from this file.

We also expect to have reserve processing driven from the Meyer Inventory File. We might possibly have reserve circulation driven from it as well, but this has not yet been decided.

There are two categories of system software in an on-line system. The first is supervisory software or generalized software. Examples of modules or module groups in this category are the on-line supervisor which operates under the auspices of an operating system. Terminal service routines, core allocation, and de-allocation routines, data management routines, and recovery procedures. The second category subsumes the transaction processing functions. A transaction is a unit of work as seen from the viewpoint of a user. That is, one file update, one file search, one operation which accomplishes something. Let us take as an example, a series of CRT screens which has been specifically designed to update the in-process file. For that unique set of screen formats there would be a unique set of programs which would perform operations specific to the data on those screens: editing and interfacing with file management routines.

No on-line system can exist without some batch processing support. There has to be a file building function in the batch mode. We plan to take the MARC tapes which come in weekly, convert them to our Stanford file building format and add them to the on-line MARC file. We expect at any one point in time to have approximately 52 weeks of MARC information on-line. This requires approximately 25 million characters of storage, and on an IBM 3330 this would cost approximately 250 dollars a month. We would expect a slightly higher figure for the In-Process File but not very much more. The In-Process File would be roughly the same size.

Another batch facility includes print routines which extract data from the files that I described previously. Printed products will include purchase orders, claims, cancellations, NPAC notices, as well as cataloged data slips, catalog cards, spine labels, and machine readable book cards.

There exists yet another class of routines which I consider to be the most important of all and those are the ones that provide system recovery. Machine crashes are inevitable no matter what kind of a configuration one has. Program bugs are inevitable no matter how good one programs. Users are going to manage to put little "glitches" into the operation because they will do something that we didn't anticipate. So, there has to be a class of routines which are perfectly de-bugged or nearly so on the first day of operation, and these are the ones that get the files back into operational condition after the crash occurs, if a particular file has been damaged. Our goal is to provide no more than twenty minutes of down time for any one file. We feel we must meet this goal because we don't feel that we have the right to call BALLOTS II a production system if we can't provide continuous service in support of the library.

III. Phasing and Scheduling

The chart in Appendix B shows both the system development process and the current project master schedule that Stanford is following for BALLOTS system. All work is broken down into phases. The first phase is called the pre-liminary analysis; in it we define the general boundaries and goals of the system. The result of each phase is a document which is jointly signed by the program-ming area and the library area, both the developers and the users.

The first document was called the Scope Document and came out in January 1970. We are currently in the detailed analysis phase of BALLOTS II. We have broken the detail analysis phase into several pieces: acquisition, cataloging, cir-culation, and reserve processing.

In the acquisition system, we have broken the system down into what we call processes. Ordering is one process and the 700-page document that Mr. Veaner showed before is the document that came out of the detailed analysis phase for ordering.

The object of this document or specification is to exhaustively define the system from the user's viewpoint. We call this an external specification. We show every document input and output in the system, every processing rule, all the activities that occur against the data elements and everything that the system is supposed to do for the user and this is in a sense the top of the iceberg. We must design and program many procedures and activities that the user is not aware of, such as file recovery.

The next phase is general design, where we define in general terms what the system is going to do, the approach, the configuration, and some of the ground rules about the size of the programs.

After that comes the detailed design phase and here the work splits into two areas: the library analysts worry about how the user is going to react to the sys-tem and the programmers begin to worry about how the programs are going to be defined. The programmers write program module specifications for every single program, its purpose, what it's to do, some general logic, and its interface with other programs. The library analysts and librarians define or write user manuals and develop training courses.

We then go into the implementation phase. Training courses are conducted; programs are developed and checked out from the programmer's viewpoint and then turned over to the library for what we call "acceptance tests."

When the system is checked out, we go into a pilot operation phase which we call installation. In this case, the users have been completely trained on both the hardware and the use of the system and we have converted the files and we have run in parallel. We run the manual system and the automated system in parallel for a period of time until the users have gained confidence that the automated system works properly. Then we discontinue running the manual system and we are in production.

This is an example of what we call a system flow chart. Mr. Veaner mentioned there are level one and level two charts. A level one chart illustrates only the functional flow of data and materials; it is intended for use of top management people. Hence, it lacks details such as head count, volume of activity, and exception routines. A level two chart is much more detailed, but is confined to illustrating the main flow of a process, not the exception routines. Level two charts define head count, the names of specific files, and broad processing functions are contained in a single box without much detail. The notation on level two charts is described below in further detail.

The level one chart for the acquisition system is a series of four or five flow charts and here is a sample of one of them. The block that I have colored in is the ordering block. This block then explodes into the order process specification book. Now, this is the level one chart. From here we go into the level two flow chart where we define every document, every process and procedure within the ordering process. Now, this is one section of one chart of the ordering document. This procedure is a manual and automated procedure where the operator would keyboard new information into the In-Process File. The series of symbols right after that are the CRT screens. And the box on the right is the purely automated process which would be a computer program and done completely by computer with no human intervention.

Each has an identification. It has a name and each different type of symbol requires specific documentation. For instance, the manual-automated box which defines the keyboarding of new bibliographic information into the In-Process File requires instructions from the terminal operator on what form to get each different data element and how to key it in and where on the CRT screen to place it.

Next is a verbal description of the box that says "Key in new IPF data." It describes the purpose, the personnel, the skills and the general functions required to input the new data.

Appendix C shows the specific CRT screen format that's going to be used. We have definite locations for every data element and we have the computer program put on the screen the names of the various data elements. The operator takes data from various forms and puts them into the appropriate place on the screen and if they don't have information on a given data element, they leave it out. This eliminates the tagging problem which arises when either a key punch or a typewriter terminal us used for input. The computer *knows* what the data element is by where it is placed on the screen.

We now have several interesting problems. One of the reasons why library automation is rather expensive is that it deals with variable length records. We cannot define in advance how long a given field is going to be, so we have to write a general routine that will handle a field of any size.

We have analyzed the MARC tapes to determine the distribution of field lengths. From this information we have laid out the screen formats to handle 90 to 95 percent of the cases for a given field. For a field which may run over, there is a plus sign at the end of the field. If that plus sign is overwritten with a number then we produce a new screen which will provide more room for that particular field. The operator overwrites the plus sign with a number corresponding to the estimated number of new lines required. This is a somewhat awkward way of handling variable length data and we are looking for better ways but we haven't found any yet.

The most important part of the system and the most detailed part is what we call processing rules. These are the rules that the programmers must use to write the computer programs. These rules are cross referenced to every data element, every screen, every process and define exactly what each program must do under what conditions against the various data elements. One processing rule might verify the check digit for an LC card number if it begins with a sever or a higher number. We define the processing rules in the most abbreviated form we can. Sometimes it's done verbally, other times it's done in a decision table format.

We have developed some specific notations, some specific documentation standards, just for handling variable length data and specializing in the bibliographic notation.

We have developed some two dozen forms to handle different types of information. What we are trying to do is to produce documentation that can communicate to three communities: the library community, the library analyst, and the programmer, and I believe the generation of these forms and the way we are using the documentation has worked quite well. The information on these forms is produced by all three groups. We have three professional librarians, all in management, living with us in our trailers defining this information. We might return them some day if we finish the documentation!

The Problem Context

The publication explosion, a compelling need for access to information, and rapid library growth are not unique to Stanford University. At Stanford, a commitment has been made to deal with the information problems of the university by improving library service and developing a campus based bibliographic retrieval system. Using the tools of computing technology and library systems analysis, computer specialists, librarians, and behavioral scientists have joined in exploring the bibliographic requirements of a major university community and creating new systems to meet those requirements.

Library automation requires a major effort in system development and sizeable expenditures for computer equipment. Computerized information storage and retrieval requires a similar investment in hardware and software. Both undertakings have common conceptual problems in such areas as bibliographic file organization and on-line searching. Each derives concrete benefits from the other: bibliographic files created in the process of library automation are available for generalized retrieval uses, and complex retrieval routines are available for searching library bibliographic files.

Spires/Ballots Project

At Stanford, two major projects have been involved jointly in library automation and information retrieval since 1968. One is BALLOTS (Bibliographic Automation of Large Library Operations Usine a Time-Sharing System), funded by the Office of Education; the other is SPIRES (Stanford Physics Information REtrieval System—informally known as the Stanford Public Information REtrieval System), funded by the National Science Foundation. The purpose of this collaboration is to create the common software required to support both the BALLOTS and SPIRES applications. The joint effort is overseen by the SPIRES/BALLOTS Executive Committee, chaired by Professor William F. Miller, Vice President for Research. Professor Edwin B. Parker of Stanford's Institute for Communication Research is Principal Investigator for SPIRES. Mr. Allen B. Veaner, Assistant Director of University Libraries for Bibliographic Operations, is Principal Investigator for BALLOTS. Management responsibility for the joint project has been delegated to the Stanford Computation Center. Mr. Hank Epstein, Project Director, holds a joint appointment with the Computation Center and the University Libraries.

ACKNOWLEDGMENT

The activity reported here was performed under:

Grant Nos. OEG-1-7-071145-4428 (095) and OEG-0-70-5237 with the Office of Education, United States Department of Health, Education and Welfare (BALLOTS—Bibliographic Automation of Large Library Operations Using a Time-Sharing System), and

Grant Nos. GN 600, GN 742, GN 830, and GN 830.1 with the National Science Foundation (SPIRES—Stanford Physics Information REtrieval System).

Grantees undertaing such projects are encouraged to express freely their professional judgment in the conduct of the project. Points of view or opinions stated do not, therefore, necessarily represent official agency position or policy.

PREFACE

This report is the result of contributions and comments from several people. John Schroeder, SPIRES/BALLOTS Manager for Technical Development, contributed material on the system development process from which the System Development section was written. The entire text was read and criticized by the following: Professor Edwin B. Parker, Principal Investigator for SPIRES; Mr. David C. Weber, Director of Libraries; Mr. Allen B. Veaner, Principal Investigator for BALLOTS; and Mr. Hank Epstein, SPIRES/BALLOTS Project Director. Miss Jennifer Hartzell of the SPIRES/BALLOTS Documentation Office made many helpful editorial suggestions.

—Douglas Ferguson, Editor
SPIRES/BALLOTS Project
Stanford, University

The Stanford project structure and system development philosophy reflect both the common uses and individual needs of BALLOTS and SPIRES. The concept of shared facilities results in system software and hardware designed to service both the BALLOTS and SPIRES applications. Two examples of common software are an on-line text editor and file-handling and task-scheduling routines. These shared facilities can service bibliographic input and specialized research files. Examples of shared hardware facilities are a central processing unit and direct access devices (making possible shared files). Combining resources in this system development effort reduces the cost of creating common facilities and provides a pool of skilled manpower resources for each project.

BALLOTS I and SPIRES I

In 1967 the Stanford University Libraries and the Stanford Institute for Communication Research began research projects with funds from the Office of Educations (BALLOTS) and the National Science Foundation (SPIRES). In 1968 the two projects came under the policy direction of the SPIRES/BALLOTS Executive Committee, thus formalizing the shared perspective and close collaboration of the projects.

Stanford University was an appropriate setting in which to initiate research and development in bibliographic retrieval. Strong interest in automation was felt in all areas of the Stanford University Libraries and especially by its Associate Director (now Director), David C. Weber, and Assistant Director for Bibliographic Operations, Allen B. Veaner. During the period from 1964 to 1966, the library had achieved a remarkably successful computer-produced book catalog for the J. Henry Meyer (Undergraduate) Library. Professor Edwin B. Parker and his colleagues at the Institute for Communication Research even then were applying to computer systems the behaviorial science analysis that they and others had applied already to print, film, and television media. The Stanford Campus Facility had an IBM 360 model 67 computer, a locally developed time-sharing system, and a first-rate programming staff associated with one of the nation's leading computer science departments. A close working relationship between the University Libraries, the Computation Center, and the Institute for Communication Research formed a firm foundation for research and development.

The combined project software development group applied themselves to writing programs necessary for biliographic retrieval. In the library, an analysis and design group worked closely with the library staff in studying library processes and defining requirements. This joint effort created a prototype system that could be used in the Main Library and by Stanford faculty and students, primarily high-energy physicists.

In early 1969, two prototype applications were activated using the jointly developed systems software: an acquisition system was established in the Main Library (BALLOTS I) and a bibliographic retrieval system (SPIRES I) was established for a group of high-energy physicists.

Centralized management of library input was handled by two newly created departments, Data Preparation and Data Control. Several terminals were installed in the Main Library for on-line searching, and a terminal was placed in the Physics Library. An on-line In Process File was created, consisting of 30 percent of the roman-alphabet acquisition material ordered by the library. A specially trained staff performed on-line searching daily during regular library hours. This prototype acquisition system operated during most of 1969, demonstrating the technical feasibility of the combined project goals. It was studied and evaluated by the library systems and programming staffs, who reviewed the human, economic, and technical requirements of a library bibliographic retrieval system.

At the Stanford Linear Accelerator Center (SLAC) Library, a file of preprints in high-energy physics was created through SPIRES I. This file is still active; records of new preprints are added weekly, and a note is made of any preprint that is published. Input is via an IBM 2741 typewriter terminal in the SLAC Library. Regular library staff at SLAC handle inputs and updating. Searching can be done by author, title, date, and updating. Searching can be done by author, title, date, and citation. The preprint file contains approximately 6,500 documents, including all the high-energy physics preprints received in the SLAC Library from March 1968 to the present. "Preprints in Particles and Fields," a weekly listing of preprints, also is produced from SPIRES I, after an initial period of support by the Division of Particles and Fields of the American Physical Society, it now is supported partially by subscriptions.

BALLOTS II and SPIRES II: System Development

The results of operating the prototype applications (BALLOTS I and SPIRES I) were encouraging particularly with respect to the advantages and practicality of utilizing common software. Under actual operating conditions, feasibility and usefulness were established and a wealth of knowledge was gained. Joining the library and retrieval application areas served by shared facilities (hardware and software) was shown to be a rewarding approach.

BALLOTS I and SPIRES I resulted from a development process in which user requirements were analyzed, programs written and tested, and prototypes created and evaluated. Librarians, behaviorial scientists, library systems analysts, and computer specialists collaborated over an extended period of time. This development process was a major accomplishment. It made possible the definition of a production bibliographic retrieval system with distinctive hardware and software requirements.

The creation of a production system for library automation (BALLOTS II) and for generalized information storage and retrieval (SPIRES II) requires continuing a comprehensive system development process. Within the framework of this process tasks are defined, assigned, and coordinated. The system development process for the creation of BALLOTS II and SPIRES II has six phases:

Phase A: Preliminary Analysis
Phase B: Detailed Analysis
Phase C: General Design
Phase D: Detailed Design
Phase E: Implementation
Phase F: Installation

Preliminary Analysis involved defining goals, describing the user environment, analyzing the existing system, selecting the system scope, and establishing the gross technical feasibility of the selected first implementation scope. These factors are described in detail in a System Scope Document that was the main output of the Preliminary Analysis Phase.

Detailed Analysis enumerates minutely the requirements that the manual-automated system must meet. In it (1) performance requirements are stated quantitatively, including response time, hours of on-line accessibility, allowable mean failure time, maximum allowable recovery time, and similar factors. (2) Record input and output are determined in terms of volume, growth, and fluctuations. Timing considerations for batch input and output are determined, in order to plan for scheduling requirements. (3) All input and output record, screen, and document formats are determined character by character. (4) Rules transforming input data elements into output data elements are formulated and tabulated. (5) The upper bounds of development and operating costs are established.

General Design encompasses both system externals (procedures, training, reorganization, etc.) and system internals (alternative hardware and software solutions to the stated requirements). As a result an overall software-hardware configuration is selected and outlined in a General Design Document.

Detailed Design completes the internal and external design, creates implementation and testing plans, and provides programming specifications. These factors are incorporated in a Detailed Design Document.

In the Implementation Phase, user documentation is created and personnel training begins. Programs are coded and checked. Testing is carried out and the results are evaluated. Programs, maintenance documentation, and test reports are prepared in this phase.

In the Installation Phase, training of all personnel is completed, files are converted, and, after the automated system has operated parallel to the manual system for a time, the changeover is made to the automated system. Performance statistics then are collected and a support plan and project history are written.

Each phase description necessarily has been abbreviated. Not all activities or outputs have been described. Activities in some phases overlap and feed back to redefine previous activities. In the installation phase, a "Wishbook" that has been maintained through all the phases is put in final form. The Wishbook is very important because it is a link to successive development iterations. It contains information on the capabilities, services, and operational characteristics whose desirability became apparent during the development process but which could not be included owing to time, cost, or technical constraints. The Wishbook also contains information on any internal (programming or hardware) and external (user or procedural) operational deficiencies that are determined after the system has been running for some time. These findings will be considered in designing new portions of the system and will aid in improving its overall design.

This outline of the system development process guides SPIRES/BALLOTS II development from the definition of goals to the installation of a fully operational system.

BALLOTS II and SPIRES II: Goals

The project goals for library automation (BALLOTS), generalized information storage and retrieval (SPIRES), and shared facilities are interrelated. The goals of shared facilities (hardware and software) support and serve the goals of BALLOTS and SPIRES.

BALLOTS

As the major information center of a large academic institution, the library must respond rapidly, effectively, and economically to the university community. The library is a complex combination of people, machines, and records that organize and open up the major bibliographic resources of the university to students and faculty. It reflects the needs and priorities of a changing university environment. The university library is also part of a larger network of information sources that includes other research libraries, the Library of Congress, and specialized information storage agencies.

The essential goals of BALLOTS are found in a library sytem (both manual and automated sections) which is: USER RESPONSIVE. The system adapts to the changing bibliographic requirements of diverse user groups within the university community. COST COMPETITIVE. The system provides fast, efficient internal processing of increasing volumes of processing transactions. GENERALIZABLE. The system is not just an attempt to automate portions of the existing manual system. It is based on the actual operating requirements of library processing; it is not completely dependent on the existing procedural, organizational, or physical setting. PERFORMANCE ORIENTED. The system provides the library and university administration with data which are useful for measuring internal processing performance and user satisfaction. FLEXIBLE. The system has the capability to expand in order to embrace a broader range of services and a wider group of users. Service via terminals will be available throughout the campus. The system will be able to link up with and serve other information systems and use effectively national data sources.

Thse goals will be expressed in specific capabilities which will, among other things, minimize manual filing; eliminate many clerical tasks now performed by professionals; increase self-servce efficiency; and provide mechanisms for recording the user's suggestions. The effect of these computer capabilities will be to reduce drastically errors associated with manual sorting, typing, and hand transcription; to speed the flow of material through library processing; to aid book selection by providing fast access to central machine files; and to enable librarians to advise a patron of the exact status of a work about which he is inquiring. In summary, responsiveness to library users, efficient operation, generality, performance monitoring, and flexibility for future improvement are the essential goals of library automation.

SPIRES

The SPIRES generalized information storage and retrieval system will support the research and teaching activities of the library faculty, students, and staff. Each user will be able to define his requirements in a way that automatically tailors the system response to fit his individual needs. The creation of such a system is a major activity involving the study of users, source data, record structure, and file organization, as well as considerable experimentation with facilities. The SPIRES system will be characterized by flexibility, generality, and ease of use. SPIRES goals are related to five specific areas: DATA SOURCE AND CONTENT. A generalized information storage and retrieval capability will store bibliographic, scientific, administrative, and other records in machine-readable form. Collections will range from large public files, converted from centrally produced machine-readable data, to medium-small files, created from user generated input (faculty and student files). SEARCH FACILITIES. The system will provide the capability for searching files interactively (on-line), via a computer terminal; on a batch basis, by grouping requests and submitting them on a regular schedule; and on a standing request basis, in which a search query is routinely passed against certain files at specified intervals. FEEDBACK. Reports will be provided on how frequently various sytem elements are used. These will include statistical analyses of user difficulties and system errors. RECORD MODIFICATION. Update and edit capability will be provided on a batch basis or on-line; options for update will come at the level of record, data element, and character string with a data element. COST AND CUSTOMERS. The cost of the services provided should be sufficiently low to enable a wide ragne of customers to cost justify their use of the system. The variety of services should be sufficiently great to encourage a growing body of users. A range of services at various cost levels must be offered to permit users to select the type of service which meets their needs within their financial limiations.

BALLOTS and SPIRES Shared Facilities

Shared facilities are hardware and software designed to provide concurrent service to BALLOTS and SPIRES applications. Since the sharing of such resources represents a substantial saving to all applications served, maximum attention will be given to the sharing concept. Whenever possible, advantage will be taken of the economies gained through providing major facilities for multiple applications. HARDWARE. The hardware environment will provide reliable, economical, and flexible support of the applications it encompasses. SOFTWARE. The software, which will consist of an operating system, an on-line executive program, a terminal handler, a text editor, and many other facilities, will be used jointly by various applications. GENERALITY/EXPANDABILITY. The shared facilities will be designed to allow current applications to be expanded as well as to allow new applications to be added without modifying previous ones.

Toward an Information Facility

The work of SPIRES and BALLOTS has potential beyond bibliographic retrieval and library automation applications. There is a growing need for computer and other information retrieval services in support of socially significant research. Such research is being conducted in the developing fields of ecology and urban studies, to name two areas.

Several capabilities and services are required. Data banks of biliographic and other information are needed for studies that draw upon several disciplines. Strong disciplinary information systems (*e.g.*, psychology) and centralized national systems (*e.g.*, Educational Resources Information Center—ERIC) produce large amounts of data on magnetic tapes. In addition, at Stanford, data are generated in on-campus research and at nearby centers. An information facility with large-scale storage equipment and sophisticated program capabilities could create and maintain data banks derived from such input sources.

Data selected from large machine-readable files could be subjected to further computer processing. Programs that perform mathematical or statistical analysis could be used to produce evidence for a problem solution that may not have been considered when the data were first gathered. Fresh insights often can be obtained without the necessity of generating large amounts of new data. Similarly, new data could be added to an existing file and up-to-date analyses performed to confirm or extend the conclusions of previous studies.

In addition to the large amounts of information now in machine-readable form, even larger amounts are now available in microforms. These include microfiche, microcards, and microfilm. Computer-generated on-line indexes to massive microform files are a form of information retrieval that an information facility could provide.

In social research there is an increasing premium placed on providing information quickly and at the site of research—which is often beyond the university campus. A computer information facility can meet these time and distance requirements. Remote terminals in a nearby city can access a Stanford computer. Direct-access storage devices operating with time-sharing software can provide immediate interactive response. Stanford has several years' experience in operating a multi-user interactive system with a network of users in the San Francisco Bay Area.

An information facility based on SPIRES and BALLOTS would combine production operating characteristics and sophisticated search and retrieval capabilities. Reliability, security, fast recovery, and cost acceptability are required to support library and administrative operations. Ease of use for people with nontechnical backgrounds (faculty or students) and extensive search request capabilities are needed by the SPIRES users. Through a combined facility, librarians would be able to use one or more search programs and a researcher would be able to access library files. Both of these activities could be carried out simultaneously from different locations. Common software such as a terminal handler would serve all user groups.

In a sense, a comprehensive information facility is an "extended library." The boundaries of this library are not terminals. A researcher will not need to go to the library catalog to search for material—a "catalog" will be as close as a terminal.

Such an information facility would be used by several major user groups.

These groups include not only librarians and university administrative personnel but also researchers at Stanford and in nearby locations. In the past, and even now, no one of these user groups could afford to have a computer facility devoted to its own information needs. As an information facility is designed to serve the daily operational needs of the university and the special information needs of various research groups, computerized information services can be offered at a favorable cost-benefit ratio.

Bibliography: Publications and Reports

(NOTE: ED numbered documents are available from ERIC Document Reproduction Service, 4936 Fairmont Avenue, Bethesda, Maryland 20014.
PB numbered documents are available from Clearinghouse for Federal Scientific and Technical Information, Springfield, Virginia 22151.)

Automation Newsletter: Project BALLOTS. Automation Division, Stanford University Libraries. No. 1, June 1969; No. 2, September 1969; No. 3-4 (combined issue), March 1970. (Available without charge from SPIRES/BALLOTS Documentation Office, Cypress Hall Annex, Stanford, California 94305.)

BALLOTS Progress Report 3/27/69-6/26/69. SPIRES/BALLOTS Project, Stanford University, Stanford, California. 402 pp. ERIC document number 030 777; microfiche $1.50, hard copy $20.00.

Parker, Edwin B. "Behaviorial Research in the Development of a Computer-Based Information System." Delivered at the Conference on Communication among Scientists and Technologists: The Study of the Production, Dissemination and Use of Information by Scientists and Technolgists, October 28-30, 1969, at The Johns Hopkins University, Baltimore, Maryland. To be published in the Conference Proceedings.

Parker, Edwin B. "Democracy and Information Processing." *EDUCOM* (Bulletin of the Inter-University Communications Council) 5, No. 4 (1970):2-6.

Parker, Edwin B. "Developing a Campus Based Information Retrieval System." In *Proceedings, Stanford Conference on Collaborative Library Systems Development* (Stanford University, Stanford, California, October 4-5, 1968); Stanford University Library, Stanford, California, 1969, pp. 213-30. ERIC document number ED 031 281; microfiche $1.00, hard copy $11.50.

Parker, Edwin B. "Information Utilities and Mass Communication." In Nie, N., and H. Sackman (eds.), *Information Utilities and Social Choice.* Montvale, New Jersey: AFIPS Press, 1970.

Parker, Edwin B. "Potential Interrelationships Between Library and Other Mass Media Systems." Delivered at the Conference on Interlibrary Communications and Information Networks, September 28–October 2, 1970, at Warrenton, Virginia.

Parker, Edwin B. "A System Theory Analysis of Feedback Mechanisms for Information Systems." Delivered at the FID International Congress of Documentation, September 21–24, 1970, at Buenos Aires, Argentina. To be published in the Congress *Proceedings*.

RECON Working Task Force (Allen B. Veaner, Member). *Conversion of Retrospective Catalog Records to Machine-Readable Form*. Library of Congress, Washington D.C., 1969.

RECON Working Task Force (Allen B. Veaner, Member). "Levels of Machine-Readable Records." *Journal of Library Automation* 3, No. 2 (1970): 122–27.

SPIRES Annual Reports

1967 Report, 57 pp. ERIC document number ED 617 294; microfiche $.50, hard copy $3.05.

1968 Report, 107 pp. Clearinghouse document number PB-184 960; microfiche $.65, hard copy $3.00.

1969–70 Report, 129 pp. ERIC document number ED 04 602. (The 1969–70 Report is available without charge from SPIRES/BALLOTS Documentation Office, Cypress Annex, Stanford, California 94305.)

SPIRES Reference Manual. SPIRES/BALLOTS Project, Stanford University, Stanford, California. 61 pp. January 1969. Revised July 1969.

SPIRES/BALLOTS Report. A 15-minute, color, 16 mm film giving an overview of the library automation and information retrieval problem in general and of Stanford's approach to it. Written and directed by D. B. Jones. Produced by the Department of Communications, Stanford University, 1969. (Copies may be rented from Extension Media Center, University of California, Berkeley 94720. Rental charge, $15.00 for 24 hours; purchase price, $180.00.)

System Scope for Library Automation and Generalized Information Storage and Retrieval at Stanford University. SPIRES/BALLOTS Project, Stanford University, Stanford, California. February 1970. Second printing, April 1970. 157 pp. ERIC document number ED 038 153. (Available from the SPIRES/BALLOTS Documentation Office, Cypress Hall Annex, Stanford, California 94305, for $7.50 prepaid.)

Veaner, Allen B. "The Application of Computers to Library Technical Processing."
    College and Research Libraries 31, No. 2 (1970):36–42.
Veaner, Allen B. "Major Decision Points in Library Automation." Delivered at
    the 75th Annual Meeting of the Association of Research Libraries, January
    17-18, 1970, at Chicago, Illinois. *College and Research Libraries* 31, No. 5
    (1970):299–312. The full text as delivered appears in the published meeting
    minutes, pp. 2-33.
Veaner, Allen B. "Stanford University Libraries, Project BALLOTS, A Summary."
    In *Proceedings, Stanford Conference on Collaborative Library Systems Development* (Stanford University, Stanford, California, October 4-5, 1968),
    Stanford University Libraries, Stanford, California, 1969, pp. 42-49. ERIC
    document number ED 031 281; microfiche $1.00, hard copy $11.50.
Weber, David C. "Personnel Aspects of Library Automation." Delivered at the
    Information Science and Automation Division Program Meeting of The American Library Association, June 28-July 3, 1970, at Detroit, Michigan.

The following two charts describe the scope of BALLOTS II implementation as defined in January 1970. They are taken from *System Scope for Library Automation and Generalized Information Storage and Retrieval at Stanford.* SPIRES/ BALLOTS Project, Stanford University. (Full Document available from the SPIRES/BALLOTS Documentation Office, Stanford University.)

Stanford University Libraries

Acquisition-First Implementation Scope

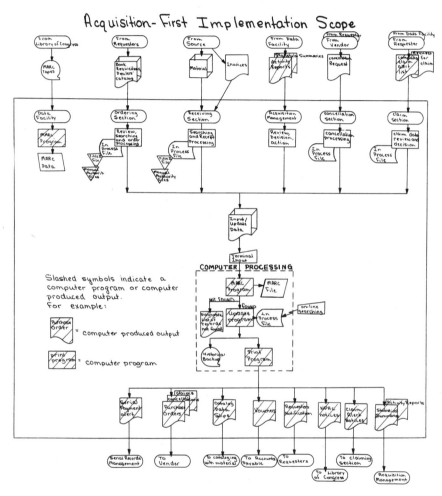

Slashed symbols indicate a computer program or computer produced output. For example:

Purchase Order = computer produced output

print program = computer program

EAM 1/27/70

Stanford University Libraries
Cataloging - First Implementation Scope

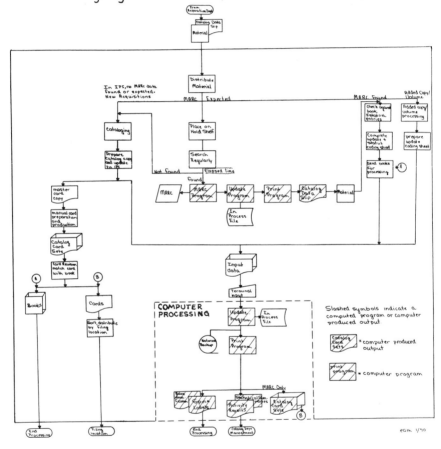

NOTES TO BALLOTS PRELIMINARY SCREEN DESIGN

1. Screen Layout

This design is oriented toward a screen of 40 lines with 52 characters in each line as used in the Sanders 720 Display System. The screen size was assumed only for preliminary design purposes and there is no assumption that this terminal will be used.

2. Screen Format

The screen display is "form-like" in that certain constant items (data element mnemonics) are displayed on the screen and the librarian types information about these items (data element values) to the right of the mnemonics. The display format is "fixed field" in that the space (field) allowed for each data element value is a specified number of positions. If more space is needed the librarian takes the action described in **Overflow** below.

3. Control Line

The first line of each screen is a Control Line that displays three kinds of status information to the person at the terminal. First is the current screen identification such as BI01, which refers to the first screen for bibliographic input. Second is the current function such as "ordering" in the case where book order information is being entered. Third is the identification number for the record being created by the person entering information on to the screen.

4. Data Input and Error Messages

The value of a data element (such as a personal name or title) is typed to the right of the displayed data element mnemonic (*i.e.*, PN or T). The first two columns of each line displaying a data element mnemonic are reserved for an error code. After the librarian pushes the "send" button, if there is an error in the data element, a code will appear in the first two columns to the left of the mnemonic.

5. Overflow

Some information on a data element may take up more space than is allowed on the screen. In that case, the librarian replaces the plus at the end of the data element field with a number or letter that asks for a given number of additional lines on an overflow screen.

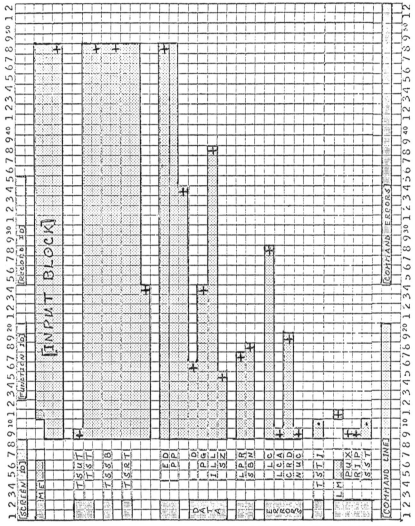

Allen Veaner   Stanford University Libraries

*(The summary that follows was actually presented on the second day of the meeting.)

My job is to summarize the preceeding discussions. We all had many hard questions addressed to us directly, one might almost say very brutally. Columbia was asked, why haven't you saved the university any money? Chicago was asked, what's the cost of keeping up with the normal manufacturer-issued changes in software and hardware? Stanford was asked why does it take such a long time to develop an on-line system? And everybody was asked, what would he do if by fiat one could have his own way and impose standardization on everybody?

Irwin Pizer made a very interesting comment about wheels having different numbers of spokes, and how these differences impeded developments in the early history of the automotive industry. I've heard of one profit-making concern that has an educational and orientation course for their middle level executives. The course is appropriately entitled, Wheel Alignment; it is intended to make sure that tope management communicates to middle management exactly what are the functions and purposes of their organization, so everyone has a unified idea of company objectives. Could we profit by "wheel alignment" in library science library administration?

Let me summarize what we have learned, what benefits we have obtained through CLSD, and take a very quick look at what the future might be.

As we have said over and over again, we have all learned that the job is a lot tougher than we thought it was. We acknowledge and recognize that there is no one person who can understand the totality of any library system, whether it's a manual system or an automated system. We have all learned that tradition is very vigorous and tough to fights, that not all the problems are visible at the start of a large and complex project, that in many instances there may have been a lack of clarity in initial objectives, and that, as time goes on, we learn to clarify and re-articulate objectives. If we don't engage in continuous reevaluation of our work, there is certainly something the matter with us. Designing a large library system is not comparable to kit building—it is a *development* process, fraught with trial and error. It is the difference between building next year's car and a totally new vehicle never before constructred, like a space vehicle.

Another thing we have learned is the peculiar and ambiguous role of the person in charge of a systems effort. The systems man is expected to be a jack of all trades, somewhat of an uncomfortable position. A systems person is often charged by the library director with cleaning up all the old, inefficient procedures. He also has to design the new system, interview, recruit and supervise the staff, document the new system, train the users, write proposals and reports, keep up-to-date with the technology, and so forth. As you can see he doesn't have very much to do! We need some clarification in defining his role, and in determining what support staff he requires.

We have also learned that to date there have been no demonstrable savings in library operations through automation; that the hardware and the software don't live up to the manufacturer's claims or to our own expectations. We have learned that on-line systems represent a whole new ball game. We know that library automation involves more than just a library staff—it immediately gets us into the political arena with the people that control the purse strings of the university and with those who are in charge of that all important resource, the computer.

We have learned the headaches and heartaches of project documentation and why systems programmers say, "I'll write my own code all over again because it's easier to recode than dig one's way through somebody else's documentation."

And finally we have learned that the CLSD project has not and cannot come up with a unified package that anyone can take home and plug into his own computer.

What are the benefits that we have achieved separately and collectively? I think Paul Fasana may have articulated the most important benefit when he said, "this collaboration has served to shatter the vertical compartmentalization that we all seem to suffer from in our libraries and has taken the flow of material and data and translated it into a horizontal flow in which everything is much more interdependent." I don't pretend that we have all achieved this but we have certainly recognized this and will be able to act accordingly in the future.

We have learned some things about "transferrability." I think we can conceive of at least three levels of transferrability. On one level, it is some kind of participation in somebody else's system, whether it's a batch or an on-line system, whether it's by contracting out work to a large batch system or whether it's by using terminals in a local network.

A second level is the delivery of a complete package of documentation to another user. As I indicated, if the system is of any size, this is going to be a very large package.

A third level of transferrability is the actual installation of a system in some other institution. External installations require significant personnel resources for training and teaching; we simply don't have those resources. But, as has been pointed out, any level of transferrability is utterly inconceivable if we insist upon tailoring the system to the environment. It seems clear that we had better start thinking of the opposite methodology: the environment must be conformed to the system and system goals must predominate. To gain benefits from true national systems, we must give up some freedom.

Future progress in library automation, as in any new and experimental endeavor, involves risk. We must follow the example of the turtle: he makes progress only by sticking his neck out.

Computer Hardware and Software for Librarians

Michael Barnett   Director of Research and Development, Wilson Company

When I accepted the invitation to speak today, I thought my paper would be called Computer Hardware and Software for Librarians, and that this would let me talk in simple terms about a few software and hardware topics, in part to bolster the morale of any library administrators among you who have to cope with "computer professionals" trying the tactics of the Emperor's New Clothes. I was told last week that most of you had already been exposed to sophisticated systems, which if anything reinforced my intention of speaking at an elementary level. The Oxford Dictionary defines "sophisticated" as "adulterated" "not pure or genuine," "falsified in greater or lesser degree," etc., and I think that this sums up a lot that is flaunted as "sophisticated" today, in the jargon that social issues oriented entrepreneurs seem to have caught, with various other things, from the military industrial complex. Even if you wanted it, I just could not provide an hour of fore front, five flush, panavistal, ultrasonic, superconductive, telemetered, photochromic, remotely localized, humanly pastelized, downright symbioticized, index sequential, non-inessential, microminiaturized, minicomputerized, midily optimized, macrocompilerized, mega buck subsidized gobblydegook.

Within the more recent non-pejorative use of "sophisticated" to mean "experienced" or "based on experience," I question, too, whether this necessarily means the most elaborate or gimmicky or what was put on the market next week. Simplicity rather than complexity may be the hallmark of experience, in the design of equipment and programs, and in the design of working procedures. So the fact that you had been "exposed" did not put me off planning to talk about a few simple topics simply, and I started to write some notes on the preparation of input, the design of records and files, operating systems, utility programs, general programming languages, and the actual development of computer programs, without looking too carefully at the conference program I had just been given. Shortly before the draft was finished, I was told that people would expect evaluation and guidance—in effect, how to out-guess the manufacturer and design for the future, whether to go mini or midi and such like, and I took a good hard look at the program, to find to my horror, that it announced a talk on "requirements . . . to meet various objectives; present hardware shortcomings; etc." I then went into a flat spin about how to talk my way out of the "requirements, shortcoming, guidance, and evaluation" angles so that I could get in what

72

I had already prepared, under the heading "etcetera," which I will now attempt. As far as your requirements are concerned, I think it would be totally presumptuous for me to attempt a summary or analysis for any single application in any one library, let alone the totality of applications in all the libraries represented at this meeting. I suppose that most of you deal largely with just a few basic processes, and I suppose there are extensive commonalities. The evolution of a structuring of activities to provide for systematic, orderly adaptation to a host of variant circumstances is inherent in the development of any profession, but the fact that activities have been structured to permit such adaptations is no ground for denying the varieties of circumstance that can arise, and which require meticulous individual analysis before "requirements" can be stated.

What about "shortcomings"? Within the possible parochialism of my own endeavors, to explore the potential use of the new technology to The H. W. Wilson Company, and also pottering along with some of my longstanding research interests that sprang from my work in quantum mechanics, my attitude towards hardware and software is conditioned by the pleasure that I derive from results of immediate concern that I can get with progressively increased ease and diminishing cost. I see the accelerated tempo of my work today compared to three years ago as progress, thanks to third generation computers; and I regard the prospect of working faster and less expensively three years hence as a prospect of further progress, rather than an amelioration of conditions to be carped at now as shortcomings. Furthermore, I see no need now to try guessing what the future may provide, as a prerequisite to present action.

Technical developments over the last twenty years have increased enormously the computer's return on my efforts, by intermittent and at times dramatic accelerations of activity. The intellectual structure of what I do, such as it is however, has not required any violent change to let me take advantage of technological developments—the structure continued to evolve, albeit faster, but the operative word has been evolution, not revolution. The real intellectual problems inherent in a computer application do not go away when the machines get bigger and faster—the "brute force" approach has proven a dismal and fantastically expensive failure in fields from theoretical physics to chess playing to mechanical translation. Waiting for science fiction storage devices to bury information, without basing its organization on scholarly insight into its contents, and the uses to which it will be put, and a recognition of the kinds of factor that influence storage and processing time whose detailed interplay may change, but which should never be squandered in a rational economy; burying information without such expert and professional organization will surely bury it and perhaps some other things besides.

As far as going mini or midi is concerned it is my belief that there will always
be a wide range of equipment, that will meet a wide range of uses. It is sad that
technological choice seems to depend so much on what is "in," that can swing
away from a worthwhile development, that has been made a fad, as irrationally
as the fad was created to begin with. Critical as I am of the "console mentality,"
and despite a past personal involvement in the mini computer field, I find a degree of oversimplification, to say the least, in the panegyrics of some glossy ads
to the free-standing virtues of their wares that free them from "the ills inherent
in time sharing." What a comedown, or comeback, from the days of project
MAC. Advances that enhance the power and cost effectiveness of large computers can enhance those of small machines too; but improvements in the economics of special-purpose computers, for some purposes, does not preempt the value
of the large machine for others. Moreover, a bad workman often blames his tools,
and incompetence proven by squandering hundreds of thousands of dollars on
one machine that is quite adequate if properly applied is no justification for seeking hundreds of thousands to spend on another.

So with requirements, shortcomings, waiting for Godot and guidance duly
disposed of, I will go on to what I wanted to talk about, in all its pristine unso-
phistication, and will come back within the hour to some comments on project
administration, software costs, and standardization that I gathered yesterday to
be of some concern.

Typing Computer Input

Most of the information that is immited to computers today is typed on keypunches and on tape perforating typewriters such as the Flexowriter and the
Duramatic. The keypunch is relatively inexpensive, but typing lower case letters
is awkward (though possible), and a separate machine (not necessarily the computer) is needed to get hard copy. The data that is punched in the card also is
printed near the top of the card, which makes a deck of cards a very convenient
medium for assembling a file of information for computer input. The cards can
be punched and printed, the printout proofread, more cards punched to replace
those that are in error, and the erroneous cards replaced by use of hand and eye,
without requiring the use of a computer, near or far. Considered as a machine,
someone doing a manual card file update can be described in pretty complicated
terms, by the time you throw in the evolution of the opposable thumb and the
nonlinear predictive extrapolation in the feedback between prehensile motor
control and retinal transducers; so by the standards of amenability to obscure
description, manual updating can be made respectable.

The Flexowriter and the Duramatic and other tape perforating typewriters are more expensive than card punches. They can be used to type in upper and lower case, they give hard copy, and after this has been proofread, the typist can put the tape into another part of the typewriter, and produce a new and hopefully correct tape by:

(i) pressing buttons to make the machine copy and correct portions of the first tape mechanically, and

(ii) typing corrections where needed

This makes it possible to produce very "clean" (*i.e.*, correct) tape for computer input, which can reduce the number of processing cycles through the computer, with an attendant reduction in computer costs and elasped time for the applications. Paper tapes can contribute to untidiness and are difficult to identify if the typist does not write an identifying comment on each tape, and file the hard copy systematically. Such actions, however, are within the realm of human competence. Getting information from a paper tape into a computer that is not equipped to read paper tape can be an incredible nuisance. If the computer installation is equipped with a paper tape reader, however, the operation is completely trivial, provided certain information, called the DCB parameters, which I'll come back to later are known. Some computer installations have paper tape readers and staff who will tell the users what DCB parameters to use.

Several other brands of paper tape typewriter are on the market, and also several keyboard machines that put information directly onto a magnetic tape, that in some cases can be fed directly to a computer, but in most requires a further piece of equipment to transfer the data to a tape that a computer can read. Consoles that are on-line to a computer can also be used to enter information. Whilst I question the economics of bulk input to a large general purpose computer from remote on-line keyboards, relative to off-line keyboarding costs, there is another development, illustrated by the Key-Edit, Key-Logic and similar machines that should be mentioned. These machines consist essentially of a bank of keyboards connected to a small computer that serves simply to feed onto different regions of a magnetic drum the data that the operators type. Periodically, the data is transferred en masse from the drum to magnetic tapes that then serve as input to the larger computers which are used to process the information. The small computer to which the keyboards are attached can perform a variety of formatting and checking operations that are economically advantageous in commercial computer installations that process voluminous data, and I think this approach merits consideration for some library and related situations.

Optical character recognition provides another input route. Several makes of OCR machines now put information onto magnetic tape from typed or handprinted documents. In simplisitic terms, increased variability of font and reliability of recognition can be achieved by some combination of increased cost, dependence on preprinted forms, and rigidity of format. This puts an organization that keyboards bulk information at the relatively happy end of the expense-reliability scale, since it can restrict typing to a single font and impose format constraints. A simple free-standing typewriter then can be used as the keyboard device, at the expense of using the optical scanner to produce magnetic tape from the typed copy.

I must stress that I have not explored the detailed economics of the last two kinds of equipment myself, but merely stated them as possibilities. The selection of an input route from any of those I've mentioned depends on an interplay of nitty gritty items of major economic significance such as the benefits of clean input to the computer, and the factors conducive to, or necessary for, fast accurate typing (*e.g.*, should hard copy be produced on the keyboard device or on a separate printer?). This interplay may be quite intricate and subtle but it can be discussed largely in common sense terms freed from pseudo-esoteric jargon, and as such, it can provide an interesting forum for getting people taped, in more senses than one.

Record and File Design

The design of records, the design of self-contained files, and the design of cross referenced files are now major elements in the course that I teach at Columbia on Computers and Librarianship. I start with a simple punched card file about Presidents of the United States, one card per President, that contains the President's surname, given names, enumeration, vital and office dates, party abbreviation and college of graduation (if any). The enumeration is punched in columns 1-2 of the card; the surname in columns 3 et seq, extending at most to column 12. If the surname doesn't reach this far, the columns of the card through column 12 are left unpunched. The first given name starts on column 13, and is followed by a space and the middle initial if there is one and, if necessary, further spaces to reach column 25. His year, month, and day of birth are punched in turn in columns 26-33. If he is still alive, columns 34-41 are left unpunched, otherwise his date of decease is punched in a similar manner, and so on (see Figure 1).

The cards that I am describing are said to be punched in fixed format, or fixed field format, because the field that contains a particular kind of item, such as a President's surname, occupies the same columns in each card. The deck of cards thus corresponds to a columnar table, from which the slashes between the year, month, and day numbers in the dates, and the spaces between the right edge of one (printed) column and the left edge of the next have been elided.

The computer has to do very little work with a file of this kind to print tabular displays. Thus, the successive lines in a table that lists surnames and dates of birth can be printed by the instruction

Print the 3-rd through 12-th characters of the record then " "
then the 30-th through 31st characters of the record then "/"
then the 32-nd through 33-rd characters of the record then "/"
then the 26-th through 29th characters of the record.

This statement is expressed in the language that I use for teaching purposes. It has equivalents in other programming languages, though these tend to be less like

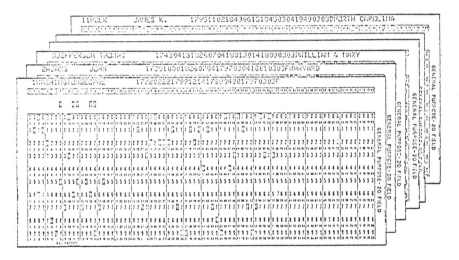

Figure 1

English. Very little time is needed to process the characters whose positions in the record are known in advance, and specified explicitly in the instruction. The computer takes a little longer, however, to extract from the file and incorporate surnames (and other items that vary in length from one person to another) in text messages such as "George Washington lived from . . . until . . ." without leaving redundant spaces after the given name and surname. The computer can do it easily enough by starting at the beginning of the given name field and testing successive characters until it encounters a space. This betokens the end of the first (or only) given name, and the computer keeps note of where it is. Similar tactics may be used to find the end of the surname. The computer can then print successive characters from the given name field, starting at the beginning of the field and stopping at the first space in it, and then print successive characters from the surname field, stopping at the first space which this field contains. The computer does this using the positions of the spaces which it had noted in the character-by-character scan to control the printing operation. The word "scanning" is used here for character-by-character testing within the computer. It has nothing to do with optical character recognition that is often called optical scanning. The kind of character-by-character scanning that I am talking about now is extremely useful. It has been central to much of my own work over the last ten years, but it does take time and it does cost money that should not be glossed over.

The Presidential data deck can be read into a computer and stored under a name that a user wishes to give to it for future reference, by simple tactics that I will describe shortly. For the moment I would like to develop the subject of record design a little further. Incidentally, I find that my class likes to have definitions of "record" and "file"; and I define them in the following way: a record is a body of organized information concerning a physical or abstract entity, and a file is an organized set of records that contains corresponding information about a set of entities of the same general kind. These entities were Presidents in the file that was just considered. They are magazine articles, in the file that is turned to next.

In my work at the H. W. Wilson Company, I am involved in some experiments to see if the new technology has any potential place in the production of Wilson Indexes. To this end, we have some programs that

    (i)   read bibliographic data about articles, poems, short stories, etc., which have been recorded on paper tape using a Dura machine,

    (ii) construct index entries from this data,

    (iii) sort the entries, and

    (iv) print them.

The experiments are still in an extremely elementary and inconclusive stage, and I mention them only because they come to mind as a convenient source of a second example of record design.

When input is typed for these experiments, each bibliographic datum is preceded by a number sign and a two-letter abbreviation, such as AR before the title of an article, AU before the name of an author, LO before the locator of the article, and so forth. The number sign together with one of these abbreviations constitute a precedence code, so called because it precedes the item it identifies. An @ symbol is typed at the end of the data about each article and poem and other published piece. This data constitutes a record, and a succession of these records for some corpus of indexed magazines constitutes a file. A few of these records are shown below, together with some of the index entries that were generated from the file in which these records occurred (Figures 2 and 3). A file of bibliographic records can be stored on disc by elementary use of the operating system. The computer can process the records systematically, finding the end of each record in turn, by testing the characters one by one until it comes to an @ symbol, which is called a delimiter in this context, since it delimits a body of information. The individual fields in a record that contains, for example, the title of an article or the name of an author are delimited by reference to the fact that each starts with a precedence code and is ended by the next such code, or by the terminal @. Some of the fields, moreover, are broken down into subfields by reference to internal punctuation, such as a comma between a surname and the given names in a personal name field, a slash after each item in the list of subject headings, and so forth. The scanning is performed by a particular type of program called a syntactic analyzer, or parser, that refers to a tabular description of the possible variations in structure of the records, which is very convenient during development work when this is likely to change. The purpose of this dissection of a record is to permit the construction of index entries in accordance with the appropriate cataloguing rules that are expressed by another table that a synthesizing program refers to (see reference (3), p. 142).

The Presidential data deck and the bibliographic tape differ conspicuously in that one is on cards and the other on paper tape. Moreover, one is typed using just capital letters, and the other is typed in upper- and lower-case. These are relatively superficial differences, however. The data on the tape could be transferred to cards by suitable equipment, if need be, and the information then read from the cards as a continuous stream. Conversely the information from the cards could be punched in a tape that had a carriage return every 80 characters, and faithfully mirrored every column of the card, complete with space codes in the tape for every column of a card that was not punched. The significant differences between the Presidential data deck and the bibliographic tape are twofold. Although Andrew Jackson did not go to college, space is provided all the same for the college field on his card—it is just left unpunched. No space, however, is left on the bibliographic tape for an unknown author when the author of an article is not known. The field that contains the title of the article is followed immediately by the precedence code for the next item which applies, such as the locator. The structure of the record in the Presidential data deck is fixed as regards the items for which fields are provided. Space is just left unoccupied if non-applicable. The structure of the record in the bibliographic file, however, may vary from one article to another. Fields are included in an individual record for just as many items or just as few items as apply, and the nature of each item is shown by the precedence code that precedes it.

There is a second difference. In the Presidential data deck ten columns are provided for the President's surname, whether he is Washington and needs them, or is an Adams and does not. No redundant space is left in the bibliographic tape, however, between items; the end of each is delimited by the number sign that begins the next precedence code.

The fields in the Presidential data deck are of fixed lengths that are maintained by padding with extra space when their contents vary in length. The obvious disadvantage of a fixed length field is that it can waste space, if the items punched in it for most of the records are much shorter than the longest. Since the computer can scan character-by-character for delimiters, this waste can be eliminated on cards as on tape by simply using variable length fields, and punching from left to right across the card, with a comma separating each item from the next. To print the sixth and third items from each successive record the computer can be instructed to scan for the fifth and sixth commas, then for the second and third commas, and to print what falls between these pairs of commas. Of course, the program that is dealing with the variable length items can be designed to keep tabs on all the commas that it passes, to avoid a rescanning such as just described, but this is not always done, and scanning times and costs can build up. Also, what do we do about people in the Presidential data deck who are happily still with us? If the computer is looking for an inaugural date between the fifth and sixth commas, willy nilly, it had better be there, whether or not there is a date of decease to go between the fourth and fifth commas. Put another way, there has to be the correct number of commas, even when there is nothing to go between some of them. Apart from contravening The H. W. Wilson prohibition of double punctuation it is very easy to lose or gain a comma when typing several in sequence with nothing between them, and this can make the computer treat one item of information as if it were an item of a completely different kind. Items whose significance is implied by their position within a sequence that is punctuated in this way are called positional parameters. The hazards of casting off commas can be avoided by the use of precedence codes, as illustrated by the bibliographic file I discussed before. This can be a mixed blessing, however, since it can lead to traps in which the computer, instead of testing each character once to determine if it is, say a comma, tests whole groups of characters against several different alternatives, and this can take very much longer.

It should be stressed then that there is no absolute merit to fixed length fields or to variable length fields, to positional parameters or to precedence coding. Each has potential benefits, and potential snags; and whilst deciding what is best in a particular situation may be extremely complicated, it is not a hopeless task, but one that an administrator can and should control. I will try to get back to this later, but while I am on the subject of record design I would like to complicate the picture just a little bit more by reference to the use of precedence codes in fixed length fields, and to a couple of terms I'm sure many of you have heard, heading counts and pointers.

At present, when the bibliographic data tape is typed on the Dura machine the typist presses the carriage return as soon as she wants to start typing another line, and it seems in some sense more "natural," both for typing and reading, to start a new line whenever a precedence code that starts a new field is encountered. Now the hard copy would look just the same if the typist spaced to a fixed right margin before pressing the carriage return, providing a fixed number of characters (including spaces) between successive carriage returns. Then, corresponding to the successive padded lines of input, each successive string of 50 characters would either

(i) begin with a # sign, when the line started with a precedence code, or

(ii) would not begin with a # sign, when the line simply continued an item from the line before.

It then would be necessary for the computer to look for a precedence code every 50 characters, without spending time scanning the characters in between. (The computer can skip a preset number of characters as quickly as it can move to the next.) Several other factors bear on whether this could save time; but if it could, how would the padding characters be provided? Certainly not by making the typist press the space bar. However, padding of this kind is completely standard in commercial keypunching operations, where it is controlled mechanically by a specially punched card that is wrapped around a small drum at the top of the keypunch. It is provided on the Key Logic kind of machine I described before without delaying the typist at all. Who knows but what it might be provided by a future model of the paper-tape reader that used a plugboard to extend the capability to recognize the end of a record that is set at present by switches.

On now to pointers. Character by character scanning can be avoided by giving the numbers that specify the positions of the ends of the successive items within a record to the computer. The positions are specified by imagining the characters that make up the record to be numbered 1, 2, and so on, from beginning to end. These numbers are known when instructions are written to process fixed field records, and they can be included in the instructions explicitly. When fields vary in length from one record to another, however, their positions cannot be included in the instructions, but they can be provided at the beginning of each record as a kind of "table of contents." If all the records in the file contain the same number of items, even though the lengths of the individual items vary from record to record, the table of contents of each record can consist of just the pointers to its constituent items (*i.e.*, the positions in the record of the first character of each item) without any further indication of what these items are. (An analogy would be the lists of page numbers at which sections start, in issues of a magazine which always has the same complement and arrangement of sections. If this is known to all the readers, the lists of page numbers serve as tables of contents of the issues, even though the lists omit the names of the sections.) If a file consists of records with varying structure, the lists of pointers can be expanded to include the nature of each item (*e.g.*, if it is a title of an article or an author), along with its starting position. Then to find an item in the record, the table of contents is examined, row by row, until a row is found that pertains to an item of the requisite kind. The pointers in this row and the next then can be used to get at the item itself. This approach has many refinements, that are often beneficial.

The table of contents principle can also be applied at a higher level to entire files. The time needed to perform many file handling processes can be reduced considerably by reference to a table of pointers to the natural subdivisions of the file, *e.g.*, the groups of records that have the same first letter in the key that is used to sequence the file. The pointers may be constructed by counting records within the file, or by counting individual characters. Some situations warrant a short table of contents to a more detailed table of contents of the entire file. Another variation of the table of contents principle uses "heading counts." This tactic is analogous to a book that had no table of contents, but started each chapter with a statement of the number of pages that the chapter contained. To find the beginning of chapter 10 a reader would proceed from the beginning of chapter 1 to the beginning of chapter 2, thence to the beginning of chapter 3, and so on. There are situations in which the computer equivalent of this is useful. It is somewhat tedious for the people who prepare and type data to provide the tables of pointers and heading counts, so the ability of the computer to count is usually employed to add this information to records that are typed without it to save enough time, when the files are used subsequently, to justify the cost of adding it.

Record and file design offer vast scope for variation, ingenuity and complexity, when all the stops are pulled and the full panoply of fixed and variable length records, table of pointers, heading counts, precedence codes, and worse have been included. The relevance of librarianship to this activity goes far beyond bibliographic data per se. The students in my course at Columbia are asked to design files of reference information (that is not exclusively bibliographic) on topics of their choice. I think that some of the traditional elements of librarianship, such as descriptive cataloguing and filing rules, are central to the effective use of computers in information systems. The extent of these rules provides a salutary indication of the magnitude of descriptive and filing problems to the uninitiated, and the rules themselves can serve as prototypes, or in some cases be used directly in the design of data bases. I am trying to develop a systematic approach to teaching record and file design and have enumerated some very elementary tactics in a recent paper. I do not know any simple guiding principle, except perhaps the use of common sense, and an awareness that intricate designs tend to be self-defeating. This does not mean, however, that simplicity excludes inefficiency. Some elaborate record and file designs, and the programs to deal with them, remind me of an old music hall sequence, in which the comic struggles around the stage, in a state of horrible contortion, supposedly imposed by his suit. After a long tirade about the tailor who made it, the comic delivers the punch line—"a man rushes over and asks who is your tailor—he must be a genius to fit a cripple like you." This may be a good time to change the subject.

Programming Languages and Tactics

As everyone knows, the computer has to be given instructions, and a set of instructions to make it do something constitutes a program. The computer manufacturers provide standard programs for certain processes that are widely used, such as putting files of data into the computer, updating these files, and printing them. These programs are called "data set utilities," in accordance with the use of the term "data set" for a file, which clashes unfortunately with its other use for a piece of equipment that sends data over a telephone. Standard program "packages" are also provided for standard scientific computations, such as the interpretation of certain kinds of experimental data, and for various commercial computations, such as occur in banking and insurance. A utility program or "package" requires the user to specify the details that characterize the job in hand, within the particular class of problem for which it was designed. In general these details are more numerous, the larger the class. Most packages and utilities are designed now to take certain things about a job for granted, unless the user actively specifies a departure from what exists as the norm in his working environment. The term "default option" is used in this regard—it is what happens if you keep quiet, and can differ from place to place, to meet local needs or traditions. For example, unless I wrote "Do not erase" on my blackboard at RCA it was erased. At The H. W. Wilson Company, unless I write "Please erase" it isn't.

The mechanics of using a standard utility program or package can be completely non-traumatic. In general, a "third generation" computer installation keeps a goodly collection of the utility programs, standard packages, compilers (which I'll explain shortly) and specialized programs of local interest in its magnetic archives—usually disc storage devices together with a catalog of where these programs are. A lot can be done with just a few of them. The general tactics may be illustrated by reference to a standard utility, that has the name IEBGENER, which is really no more repellent than the names of many of the books in your libraries. IEBGENER can read the data in a deck of cards and make the computer print it, or punch a duplicate, or record it on magnetic tape, or in the computer's magnetic archives; it can also make the computer take the data from a file that is already on a magnetic tape or in the magnetic archives and print it or punch it or write it afresh on tape or disc. About half a dozen cards are needed at worst to use IEBGENER for any of the processes I've just mentioned, in any IBM 360 installation that maintains the operating system in any semblance of normalcy. The cards that I use at the friendly neighborhood computer to print a deck are shown in Figure 4, and should require only trivial changes at most, to

```
//TRYGEN01 EXEC PGM=IEBGENER
//SYSPRINT DD SYSOUT=A
//SYSIN     DD DUMMY
//SYSUT2    DD SYSOUT=A,DCB=BLKSIZE=80
//SYSUT1    DD *
THIS PARAGRAPH, STARTING WITH THE PRESENT SENTENCE, AND ENDING WITH THE NEXT
LINE OF ASTERISKS, WAS PROVIDED ON PUNCHED CARDS IN THE INPUT STREAM, AS THE
INPUT DATA SET (SYSUT1) OF A JOB STEP (TRYGEN01) THAT USED IEBGENER TO PRINT
IT. THE SYSUT1 AND SYSUT2 DD STATEMENTS ARE:
 //SYSUT2 DD SYSOUT=A,DCB=BLKSIZE=80   AND   //SYSUT1 DD *
************************************************************************************
/*
```

Figure 4

run elsewhere. The first card* heralds the beginning of a job, by the presence of two slashes in columns 1 and 2, and the word JOB in columns 12-14. It requires the account number and the name of the user, and perhaps some innocuous gobblydegook that you can take for granted. The card is called, not too surprisingly, a job card. The next carries the message

Execute the program called IEBGENER

abbreviated to

EXEC PGM=IEBGENER

which likewise isn't too much to swallow. The slashes on columns 1 and 2 identify this card, like the JOB card, as one that communicates with the operating system. The abbreviated message to execute IEBGENER makes the operating system search the catalog of programs in its archives to find where the program

---

*This card is omitted from display.

called IEBGENER is stored, and having found it, to tell it to get cracking. Duly activated, IEBGENER is now agog with expectation of the so-called DD statements that are forthcoming, not so much in hope of salvation—DD stands for data definition, not Doctor of Divinity—but in order to find where it has to get the data from and send it to. The first DD statement that reads

//SYSIN DD DUMMY

is an unfortunate vestige of evolutionary development, that can just be taken for granted here. The next statement

//SYSPRINT DD SYSOUT=A

is a cryptic encoding of the fact that messages about the progress of the job (like "all is well" or otherwise) appear in the mainstream of printed output which is designated SYSOUT=A). Then come two really important DD cards—the one that is punched

//SYSUT2 DD SYSOUT=A,DCB=BLKSIZE=80

which connotes where information is to be sent to—in this case the mainstream of printed output too. (The further coded information DCB=BLKSIZE=80 is another detail of IEBGENER to be accepted, like some of the items on call slips in libraries.) The card that is punched

//SYSUT1 DD *

specifies where information is to come from. The * means the cards that follow. The end of the deck to be printed is marked by a card with a slash in column 1 and an * in column 2.

What I have just told you admittedly is technical, and a far cry from the English-like programming that I use in my course. It does provide a basis, however, for getting some first-hand experience of dealing with a computer in a way that is completely standard and which can provide some useful calibrations and insights. The coded information I have been describing is expressed in "job control language" or JCL for short. Within its somewhat weird conventions the mainstream of punched output is called SYSOUT=B; so to duplicate a deck of cards instead of printing it, simply replace the card

//SYSUT2 DD SYSOUT=A,DCB=BLKSIZE=80

by a card with B instead of A in the setup shown in Figure 4. To record the data in the cards on disc, the SYSUT2 card is changed again, to specify

(i) the unit on which the data should be recorded,

(ii) the space to be allocated for it,

(iii) the size of the records and the "blocking factor" that affects how
quickly it can be read back for processing (these constitute, in part,
the data control block (DCB) parameters), and

(iv) a name to refer to the file in subsequent jobs.

To print a file that has been put on disc in this or any other way, IEBGENER
can be used with a SYSUT1 card that specifies the name that the file was given
when it was catalogued, and a SYSUT2 card with SYSOUT=A. To punch a file
that has been catalogued on disc, use a SYSUT2 card with SYSOUT=B.

Suppose now that you often want to print decks of cards, and files that have
been written on magnetic tapes. The SYSIN and SYSPRINT and SYSUT2 cards
will not change, and can be eliminated by creating a "catalogued procedure."
The information in the set of JCL cards is given a name, say MYPRINT, and put
into the magnetic archives of the computer by a standard operation that is quite
trivial. A file can then be printed by a card that is punched //EXEC MYPRINT
and a //SYSUT1 card that identifies the file. The information called MYPRINT
constitutes a "catalogued procedure," since it is a procedure that is stored and
catalogued in the computer.

A program or a catalogued procedure can be executed several times within a
job. Several different programs and/or procedures can also be executed in a job.
Each execution is called a job step, and is triggered by an appropriate EXEC
card. This provides a convenient starting point for administrative control of computing expenses. The operating system allows a user to punch, on the EXEC
card, a limit on the time for which a step may run.

The execution of individual steps can be made contingent on the success or
failure of previous steps. The operating system can print meticulous records of
the time, and storage and other salient items used by each step, and by the entire job, and the cost computed in accordance with the rate structure of the installation.

The ability of the system to run a succession of job steps in the ways just described makes it possible to segment a big problem into steps that are each quite
short, and which can be tested individually, and often concurrently. Segmenting
a large job, moreover, can preclude the kind of waste that occurs all too often in
which the computer is left to run for an hour or two, on data that should take
this long to process, but because of an error in the program, triggers an hour or
two of futile cycling. The accounting information for successive job steps also
shows where improved efficiency can be most beneficial.

A utility or "package" program is used by specifying the characteristics that
define the individual problem in hand within the class of problems for which the

program has been written. Despite the power of many of these programs, an organization that uses computers usually needs some further programs that are specific to its activities, which have to be written in a general purpose programming language. A very simple program, written in the language called SNAP that I developed for teaching purposes is as follows:

Call "You cannot err or make a bloomer with the wares of ancient Sumer" the tag.
Print "Drinking mugs for the longest thirst." Print the tag.
Print "Chariots of distinction." Print the tag.
Print "Mosaics for porch or patio." Print the tag. Execute.

This makes the computer print two-line display labels for the Mesopotamian Merchants Mart at the Pax Romana Trade Fair. It saves human effort since the instructions that the user types contain fewer key strokes than the labels that the computer prints. The grammatical elements of SNAP that are used in this example also permit the production of personalized form letters, catalog cards, index entries, and processional scenes of stylized animals and vistas of palm trees and desert islands (which illustrate a non-frivolous technical point). The SNAP procedure just given consists of statements (*i.e.*. sentences) that begin with imperative verbs. A SNAP procedure, in general, contains a succession of imperative sentences that begin with verbs such as Print, Call (in the sense of give a name to), Read, Copy, Insert, Delete, Overwrite and Append, whose objects are strings of characters, and Set, Increase and Decrease that operate on numbers. A SNAP procedure also may contain conditional sentences that consist of:

(i) the word IF,
(ii) a condition to be tested (*e.g.*, "the 5th and subsequent charcters of the record are the same as the reference key"),
(iii) the action to be taken when the condition is met, and
(iv) the word OTHERWISE and the action to be taken when the condition is not met.

The computer executes the statements in a procedure one by one in sequence, until it comes to a "branch instruction" that sends it to a statement somewhere else, in a manner analogous to a taxpayer filing a tax return. Lines on an income tax form are identified by number. A statement in a SNAP procedure is identified by a parenthesized name that precedes it, for example, "last ditch action," that is cited in statements such as "continue with the last ditch action." A SNAP procedure may also contain indicative mood statements that define, for example, the structure of input material to be dissected for processing.

A program written in a "manufacturer's" language such as FORTRAN, COBOL, ALGOL, or PL1 looks somewhat different from one in SNAP, but the

basic principles are much the same. These languages are called "high level," in
contrast to the "lower level" (or "assembly") languages which are closer to the
"machine language" which the computer's circuits decode and act on directly.
The manufacturers' high-level languages contain many more elements than SNAP
does at present, and permit more efficient use of the computer for most purposes,
but SNAP is useful pedagogically, and some practical use of it is beginning. The
manufacturers provide special programs called compilers and assemblers to translate programs into machine language from high- and low-level languages, respectively. I have written programs exclusively in FORTRAN, since it became available. The SNAP processor is written in FORTRAN, as were the typesetting and
other text processing programs that I developed previously. I do not want to argue the merits of one high-level language over another—such arguments are often
just rationalizations of confidence in the familiar, and unawareness of the capabilities of the unfamiliar. The use of FORTRAN has enabled me to transfer programs from one computer to another untrammeled by differences of model (even
generation) or manufacturer (even nationality), per se, and relatively untrammeled by differences of operational ritual between installations of the same
model of computer. The continued availability of FORTRAN and COBOL compilers on future computers seems assured by the extent to which these languages
are used at present. The merits of using high (as opposed to low) level languages
to program computer applications have been argued extensively (see, e.g., reference 5, p. 218). In addition to transferability and stability of programs there is
the relative ease of learning to read and to write programs in a high-level language,
and actually reading and writing them. Writing programs with an eye to intelligibility and providing good documentation are factors conducive to effective use
of personnel and equipment, when the programs are written, when they are
copied, and when they are modified, for use in the same or in another environment. Of course the level of a language does not in itself ensure intelligibility,
and some programmers tend to use "powerful" constructions of "sophisticated"
high-level languages to perpetrate miracles of unintelligible inefficiency. A simple
style can be very effective in programming, as in ordinary writing.

In contrast to high-level languages such as FORTRAN, a low-level language
(i.e., assembly language) permits actions to be expressed in terms of actual machine operations, that may provide higher speed, or be essential to using special
attachments to a computer. There can be merit to encoding a highly repetitive
element of a computer application in a low-level language as a "sub-program"
that is invoked by a high-level program for the overall application. Doing this,
however, is often best deferred until programs that are written in a high-level
language, and easily changed, have been used to explore the overall logic ade-

quately, since it is possible to lavish effort streamling an operation that can be made a non-critical element of an application by reorganizing the overall approach. The high-level language PL1 does permit reference to machine functions (so did FORTRAN III), but I do not think that this has closed the door on conjoint use of say FORTRAN IV and assembly language subprograms.

The effects of varying the overall design of a program, and the design of the records and files that it processes, can be explored both experimentally and theoretically, to determine which provide the "optimum," *i.e.*, best way to proceed. This is called optimization. Timing and related information can be recorded by the job accounting capabilities of the operating system that were mentioned earlier, and at a greater level of detail by including, within the user's program, special instructions to record the duration and frequency of constituent processes. Theoretical analyses offer vast scope for the application of certain mathematical notations and techniques, that are now grouped under the general heading of "finite mathematics," and known more technically as "combinatorial mathematics" and "graph theory." This material is presented for humanists already in some university courses and texts.[4] I hope that it will gain acceptance in library school curricula before long.

I have tried to talk a little about the various matters I was supposed to address, and I see that standardization, on-line debugging, software costs and project administration are still on the list. A wealth of standard equipment and software is now available and should be used wherever possible. Statements concerning its unusability should be reviewed critically, and reinventing the wheel at vast expense should be discouraged. So should measures that force an installation out of compatibility with others by departing from widely used standards. Commonality of library operations should be made the basis of standard program modules, where this is reasonable, but doctrinaire pursuit of standardization where it is inappropriate can be very destructive.

As regards on-line debugging, the prospect of latter-day infant Schuberts doing keyboard improvisation at a console has long filled me with profound unenthusiasm, and it still does. We hear a lot about the dangers of frustration if a programmer cannot get an instantaneous response from the computer, and the dangers of frustration if the research student cannot get an immediate answer from a data bank. I debug my programs using batch processing in commercial installations where the turnaround time varies from a few minutes to a few hours. I try to submit jobs that each test several features of a program, and to have several such series of tests going in parallel. Most runs produce a volume of output that is inspected most conveniently as hard copy from a line printer, rather than by looking at a console display.

Designing a series of programming tests takes some effort and concentration. So does designing a scientific experiment, and setting it up. In a serious literature search, time has to be spent reading, comprehending implications, and deciding what to seek next in an orderly, organized manner. Has low frustration tolerance been a conspicuous characteristic of successful scientific or humanistic research of the past? I wonder to what extent the avowed needs of the users and the implementers of some computer applications today are just posturings, perhaps encouraged or even initiated by the debasement of the words "research" and "creativity" in the grade schools. Some rather vast expenditures seem to have rather flimsy premises. On the general matter of software costs, the attitude seems quite rife that nothing significant can be done—not even a feasibility study of a major application—without spending hundreds of thousands, perhaps millions, of dollars. I think that these sums should be measured in the tens of thousands.

As regards project administration, I know of no panacea, in computing or in any other area of professional activity. Having confidence that you can understand what goes on, and putting this to the test of asking questions, and persisting until you are satisfied that the answers really make sense, can be a large part of the battle. I hope today's talk will lead some of you to ask some questions.

References

1. M. P. Barnett, Computer Programming in English, Harcourt, Brace, and World, New York, 1969.
2. M. P. Barnett, SNAP—A Programming Language for Humanists, Computing and the Humanities, 4 (4), 225, 1970.
3. M. P. Barnett, Teaching Humanists to Use Computers with SNAP, Proceedings of the World Conference on Computer Education, III/137-144, International Federation for Information Processing, Amsterdam, 1970.
4. See, for example:
   Charles K. Gordon, Jr., Introduction to Mathematical Structures, Dickenson Publishing Company, Inc., Belmont, California, 1967.
   Marvin Marcus, A Survey of Finite Mathematics, Houghton Mifflin, Boston, 1969.
   F. Harary, R. Z. Norman, and D. Cartwright, Structural Models: An Introduction to the Theory of Directed Graphs, Wiley, New York, 1965.
5. M. P. Barnett, Computer Typesetting—Experiments and Prospects, MIT Press, Cambridge, 1965.

```
#CO
#AR Introductory essay
#AU Millikan, Max Franklin
#LO Int Org 22:1-15 Wint'68
#AR United Nations as an instrument of economic and social development
#AU Kotschnig, Walter M.
#LO Int Org 22:16-43 Wint'68
#SB United Nations
#AR Role of trade in economic development
#AU Frank, Isaiah
#LO Int Org 22:44-71 Wint'68
#SB Commerce
#AR General agreement on tariffs and trade
#AU Evans, John W.
#LO Int Org 22:72-98 Wint'68
#SB General agreement on tariffs and trade
#AR United Nations conference on trade and development
#AU Gardener, Richard N.
#LO Int Org 22: 99-130 Wint'68
#SB United Nations conference on trade and development
#AR International monetary fund
#AU Bernstein, Edward Morris
```

Figure 2   Input Stream

O ⎯⎯ Animal mechanics--Early works to 1800
O ⎯⎯⎯ De motibus animalium; ed by H. Shapiro and F. Scott
⎯⎯ J. Buridan. Isis 58:533;52 Wint'67

O ⎯⎯⎯⎯⎯⎯⎯⎯⎯⎯⎯⎯⎯⎯⎯⎯⎯⎯⎯⎯⎯⎯⎯⎯⎯⎯⎯⎯⎯⎯⎯⎯⎯⎯

Asher, Robert Eller
O ⎯⎯ International agencies and economic development: an
overview. Int. Org 22: 432-58 Wint'68

O ⎯⎯⎯⎯⎯⎯⎯⎯⎯⎯⎯⎯⎯⎯⎯⎯⎯⎯⎯⎯⎯⎯⎯⎯ ⎯⎯⎯

O ⎯⎯ Auden, Wystan Hugh and Taylor, Paul B.
(trs) Skirnir's ride (poem). Mass R 9:241-6 Spr '68

O ⎯⎯⎯⎯⎯⎯⎯⎯⎯⎯⎯⎯⎯⎯⎯⎯⎯⎯⎯⎯⎯⎯⎯⎯⎯⎯⎯⎯⎯⎯⎯⎯

O ⎯⎯ Bernstein, Edward Morris
International monetary fund. Int Org 22:131-51
Wint'68

O ⎯⎯⎯⎯⎯⎯⎯⎯⎯⎯⎯⎯⎯⎯⎯⎯⎯⎯⎯⎯⎯⎯⎯⎯⎯⎯⎯⎯⎯⎯⎯⎯

O ⎯⎯⎯⎯ · ⎯⎯⎯⎯⎯⎯⎯⎯⎯⎯⎯⎯⎯⎯⎯⎯⎯⎯⎯⎯⎯⎯⎯⎯⎯⎯⎯
Bloch, Henry Simon
Regional development financing. Int. Org 22:131-51
O Wint'68

O ⎯⎯⎯⎯⎯⎯⎯⎯⎯⎯⎯⎯⎯⎯⎯⎯⎯⎯⎯⎯⎯⎯⎯⎯⎯⎯⎯⎯⎯⎯⎯⎯

⎯ Blough, Roy
O ⎯⎯ World bank group. Int Org 22:152-81 Wint'68

O ⎯⎯⎯⎯⎯⎯⎯⎯⎯⎯⎯⎯⎯⎯⎯⎯⎯⎯⎯⎯⎯⎯⎯⎯⎯⎯⎯⎯⎯⎯⎯⎯

Buridan, Jean
O ⎯⎯ De motibus animalium; ed by H. Shapiro and F. Scott
⎯ Isis 58:533-52 Wint'67

O ⎯⎯⎯ · ⎯⎯⎯⎯⎯⎯⎯⎯⎯⎯⎯⎯⎯⎯⎯⎯⎯⎯⎯⎯⎯⎯⎯⎯⎯⎯⎯⎯

O ⎯⎯ Coffin, Frank Morey
Multilateral assistance: possibilities and
prospects. Int.Org 22:270-87 Wint'68
O

O ⎯⎯⎯⎯⎯⎯⎯⎯⎯⎯⎯⎯⎯⎯⎯⎯⎯⎯⎯⎯⎯⎯⎯⎯⎯⎯⎯⎯⎯⎯⎯⎯

Figure 3   Output Display

Administrative Commitment and a Course of Action: A Panel Discussion

Moderators: Warren J. Haas
Director of Libraries
Columbia University

Panelists: David C. Weber
Director of Libraries
Stanford University Libraries

John P. McDonald
Director of Libraries
University of Connecticut Libraries

David Kaser
Director of Libraries
Cornell University Libraries

Carlos A. Cuadra
Manager
Library and Documentation Systems Department
System Development Corporation
Santa Monica, California

Introduction

Warren J. Haas   Columbia University Libraries

This is the administrator dominated portion of the program in which we hope to shed some light on administrative concerns. The members of the panel will consider the advantages and disadvantages of several alternate courses of action that might be selected to carry out a decision to automate a substantial segment of library activity.

We hope that the three library directors on the panel will focus their most critical administrative attention on an appraisal of the approaches they have taken, indicating shortcomings as well as advantages.

David Weber will concentrate on what might be called independent development by looking at Stanford's experience of throwing a massive institutional capability into an automation effort. John McDonald will focus on the NELINET project, where several libraries have joined together to hire a commercial firm to carry out the automation objectives of the consortium. David Kaser will report on a different approach, one where five academic libraries in New York State's clean air district have joined to create an organization to carry out common objectives. Our fourth panelist, Carlos Cuadra, is involved with library operations and appraisals of library efforts on many fronts in his work. He will consider the prospect of commercial services for research libraries. He will look not only at the advantages but the disadvantages as well.

Before turning to our panelists, however, I would like to spend a minute or two recording observations on some topics that might in any reasonable world be acknowledged to be at least pertinent for consideration before committing a library to a major automation program.

There are many reasons why libraries have moved to adopt computers. They have acted in some instances because of convictions held in certain circles that computers obviously offer the only hope for salvation and operating efficiency. In some cases libraries have moved to automate because of faculty and administrative pressure, sometimes for reasons of prestige, and, on occasion, even because of an institutional computer capacity that's not being fully used. Others have gone ahead because of a feeling that computers represent a capability that will be required in the future, although the purposes to which that capability might be put are far from clear.

It's impossible to know for sure, but I doubt that automation activity has commonly grown from analysis of specific library service objectives, an appraisal of the relative importance of those objectives, and, finally, a review of all realistic alternative ways to those established goals. While this kind of careful decision making process has not always been followed in the past, it is essential that it begin now. The time has come when all library activities, including automation programs, must be carefully scrutinized in the context of academic objectives and library obligations.

But let us assume that a decision to move into a major program of automation is in fact the result of a rational process. What are the implications? In thinking about this topic in recent weeks, we have listed quite a few items that are obviously inherent in such a decision. We have also come upon some that should perhaps be more prominent in our minds than they are. In the next few minutes let me simply identify some of these implications of automation that should enter into the thinking of administrative affairs.

First is the matter of cost. Perhaps it's not fashionable to be concerned with such details but believe me, the topic has taken on a new reality. Paul Fasana distributed yesterday a summary of Columbia's true costs.[1] Some of the elements are estimates to be sure, but the figures for five years of efforts still add up to more than a million dollars. They indicate a current level of expenditure of more than three hundred thousand dollars and they suggest that even after five years, about 75 percent of expenditures are still in the development column and only 25 percent are producing products pertinent to operations.

From what we have heard, the picture is not much different at Stanford or Chicago. I'm not judging these facts. The evidence is simply that at the stage of development being reported here, library automation is expensive. This is not an implication—it's a fact to be reckoned with by any responsible administrator. The costs described have to be accepted and budgeted for, and ways have to be found to reduce costs and still produce results. The implication is that the library or the university will do without some of the things that automation support money would have bought.

Second, I would say if the reasons for proceeding are sound and the costs acceptable, there are still some implied administrative obligations. It is not enough to say, "go to it . . . call me when we are automated." Administrative officers have a responsibility to monitor progress, they have a responsibility to assess the products in the light of the promises, they have a responsibility to promote full utilization of developed systems, and they have an obligation to insist that every possible benefit be squeezed out of automation activity. For example, computer based circulation systems that don't automatically provide sophisticated statistical information about use of the collections are less than perfect automated systems. The same might be said of processing systems that fail to measure and assess the flow of materials through the system.

Now, let me bypass some lesser concerns and concentrate on a category of implications that I might characterize as "new dependencies."

The process of automation generates a new, important, and complex series of dependencies for library administrators and library users alike. I would never suggest that any library staff should be composed of interchangeable parts, but somehow the departure of a reference librarian with a background in American history who is replaced by one with a background in English literature does not seem to generate the shock waves that inevitably come when a senior systems analyst with the acquisition system fully documented in his mind elopes with the junior programmer who is half way finished with a new fiscal control system and both move to Aspen, Colorado. I don't think I resent the impact of this kind of defection as much as I feel concerned about the lack of an equal effect occasioned by the departure of the fully competent bibliographer. In any event, I wouldn't underestimate the extent of this new dependence, which is inversely proportional to the size of the systems staff.

There are dependencies on other levels as well. For example, library performance suddenly becomes a function of computer center performance, which is in turn hardly affected at all by libraries. Even more complex is a new kind of dependency that develops when individual librarians commit themselves to design their systems to that they will be integrated with and functionally dependent upon the performance of regional or national systems.

Each new level of system integration implies a greater dependency. It is possible that individual libraries are getting into an awkward position of assuming new responsibilities while at the same time they are reducing their ability to guarantee the quality of their own performance. There seems to be only two possible ways out of this dilemma. Either we develop a new operating philosophy that actually fragments and distributes operating responsibility among a number of service activities, or else we find effective ways for individual libraries to actively take part in the process of setting objectives and priorities for the central agencies on which we depend for our own performance.

I could talk about more implications inherent in automation decisions—the commitment of time which in the end is the same as the commitment of money, not doing things that would otherwise be done, a real reduction in operating flexibility growing out of the shadow of major investments, the need for new staffing patterns, and new staff responsibilities, etc. But I will stop here with a story about an English speaking lecturer addressing an audience that understood only Chinese. He had made arrangements for a crude kind of translation. The translator was to write the appropriate Chinese characters on a blackboard. The speaker started to talk, and talked for some time. The translator did nothing. Finally, the speaker stopped and said, "Why aren't you writing?" His translator said, "Chinese characters represent ideas, not words, and I'm still waiting."

I hope there might by now be one idea on the blackboard and that the panel will fill it.

References

1. See Section I, *The Columbia Experience*, by P. Fasana.

Independent Development

David C. Weber Stanford University Libraries

What has been the exact nature of Stanford's commitment given the style and pattern of development that Mr. Veaner and his colleagues described earlier in this conference? In retrospect it is clear that the Library and the University did not at first recognize the magnitude of its commitment. Partly due to our striking success with the book catalog design, we thought we fully understood the complexities of a major library system and we further thought that the computer specialists had grossly and totally underestimated the effort required. In fact we underestimated it almost to the same extent that we thought the computer specialists underestimated it. A dependable on-line system is *many* times more complex than any off-line system. It is difficult to scale this difference numerically, but at various times we have estimated that the BALLOTS system is 20 to 50 times more complex than the batch system used to produce the Meyer Library book catalog. So here we are three and a half years later, committed to achieve a successful design; and we now finally have in sight a sound and reasonably economic system.

There are three kinds of commitment.

The first commitment that can be mentioned is that of *manpower.* The staff effort in the Automation Department has varied from nine persons at the earliest time up to some twenty-five at the peak. In addition to this, the regular library departments and administrative officers have made major contributions of staff time, from professionals as well as library assistants, an amount which provided an additional 18% beyond the full-time staff. This effort has had a significant effect on manual operations—productivity and output have been maintained with difficulty. The Director of Libraries rather consistently has devoted 15% of his time to participating in this effort. One notes a sharp increase in staff effort as we progress from the prototype operating system, which was demonstrated in the spring of 1969, to the greater efforts to design the production system in which we are now in midstream.

This commitment of manpower also means convincing individuals that it is worth the effort. It takes time at Administrative Conferences, at Staff Association meetings, at regular automation briefing sessions, at coffee breaks, and at employment interviews. It requires that project leaders and department chiefs can describe the rationale behind the effort and how all staff members participate in one way or the other. Personnel at all levels of the organization must be convinced of the desirability of the enterprise. The long-term nature of complex development projects also means putting up with long periods of frustration at lack of immediately useful results and continuously convincing the staff that the effort is worthwhile.

Furthermore, it takes conviction from the budgetary officers, the Computation Center, Administrative Data Processing Center, fund-raising staff, and it is a help to have a faculty advisory committee which understands and supports the promise of library automation.

Stanford was fortunate in having as Associate Provost for Computing, Professor William F. Miller, now Vice President for Research, who had extraordinary national stature in the development and management of computational facilities and a conviction that there was utility in and need for library automation. Without his help, and the collateral support from the Vice Provost and the Director of the Computation Center, we could never have made the strides that have been made.

Another commitment is that of local *dollars*. This takes two forms. One of these is the matching expenditure commitment under the terms of the USOE grant, which includes the continuing general funds support for the Automation Department's core efforts. This financial support is essential so as to demonstrate to the library staff, to budget officers, as well as to funding agencies that the University is deeply serious in achieving an effective and operational system. In Stanford's case this total library cost-sharing contribution has approximated half of the direct project personnel expenses.

The second kind of dollar commitment is University long-range financial planning in support of the conversion to an operational system. This takes some boldness on the part of the University's Provost and Vice President for Finance so that in long-term budget forecasts there can be reasonable funding earmarked for that purpose. In days when universities are having exceedingly difficult financial times, one can appreciate the magnitude of such a commitment. The incremental cost of putting up a major on-line system may be from $250,000 to $450,000 per year depending on many local factors. The investment required to convert basic library operations to a heavily on-line machine system is in the range of one or two million dollars.

A third kind of commitment is that of *space*. Stanford started with three rooms of 1600 sq. ft. The staff somehow survived in this space throughout the prototype system development, but then moved to two "portable space" trailers of 2100 sq. ft. This additional room was needed as the work moved from system analysis into system design and programming so that the staff could be near the Computation Center. This new space annually requires University general fund support from the Library's automation budget. In plans for Stanford's new library building 4,500 sq. ft. are reserved for the computer, staff, data storage, etc.

Let me emphasize that the project has succeeded as well as it has due, in my judgment, to the extraordinary efforts and convictions of several key individuals. There has been the top library administration which I suppose carries some of the credit for the esprit de corps and administrative backing. There certainly is the Assistant Director for Bibliographic Operations who has often faced exceedingly discouraging conditions and maintained unstinting efforts to assure success. There are the department chiefs of acquisition, cataloging, government documents, and circulation who have given strong support. In planning the data computer facility on which the Administrative Data Processing and the Library will merge their operations, there is the Associate Controller who helped greatly in the Meyer Book Catalog and is a strength in realizing the importance of library automated operations and the soundness of progress to this end. Professor Edward B. Parker, as Special Assistant to the Director of Libraries for Computer Applications, has provided crucial assistance. The Vice President for Research, as mentioned above, was a key individual from his position as Chairman of the BALLOTS/SPIRES Executive Committee.

Let me now allude to some of the advantages and disadvantages in the kind of approach to library automation which has been followed at Stanford. Some of these may also have been referred to in presentations of the preceeding speakers; I trust our discussions may help clarify the fine points which make one factor an advantage or disadvantage, or perhaps a mixed blessing, in one or another type of automation project.

First, the four *disadvantages* that can be discerned. These include the fact that the rate of progress is constrained by the local hardware and the system software. If the Computation Center or Administrative Data Processing is designed for batch jobs or for massive computational tasks it may be wrong for the library. Work on somebody else's special-purpose machine may be far better.

Secondly, funding is more risky if you proceed alone than if you work as part of a consortium. This is partly because of the views of funding agencies which may find it more attractive to work with groups instead of singling out one institution.

Third, in a large and complex project, there is the ever-present danger that the many parts of the total effort cannot be coordinated towards achieving an operational system. Without an experienced and determined technical manager, much effort can be dissipated along the bypaths and backwaters of interesting research problems not altogether relevant to implementation. Only the largest projects offer professional challenge to the scarce top talent.

Fourth, there is an increased risk that a system developed solo may have less transferability, have reduced compatibility with national standards, and fail to see local peculiarities that consequently get built into the automated design.

Turning now to six *advantages*, and I suspect that these will also be found in some shape in projects of a different structure. One point is that the program can be attuned to local priorities within the library system. Thus if Stanford believes that a cataloging system should come first, it can do so without having to convince others; or it can choose the undergraduate library as a first cataloging implementation whether or not other participants have an undergraduate library; or it can eliminate the main entry concept and fully accept the Anglo-American code and alter filing rules in order to affect computer applications without compensating to the constraints of other organizations. This is a very substantial advantage of an organization "going it alone." You have only yourself to blame if you have not chosen the right targets or moved at the right pace.

A second advantage is that the design can be most soundly constructed by those who will actually operate it. Daily in-person consultation between, for example, cataloging staff and design team, produces effective results.

Thirdly, staff communication will be clear and rapid. This goes without saying, perhaps, yet one must not understate the importance of facilitating frequent spur-of-the-moment talks to review a document or see a flow chart. The weekends seem frequent when I've received a lengthy draft document and reacted by Monday morning.

Fourthly, a system will be thoroughly understood and supported by the staff that participated extensively in each element of the design, and this has major impact in rapid implementation and effective use of the new system.

Fifth, the rate of progress will not be held back by the weakest among a group of collaborating institutions. This gain also includes the time that may be required to prepare special reports or special presentations to provide tutorial help from the strongest to the others.

Sixth, it will generally, although not necessarily, be less costly. In working by oneself, there is, of course, no commercial profit that needs to be earned, and neither is there the extra cost of transportation or communication with organizations a mile or more distant. (This may, of course, be offset if one needs to use consultants for talent not available on campus, or if the local computer is not suitable and it requires going to and taking data files to another computer.)

One might generalize by saying that, considering all disadvantages and advantages, a decision to proceed on one's own is sound only if there is the proper mix of adequate money, manpower, space and specialized talents. In institutions where these exist, an independent advance into library automation would seem on balance the most effective and efficient means.

NELINET: One Approach to Library Automation

John P. McDonald   University of Connecticut Libraries

As I understand it, my function is to discuss the implications of an administrative decision to automate library operations by means of an interinstitutional
cooperative, more particularly, a regional association involving medium-size university libraries. I suspect that there is no one in this room who has not heard of
NELINET, and some of you may know more about it than I do myself. But on
the off chance that the growing NELINET bibliography has escaped your notice,
I shall describe the project briefly. To this end I am doing a bit of paraphrasing
of the January 1969 issue of The New England Library Association *Newsletter.*
In that issue Samuel Goldstein, then NELINET project director, wrote somewhat
as follows: "The New England Library Information Network (NELINET) is a regional center for the provision of computer-aided services in New England libraries. Sponsored by the New England Board of Higher Education, funded by a series of grants from the Council on Library Resources and the U.S. Office of
Education, and implemented by Inforonics, Incorporated of Maynard, Massachusetts, NELINET has progressed from an initial systems analysis of the six New
England State university libraries to a pilot operation in which five of these libraries receive customized cataloging products, conventional catalog cards (with call
numbers and overprinted headings) and book labels. Additional services now being developed or planned include acquisitions (searching, order control, processing, and accounting); accession list, and bookform catalog production; circulation
and interlibrary loan control; library management information; and remote data
base interrogation."

That is what NELINET is and hopes to be; now let me describe from the
point of view of the University of Connecticut Library what I see as some of the
results of our decision to automate by way of the cooperative route.

First I must tell you very briefly what the University of Connecticut Library
is like. It is what I call a "nouveau riche" library. By that I mean that it has more
than tripled its holdings over the past decade, has increased eightfold the number
of volumes added annually, and has annual operating expenditures in 1970 of
more than 2.2 million as compared with almost exactly one tenth that amount in
1960. It serves 15,000 undergraduate and 5,000 graduate students now as compared with 9,000 undergraduate and 2,000 graduate students in 1960. Depending
upon how you look at it, this is a gratifying or horrifying record. In either case
we see a very young library with a range of problems brought on by rapid growth

NELINET: ONE APPROACH TO LIBRARY AUTOMATION 103

upon which it did not seem wise to place the added burden of inhouse automation. Because similar conditions existed within the other New England state university libraries, in 1964 the directors of these libraries began seriously to discuss how they could make a common attack on operating problems through the use of the emerging computer technology. NELINET today is the result of those early discussions, and that phase of the development of the project is well described by Donald Vincent, director of the University of New Hampshire Library, in the June 1967 *ALA Bulletin.* So much for the background.

What are the effects within the participating libraries of the decision to take a cooperative approach towards automation?

These effects can, I believe, best be seen in terms of varying sets of relationships. I would mention first *over-all relationships,* involving the participating libraries, the prime contractor, the central project staff, and funding agencies. Next are what might be called *internal relationships* having to do with how the cooperative project is viewed by the library staff, the faculty, the university administration, and students. (Nowadays one must not fail to take into account the attitudes and interests of students.) The third set of relationships are those which develop between the cooperative project and *the larger library community.* I have in mind regional planning groups such as the New England Library Association's Regional Planning Committee, the library development branches of state libraries, or the commonly-found development committees of state library associations. In this category one might place the State commissions of higher education; other networks and consortia, both local and regional, as well as other libraries which may aspire to membership in the network.

To develop this outline completely would take far more time than I have at my disposal; therefore, let me only mention within each of these sets of relationships one or two problems that seem to me typical of the many that we have encountered in the development of NELINET. Within the first category I would observe that relations among the participating libraries have on the whole been excellent, but differing degrees of commitment to the project are always perceivable. These may derive from differing conceptions of the network and its services; they may derive from impatience with the pace of cooperative development; or they may derive from differences in institutional ability to go-it-alone in some aspect of automation. On the other hand a project such as the one in which we are involved, which uses an outside contractor for research and development, has at least one distinct advantage. It avoids the suspicion that any one institution is dominating the system and is imposing its methods and procedures on the other participants.

Relationships between the participating libraries and the project staff and the prime contractor have usually been smooth, but from time to time it has seemed to the head librarians that the staff and the contractor tend to lose sight of local needs because they are not involved on a daily basis in any ongoing library operation. On the other hand, it could be argued that this very condition makes possible a greater objectivity as the project staff and the contractor choose among the available alternatives for technical development.

As for the relationship between the project staff and the prime contractor, I think it is no secret that the most serious problem we in NELINET have faced lies in the area of proprietary rights to programs and other softwear. Such problems will arise where a project uses an outside contractor who is involved in similar work for other clients. In this situation it is difficult for the contractor to say with complete certainty "this is yours and this is mine." What he is more likely to say is, "This is ours."

Let me turn now to the second category, that of the internal relationships which come to light within a member library. First I would note that for every library that is involved with a remotely-based automation effort, a sharp difference can arise between the degree of commitment of the administrative staff on the one hand, and of the technical services staff on the other. The separate outside project does, I believe, make it more difficult to achieve local commitment from the operating or line staff. Further I would say of a project such as ours, which at the moment provides only a fraction of our cataloging, that it is difficult to achieve good articulation between the local services and the remotely-derived services. Counterbalancing these problems, however, are a number of salutary effects that arise from the necessity to reach cooperative decisions. Take red subject headings for example. The library that is involved in inhouse automation and has always used red subject headings is more likely, I suspect, to retain them than the library that is automating cooperatively and must abide by a group decision. At this point let me state somewhat parenthetically my belief that cooperative automation may have the effect of reducing internal consistency within the records of an individual library. On the other hand it should have the effect of bringing about greater consistency with *national* bibliographic standards. Working cooperatively the NELINET libraries have had a high degree of awareness of developing national standards, and we hope very strongly that NELINET will achieve the kind of symbiotic relationship with the RECON Project and other national efforts that it has so far enjoyed with MARC.

I should like to mention one other local effect of a remotely-based automation project. Such a project is an extremely convenient answer to those members of the faculty and administration who exert great and usually premature pressure to automate library operations. These are the people who actually expect an answer when they ask you the question, "When are you going to computerize your library?" To be able to point to a cooperative project can be a very good and useful thing in the library with an undersized and undertrained staff. This tactic is only permissible so long as the cooperative is not allowed to become window-dressing, but is instead vigorously promoted in an effort to secure local support.

Now just a word about the relationship of the cooperative project to the larger library community. The example that comes most readily to mind involves the relationship between the project and other plans for regional library development. If, like NELINET, the project appears to be successful it will probably create a certain amount of envy, and envy will in turn breed a certain amount of criticism. For this reason it is vital for the project staff and the participating libraries to take pains to design the project so as to complement other cooperative activities and to avoid duplication of effort in a field in which there is so much to be done that competition cannot be accepted.

By way of conclusion, I want to make one or two general observations about how NELINET has affected other forms of cooperation among the participants. There is no doubt in my mind that the NELINET experience has encouraged us to undertake a variety of cooperative enterprises that might not otherwise have been attempted. Once the head librarians learned that they could work together, then the reference librarians, the documents librarians, and the acquisitions librarians found that they too could work successfully on common problems. As a result, the NELINET libraries have published a joint list of major microform holdings, have reached a formal agreement for joint use in line with the requirement of the U.S. Office of Education for a Title II-A Special Purpose Grant, have developed a regional interlibrary loan code, and have established procedures for using the NELINET teleprinter circuit to expedite interlibrary loans. As a group the head librarians have met with the graduate deans of participating institutions to consider the possibility of specialization in academic programs as a means of reducing library commitments. Nothing much has yet come of this attempt but it remains one of the most important avenues of future endeavor.

As I think of other possibilities for future cooperation I become increasingly convinced that those of us who are concerned with NELINET can have no better goal than to find ways to work productively with other regional networks. This is where a part of the future lies and I believe that we may be uniquely equipped to pursue this purpose in the years immediately ahead. I say this because NELINET has just been successful in recruiting Ron Miller to the position of Project Director as of this coming January. I am sure you will agree that he is the kind of person who can help fashion the links that will allow networks to function effectively together in the future.

FAUL: A Consortium Approach to Library Automation

David Kaser Cornell University Libraries

My assignment is to describe how we have attempted to seek joint systems analysis and design through the Five Associated University Libraries (FAUL), which is a consortium comprising the SUNY units at Binghamton and at Buffalo, New York, the University of Rochester, Cornell, and Syracuse University. It was banded together in August of 1967. The stated purposes of FAUL were to "work toward a coordinated policy of long-range library growth and development with coordinated acquisitions policies, shared resources, the development of compatible machine systems, provision of easy and rapid communications systems among the membership, the provision of shared storage facilities, and exploration of other areas of cooperation."

During the first two years of FAUL's existence, many relatively undramatic cooperative ventures were initiated, some of which were successfully accomplished and others of which were ultimately laid aside. Only two of these early projects utilized machines. These were called MASFILE I and II and the establishment of a MARC Processing Center. The former were pilot projects toward the development of a machine-based union catalog of FAUL holdings, and, although these projects were successfully completed, the ultimate goal was finally tabled as being too expensive for the present time. The MARC Processing Center was run for a year and then discontinued, except for simple receipt of the tapes, when it was observed that none of the FAUL members were using or planning immediate use of the MARC data directly.

Both of these machine efforts were conducted for FAUL under competitively bid contract by the Technical Information Dissemination Bureau at SUNY-Buffalo. This kind of employment of a service bureau to do machine work jointly for a consortium under contract was, from the FAUL standpoint and apparently also from the standpoint of the contractor, highly successful. The work was done promptly and well by people who were knowledgeable and experienced in the building of biliographic data bases, and with strong and competent advisory input from a monitoring committee of FAUL librarians. I believe there was consensus among us that use of an outside contractor, rather than of computer facilities and expertise from any one of the member libraries, assured a valuable and disinterested detachment and perhaps sounder decisions than might have been obtained otherwise. At any rate, the concept of service bureau utilization under contract was well received by FAUL members.

Meanwhile, two members of FAUL, Cornell and the University of Rochester, arrived concurrently but separately at the conclusion that their circulation systems were in need of careful scrutiny with a view toward their possible mechanization. After bilateral discussions, not through the consortium, these two institutions decided to engage in analysis of their systems jointly rather than singly on the assumption that they could thereby eliminate some duplication of effort, thinking, and occasional costly but unavoidable error. A systems analyst and a circulation librarian from each of the two institutions formed a team which set about the assignment jointly and worked together for a year producing parallel analyses and a single proposal for computerizing both circulation departments. Again, the experience from the standpoints of both institutions was, with a couple of lapses, a happy one, and the concept of joint analysis began to gain favor in the FAUL community.

Still a third concurrent development was taking place in FAUL which was to point toward joint systems analysis and design. Early in 1969 the FAUL Board, which incidentally comprises the directors of libraries in the five institutions and the academic vice presidents, concerned about the difficulties of long-range planning within the consortium, assigned to one of its members the task of conceptualizing a long-range program of cooperation that could save rather than cost money.

The concept which was suggested under this charge was that over the long future FAUL develop a service bureau of its own, with its own staff, a single set of software systems, and a dedicated hardware configuration which would render under contract to each of its constituent libraries the fulfillment of all of their technical and machine needs. Presumably this bureau would ultimately maintain a single, monolithic serial inventory, all accessible through terminals in each of the libraries, a similarly single merged order file, one massive circulation record, and a single, monlithic serial inventory, all accessible through terminals in each of the member libraries. This concept was hardly developed out of individual or collective virginal naivete, because each of the member institutions had already spent substantial amounts of money on computerization efforts unilaterally. Buffalo and Syracuse had mounted large shelf-list conversion projects: Cornell was operating an advanced acquisition system (I planned to say "sophisticated" there, and although I am sure that "advanced" is equally imprecise, I will use it nonetheless), an advanced acquisition system; and Binghamton had an automated circulation system. Although each institution was also planning to spend substantial additional sums unilaterally over the next decade for further computerization, there was growing discomfort among us about the enormous costs of doing so. None of us have enjoyed any mechanization money from outside sources. The rationale behind the proposal to develop a FAUL service bureau therefore assumed that the needs for such services in research libraries probably have considerably more similarities among them than they have differences and that substantial savings should therefore accrue from elimination of obvious overlapping efforts that would occur if each constituent institution were to walk the path alone.

The alluring over-simplicity of this scheme of course bred considerable caution, if not downright distrust, in the minds of some members of the FAUL Board, and they convoked a meeting of themselves and their five computer center directors, so as to gain some technical advice. The computer center directors lent it cautious support, but many concerns were raised in the lengthy discussions that ensued. Eventually, although modified—indeed perhaps "battered and bruised" would be a more appropriate phrase—the concept did survive. The FAUL Board never did fully adopt the scheme, but neither did if fully kill it. First efforts to implement it, however, failed abysmally. A contract was let to a service bureau to survey the technical services activities in the five-member libraries at a fairly high level of generality and to produce a kind of template that would reveal areas of commonality and areas of uniqueness. Unfortunately, inadequate funds were allocated to the project, personnel problems arose, the time frame allowed proved to be too short, and, finally, the service bureau itself went out of business. It was a bad trip.

Nonetheless, three of the five-member institutions decided to engage in a program of joint systems design as a kind of experimental commitment, if those terms be not contradictory. Cornell, Rochester, and SUNY-Buffalo first agreed to utilize the joint approach, and then set about to decide what specific systems they should devote first attention to develop. Internal staff studies revealed that the highest priority need for systems improvement at Buffalo was in serials control and the second priority need was for improved circulation control. The same priority sequence obtained at Rochester, although the reverse sequence was identified at Cornell. In an admirable spirit of cooperation, Cornell subordinated its parochial concerns to the wishes of the group, and it was agreed that a joint on-line serials control system would be attempted first.

Several months ago these three institutions, working through FAUL, retained a systems team under the project direction of the FAUL coordinator Ron Miller to develop a single serials control system to meet the needs of all three participants. Following the decision the three institutions contracted to three phases of a proposed five-phase project with the several phases described simply as follows:

1. Analysis of the serial system needs of the participants.

2. Evaluation of existing and possible serials control systems appropriate to those needs.

3. Design of basic system modules.

4. Pilot implementation and testing of the proposed system.

5. Operational implementation.

Phases one and two are now well under way and thus far the three participating libraries are pleased with this joint approach. The personnel assigned to the task have been knowledgeable, experienced, and enthusiastic, and they have earned the initial respect of the librarians with whom they have to work closely. The three institutions are moderately optimistic that this approach will succeed.

Yet it might also fail. Cooperation when it costs nothing is easy, but when it is expensive, as this is, even among men with the best will in the world, cooperation requires of all of its participants the wisdom of Solomon, the patience of Job, and the prophetic powers of blind Tiresias thrown into the bargain. Unfortunately, there is no evidence to indicate that the directors of FAUL are any more endowed with these laudable traits than are normal men elsewhere. Regardless of whether we succeed or fail, however, we feel the stakes are such that we must continue the effort.

THE COMMERICAL SERVICE APPROACH TO LIBRARY AUTOMATION

Carlos A. Cuadra System Development Corporation

Scope of Discussion

The preceding speakers have identified and discussed two major approaches to library automation: the independent action or "do-it-yourself" approach and the approach involving multi-library automation activity. This second basic approach, as we have heard, comes in several flavors.

I would like to make two points at the outset about these. One is that neither of these major approaches precludes the involvement of commercial organizations. The second is that the best successes in the use of commercial organizations have come in those instances where the library employing the commercial organization was itself knowledgeable about automation. That may seem paradoxical, but it really isn't. The better informed the library staff is about automation, the better it can determine *whether* it needs the commercial help and *what* kind and *how much* help it needs. Also the better its own understanding, the better its ability to select a contractor that can really help them.

I plan to concentrate on three kinds of assistance the commercial organizations can provide to libraries in their approach to automation. The first kind of assistance is consultation. The second is continuing service, such as help in selecting, ordering, and cataloging library materials. The third kind of assistance involves providing libraries with ready-made, off-the-shelf computer programs—in support of the libraries' own automation efforts.

Use of Consultants and Contractors

The use of a consultant or contractor covers a wide range of activities and amounts of help, from the half-day "quickie" type of consultation, which I call the "oracle treatment," to large contracts spanning quite a bit of time. The NELINET relationship with Inforonics illustrates the latter kind of consultation.

There are a number of advantages in this kind of use of commercial firms. First, by using a contractor, the library can usually get more experienced help than they can afford to hire. To attract an experienced library systems designer (of which there are not many), the library must make the job financially attractive and offer some sort of job permanence. As we heard in the description of the Columbia experience, often it's very hard—and sometimes impossible—for a library to get the right kind of people in sufficient quantity to do the necessary

110

job on a timely schedule. Secondly, the use of an experienced contractor firm can save time. The more competent the contractors, and the wider their knowledge and experience on the kind of system you want them to develop, the more time can be saved.

A third advantage in the use of a contracor is that it can save money. How much money is a function of the time saved and the cost of the contractor's services. It is also a function of special resources that particular contractor organizations may have, for example, ready-made computer programs that may be applicable to the library's operations.

The fourth and most important advantage, I think, is that with a contractor organization, one can virtually guarantee performance. With one's own staff, there is no guarantee whatever against failure. All one can do is fire the people who fail to deliver. On the other hand, if the library works out a carefully conceived contract with a reputable organization, they are *at least* financially protected against poor performance.

Now, there are a number of disadvantages to using a consultant or contractor organization. One is that there is some risk that one will not find a highly capable contractor or talented individuals from that firm, or even if one gets a good contractor, that exactly the right people will be put on your job. There aren't that many contractors that are highly experienced in library automation, and their outstanding people may be spread pretty thin.

The second disadvantage is that contractor organizations may not make the creative investment in the design that the library staff might make. The contractor organization doesn't have to live with the system, and they may possibly do no more than fulfill the letter of the contract. Paul Fasana suggested yesterday that creative involvement may be something of a mixed blessing for a given library: the library's own programmers may become too creative and want to continue the program refinement ad nauseum. However, I still think that contractor non-involvement is a clear disadvantage and a clear risk.

The third disadvantage is that the use of a contractor reduces the opportunity for the development of the library's own staff, and it leaves the library dependent on the contractor for maintenance and system improvement and, indeed, for computer programs about which there may be the question of proprietary rights. I think that it's generally known that much systems and programming documentation is poor. In fact, it's often so poor that sensible people actually reject programs that are available from other people free, because they are aware of how much effort they will have to put into learning how the program operates and in trying to make program changes themselves. It may cost the library time and money to use the system development process as a training exercise for their staff, but it may well be worth the cost. So, the use of a contractor does pose a certain disadvantage, from the standpoint of staff training.

A fourth problem that occurred to me just this morning on hearing John McDonald's comments is that the use of a contractor may muddy the question of proprietary rights to the program that the contractor has developed. I think that this is the kind of thing that ought to be avoidable with a clear contract and a clear understanding. Nevertheless it should be registered here as a risk.

These are the major pros and cons that occur to me regarding the use of a contractor in the design and the development of a library system. I hope it is obvious, about these pros and cons and the ones I will be mentioning later, that there is no way in which one can add them up *in general* and come up with any kind of clear prescription. It really depends on what needs to be done, what the library has to do it with, and what the particular contractor offers in the way of help.

Services

Let me turn now to the second kind of commercial help, which I will call services. I'm not really sure that this is "an approach to automation"; it may really be, strictly speaking, an avoidance of automation in the sense that one is using a commercial firm to provide a service that one doesn't want to automate at a particular point in time. I include it here simply because one can use commercial services in conjunction with one's own automation efforts. One can, for example, do part of a book catalog in the library and use commercial services to do the other part. In addition, commercial services can be used for some library functions as a way of training one's staff. If one can watch over the shoulders of the commercial firm, one may get enough clues to be able to automate this same function in one's own library.

The automation-based commercial service that seems to be of major interest to most libraries is the preparation of book catalogs, probably because it is, in general, a nonrepetitive job that requires keyboarding facilities, computer programs, a computer, and printing facilities of some sort. There are about 25 to 30 firms in the U.S. today that offer this kind of service, and an increasing number of these have computer output to microfilm (COM) and/or photocomposition equipment that can provide book catalogs of high graphic arts quality.

The main advantage to libraries in using such services instead of developing their own book catalog production capability is that it helps them to avoid a large capital investment. To build a good book catalog program, one might have to invest upwards of about $30,000 in manpower for design and programming and in computer time for program checkout. One would also have to invest in keyboarding or data processing or photocomposition equipment, if these were not otherwise available in one's particular setting.

On the other hand, there are several disadvantages to the use of commercial book catalog services. For one thing, it may be more expensive over the long run. The commercial rates have to include a markup for marketing costs, overhead, and profit, a total of perhaps fifty to two hundred percent.

A second disadvantage is it makes the library rather dependent on the particular supplier, and, if the data are stored by the supplier in a unique file structure, the dependency may be even stronger. A unique formatting or file structure may not begin to pose a problem until the library begins to order updates and recompilations of the book catalog. One library system in the West that had a book catalog prepared for them later discovered that a complete three-year cumulation that they wanted would cost them $80,000, far more than they had anticipated. Unfortunately, they were not in a position to simply take their data file and go to some other supplier; they had to live with four separate catalogs for the next year.

Overdependence is also the key problem with the other major commercial service used by libraries: assistance in technical processing. I don't think I need to discuss this particular problem, for this audience.

One *advantage* of using commercial service for this kind of library activity is economic. It can be cheaper, particularly if the library doesn't have sufficient volume to afford the assembly-line type of operation and the specialized staff that are useful in some aspects of technical processing. The Columbia University talk yesterday suggested another possible advantage: that the library using commercial service is somewhat protected against surprises by the university computer center—surprises such as changing the computer without much notice. But I think the main advantage of this kind of service to many libraries is that if the library has money for books but none for people, it can still acquire and catalog the books it needs. And this is not an untypical situation. For example, the Los Angeles school district currently has quite a bit of book money but no money at all for catalogers.

The main disadvantages of commercial technical processing support, as I mentioned earlier, are really overdependence and the corresponding inability to do something if one gets less than ideal service from the supplier. There can also be a cost disadvantage if the library or library group is sufficiently large to run its own complete processing operation or its own service bureau.

That's all I plan to say about the pros and cons of commercial services for technical processing, since I'd really be embroidering on the obvious to most of you. However, I would like to add one last thought that was triggered by yesterday's discussion. As you may have noticed, I have left abstracting and indexing services out of the discussion, in particular the use of magnetic tapes produced by Chem Abstracts, NASA, ERIC, and so on. I don't think that these are of great interest to libraries now but I expect them to become of great interest in the near future. I would hope that it will not be necessary to have 25,000 Chem Abstracts files or 25,000 ERIC files, or 25,000 MARC files hanging on computers throughout the U.S. for on-line access. That would be a very silly and wasteful kind of duplication. And the kind of effort that I commented on yesterday in response to Gordon Williams' question—the effort of the National Library of Medicine to hang a large data base at one place and provide on-line service to many organizations—is reasonable proof that this can be done. And it can be done at economical cost.

Ready-Made Tools

The third kind of commercial service that I wish to discuss is quite new, so new, in fact, that it's hard to predict what its impact will be on library automation. This is the availability of ready-made, off-the-shelf computer programs. I think that this is an important development because it gives libraries one more alternative approach to automation. Some libraries can't afford to undertake independent automation efforts, either because they are not rich enough or because they don't have a grant, or because they are unable or unwilling to instigate or join a cooperative effort. They can pursue their go-it-alone philosophy if they can obtain from a commercial firm, at a reasonable cost, one or more computer programs that can do particular jobs for them.

What kinds of package programs are available? Well, it's a little hard to say at this point. A number of firms have developed programs that *they* use in a service bureau type of operation and it's not entirely clear whether they would be prepared to lease or sell them outright to a library or a group of libraries. However, there are a few computer programs that are intended for library systems or special library systems that have been formally announced as purchasable.

I'll start with the two I know best from my own company. We have announced a circulation control program that runs on a 360/40 or larger computer. The program costs $5,850 and does most of the kinds of things you would expect in a circulation program.

We have also announced a program package called ORBIT II for on-line interactive search of large bibliographic files. This system of programs costs $22,000 and runs on an IBM 360/40 or larger computer in a partition under the standard operating system—OS/MVT or OS/MFT. The system can accommodate 150 or more concurrent users.

There is also a system called Inquire, developed by Infodata. The cost of the system is $26,000. I do not know much about this system yet, but I believe that it's basically a retrieval system and that it has a quite rich set of commands.

The only supposedly complete program package to support library processing that I know about is said to be available from Input Services, Incorporated in Dayton, Ohio. The system is called LIBRICON and it operates on an IBM 360/30 or larger computer under DOS, or on a 360/40 or larger computer under OS. The cost of the program (with perpetual maintenance) is 50 thousand dollars for one location.

A fifth program or set of programs that I should probably include in this group is the BATAB System, which provides support for the acquisitions process. It prepares purchase orders, does fund accounting, maintains in-process files, produces reports, and so on. The system was developed for Baker and Taylor Co. by Stan Optner Associates and, although it hasn't been announced as a salable product, I have been told that it is available—free of charge, in fact—to libraries who are customers of Baker and Taylor.

These five programs are the only library-oriented ones that I know of that are intended for operation by the libraries themselves *on their own computers.* If anyone knows of others, I would appreciate very much knowing about them. There are a few other programs available, primarily data management systems, that do have some bibliographic capability, but they are not basically library-oriented programs and it may not be efficient to use them for library processing.

All of the other programs that I know about seem to be used for service or for internal operations by the particular commercial firms that developed them, for example, Bro-dart, IBM, Becker and Hayes, and SDC. I have not uncovered any kind of ready-made packages for serials or for book catalogs to date.

Now, having mentioned a number of available and potentially available program packages, let me state some of the advantages and disadvantages of a library's using them. The advantages are very clear. First, the programs can be purchased at a fraction of the cost of developing them. I happen to know, because my own staff did the work, that the ORBIT on-line retrieval system cost over $200,000 to develop. And it would cost about that amount for someone to try to replicate a system of this complexity. So the sales price of $22,000 could be a bargain if the program does what the particular library wants it to do.

The second advantage is that the ready-made programs are available now. One can be on the air in a matter of days or weeks, as opposed to months or years, and one can generally *guarantee* being on the air on schedule. That's very hard to do, as you have heard in the past day and a half, if one has to design, develop, and test computer programs that have any signficiant degree of complexity and power.

A third possible advantage is that the cost for maintaining and improving the programs may be fairly small, in comparison with doing it oneself. Most program packages include a year's maintenance as part of the selling price, and program improvements are likely to be made available to the program user at relatively little or no cost.

Now, what about disadvantages? The main one is that the library data processing staff, if it has one, won't know what the insides of the program are like. Although the firms that sell the program will probably provide good user manuals and good operator manuals, they are not likely to provide the kind of program documentation that would permit the using organization to modify the program easily itself. So, if the library discovers that there are serious bugs in the program beyond the warranty date, or some features that ought to be changed to accommodate the special needs of the library, the library may be helpless to make the change. On the other hand, most if not all commercial firms that sell library programs will agree to modify the program for a fee. And the fee might even be a bargain compared to the library's doing it itself. However, the lack of control really must be recognized as a serious potential disadvantage.

Another possible disadvantage, which perhaps I should simply call a danger, is that the ready-made programs may not do exactly what the library or group of libraries wants, and they may twist their requirements to meet the capabilities or the limitations of the available packages. For example, one library program that I know about does not provide for use of a five-digit vendor code or the full 12-character LC card number, so the libraries have changed their procedures to adapt to the program.

Now, how bad an effect this twisting will have on the library's operations is hard to say, in general. Each purchaser or user of a program package will have to decide how much he is willing to bend his requirements in order to take advantage of the financial savings possible in buying a ready-made program.

In spite of the kinds of limitations and hazards that I mentioned, I believe that the availability of ready-made or nearly-ready-made computer program packages for libraries is an important new development. Together with the various kinds of commercial service that I have mentioned, they provide some cost effective alternatives to the do-it-yourself approach to library automation.

Final Comment

To summarize, the commercial approach, as I've discussed it today, encompasses three things: (1) consultation and support—that is, people help; (2) use of service bureaus for some library functions; and (3) use of ready-made computer programs. Each of these has clear advantages and clear disadvantages, and the library or library group planning an automation effort should consider each of these very carefully before making expensive or irreversible commitments.

A REALISTIC ASSESSMENT OF WHERE
LIBRARY AUTOMATION IS TODAY

The purpose of this session was to review the immediate past attempting to evaluate the predictions and goals established in the early '60's with accomplishments, and to identify what steps should be taken in the immediate future.

Why We Are Where We Are

Irwin H. Pizer   Associate Director of Libraries, SUNY at Buffalo

In the centennial year of the death of Charles Dickens, it seems appropriate to quote him. His opening sentence in *The Tale of Two Cities* may well be construed to apply to the state of library automation—It was the best of times, it was the worst of times. . . .

Since I am privileged to present a subjective view of the condition of library automation, and in order to keep us from entering a profound state of depression, let us remember that Dr. Pangloss advised Candide that it is proved that things cannot be other than what they are, for since everything was made for a purpose, it follows that everything is made for the best purpose. It follows then that those who maintain that all is right talk nonsense; they ought to say that all is for the best.

I shall not tax your credulity by claiming that all is right with library automation, for we know that that is not so. It may well, however, be for the best.

Although mechanization of library procedures is correctly traced back to the work of Ralph Parker, it is only the last ten years which can truly be regarded as the beginning of the era of library automation. The sixties began bright with promise and hope and enthusiasm for the task. Schultheiss, Culberson, and Heiliger plotted a master plan for the automated university library and a brave attempt was made in Chicago to implement the design. And yet, today, neither the University of Illinois Chicago Circle Libraries nor any other university has gone more than a few steps down the road toward the accomplishment of the goals set.

After working intensively in this field for the past eight years, I believe that the reasons for the lack of success in all of our efforts, mine included, are not obscure.

A major problem has been the tendency to underestimate the depth and complexity of the library operation, especially on the part of the technical specialist, but also on the side of the librarian. In addition, the insecurity of the librarian in this new and wonderful realm, led to compromise with system needs in favor of the machine and to the detriment of the eventual success of the system. The problems foreseen by Parker with the training of library staff and acceptance of new, different, or modified ways of doing things has been real and is not solved quickly or easily.

Much projected library automation has depended on a high degree of cooperation, both inter- and intra-institutional, with the rewards being more often in-

119

tellectual than real in terms of tangible benefits. None of us is so secure or altruistic as to be able to divorce our needs and desires, whether personal or institutional, from our deliberations and actions. The policitcal problems *ARE* enormous and real; the evidence of the effect of these considerations can be seen from the national libraries, down through state systems, to regional groupings, and finally with individual libraries between departments. Whether the fear of loss of power, prestige, freedom, or control, etc., is real or imagined, the effects may be equally damaging. More than one project has come to grief because such problems played an important role. The early Columbia-Harvard-Yale medical cataloging project was one example, and we are now witnessing the rapid decline of the SUNY Biomedical Communication Network for this reason as well as the others I am discussing.

The sixties were the affluent decade for libraries; money was relatively easy to justify and obtain. But we have seen the seven fat years and we are now in the second of the lean years. The economic problems which restricted us before will press in upon us now and force us to take a much harder look at how we spend our reduced budgets.

Probably the most important problem which has served to defeat us, however, has been our inability to come to agreement on basic standards. Collectively, we represent the expenditure of millions of dollars of public and private funds but there is still no sizeable national data base for any type of material which we deal with. We still cannot exchange data in machine readable form which each of us will accept without major or minor revision, not to mention the reformatting tasks which are performed endlessly. The recent conference at Airlie House served to emphasize the distance we must still travel to reach the goal of a national network, no matter how it is designed. It also showed how wise the communication gap is between technologists, librarians and the user population, both in terms of what libraries do, as well as how, and why. Kipling's six honest serving men have not yet performed their duties for us.

New York state and its institutions have probably developed more unified plans and products than most large geographically and functionally related segments of our society. But even here we have an uncoordinated embarrassment of riches. There is NYSILL, the 3 R's program, the SUNY Biomedical Communication Network, the federally supported Regional Medical Library, FAUL, other privately supported consortia, etc., but it is only in the last month that the New York State Library took the initiative and the first meeting was held to try to find common ground between them. *The New York State Union List of Serials* is the first tangible product of cooperation between some of the groups mentioned and it heads a family of regional or otherwise related sub-group lists.

And yet, even with the large data base represented by the New York State Union List of Serials, over 55,000 titles, and holdings from more than 80 libraries, the records are not compatible with the State Library's own internal serials control operation, because of time constraints in the production of the list, and because of programming problems involving the handling of the necessary record coding. In addition, the Federal Libraries are supporting a pilot serials project dealing with science serials which chose to ignore the existing large files available in New York (there is also the Union Catalogue of Medical Periodicals of the Medical Library Center of New York, which NLM is using as the basis of its own internal system) and chose a smaller master file from the Canadian National Library. This was, in turn, reformatted with some difficulty, and provided a very limited number of data elements which had to be added to for the project's purposes.

One wonders how many times we are going to reinvent the wheel, or if we do accept someone else's wheel, insist that ours must have 25 spokes rather than his 15, or someone else's 20? How much can we force society to pay for, and how can we justify such tinkering to suit small, specialized purposes which might better be dealt with manually, or in some other way?

How long will we continue to play into the hands of such commercial firms as Chemical Abstracts or Engineering Index, who are still trying to urge the adoption of Coden as a standard serial number, even though it has been repeatedly rejected by the Federal Libraries, their professional advisory committees, the ARL, as the sub-contractor, for the serials pilot project and many thinking people who have examined the issue. We have lost several years of possible progress toward improved interlibrary communication over this point alone, and perhaps the chance to see a central federally funded agency established to assign and coordinate the number system.

The need to press for such things as the adoption of the standard serial number; effective implementation of a cataloging in publication program, together with use of the standard book numbers; widespread and wholehearted acceptance of the MARC data formats, etc., is real and urgent. Lip service to standardization has sapped our strength and our goal has eluded us. We may need to be ruthless in determining whether the cost of making our records tailor-made can be supported and continued. We must be sure of the correctness of our design and not allow the technologist to dictate the structure of the system because it is easier for him or for the machine. It is, after all, our profession, and we do know best what is needed to accomplish our work.

Let us remember Dr. Pangloss when we look back on our decade of activity and progress. There is no effect without a cause. . . in this best of all possible worlds.

What Can We Discern from Present Activities and Where Are We Going in the Immediate Future

Charles T. Payne

An overview covering much of our past experience and present activity was given in an earlier part of the program so I will restate our present level of accomplishment only very briefly before going on to future plans.[1] The University of Chicago Library has a powerful bibliographic data processing system in daily large-scale production. It is a practical and useful system. Our only real reservations at this time are economic ones. The system costs more to operate than we had hoped. We are aware of some of the primary reasons for this and are working to improve the cost-benefit picture. One reason is that because of low staffing levels during much of our project, we have been reluctant to go back and update or improve operations that worked. For example, IBM 1050 terminals have been used from the first for data input. These 1050 configurations that we have are expensive, but we have never taken the time to make a serious study comparing data input systems because what we have works.

A second factor is that we have not always utilized the system as it exists in the most efficient way. It is a complex system and at times clerical-level decisions in regard to data in files, for example—decisions made for only slight advantage to the people involved and in ignorance of the machine aspects—have caused extended periods of inefficient machine file processing.

Perhaps the major reason the system costs more than we had planned lies in the pricing algorithms of the University Computation Center which are structured to recover a lot more than equipment costs. This pricing policy of course reflects University policy but the resulting costs to the Library for computer services are well above those predicted two or more years ago. We are currently working to improve all of these conditions.

Further, we have thought during the entire course of our development that the best hope economically for a large-scale library system would be in covering the widest possible range of products and services. And this leads me from where we are to where we would like to go.

The development of the basic bibliographic data processing system at Chicago has had as a primary objective the handling of the daily, ongoing library processing operations and generating a variety of products necessary for these operations, such as purchase orders and catalog cards. The system emphasizes printed products and a successful large-scale production operation has been implemented even though the files are, in general, limited to single-key access. In our operations, this means access by record item number or, for our MARC files, by LC card number.

There is a direct relationship between the limitations of single-key access methods and the emphasis in our system on printed products. Single-key access capability can be made to work quite well for development of a system which is primarily geared to printed products for acquisitions, cataloging, and other technical processing operations, but it has two serious drawbacks. One, a by-product of the operation has been the buildup of a large data base of machine-readable bibliographic records and we cannot now effectively or efficiently make use of these data. Two, we cannot readily expand our system operations to cover other library operations such as searching, selection, and reference which would require more sophisticated file access.

In order to provide the higher level of data processing capability necessary to expand to these levels of library service, it will be necessary first to develop computer software systems—systems capable of supporting large and complex file organization, maintenance, indexing, query and response, and reporting activities—all within the context of a general purpose university computation facility.

Since 1966, the University of Chicago Library has been engaged in a library systems development project, and, in brief, this first phase of development required intensive analytical and design effort, involving library and bibliographic detail and an attempt to use available computer and peripheral equipment and operating software. Development from the first has been toward practical production-scale systems, with a goal of full implementation into library operations, and in this we have been largely successful. However, the system as developed makes use of on-line disk-held files organized by indexed sequential access method. In general, these files are limited to single-key access capability. Further indexing is available only in a limited sense for output request items.

The absence of adequate computer file organization, indexing, and retrieval capability has severely restricted the logical development of almost all computer-based library data systems as large file systems. The time has already been reached when library data bases have grown very large (the Chicago data base has over 100,000 machine-readable bibliographic records). These data bases are growing larger daily as new records are processed. Not only large, or even very large, but extremely large files could become possible in the immediate future through retrospective conversion of bibliographic records.

The sizes and growth rates of library data bases make more obvious the urgency of the needs for an adequate data or file management system. Such a system would provide new means of access to bibliographic data and more sophisticated use of the data through direct access capability. This access capability is required for on-demand file searches, for many subject or other specialized information retrieval demands, and for on-line file query and data response activity.

To provide such access capability for a moderate-sized, time-shared computer system requires prior implementation of software not now available as a package. We feel that a stage of development has been reached requiring a major shift in emphasis from library system development to computer system development. Creative development beyond the present state of the art of computer data management systems is needed.

There are some data management packages now in operation, and some partially so, and many in various stages of design. We know of none that meets our criteria. Many of them tend to be large, complex, and expensive, or require a moderate-to-large dedicated computer for their operations. A limited number of library data systems are now being, or have been, implemented on such dedicated computer systems but the majority of libraries will not have available large, dedicated computer data management systems.

There are a number of people working on a number of cuts at the large file problem at the present time, *e.g.*:

(i) special research studies using model or simulated systems;
(ii) development of special research facilities to study specific problems, *e.g.* file organization, data compaction automatic indexing, format recognition, etc.;
(iii) development or adaptations of some of the highly-generalized data management systems;
(iv) development of highly-specialized systems for small data bases—usually near the lower end of the 10,000 to 100,000 record range.
(v) development of large multi-terminal, conversationally inter-active communications and large file systems;
(vi) studies of system users' needs and reactions;
(vii) development of model-sized demonstration systems;
(viii) development of methods of building very large files as opposed to methods for using very large files.

None of the work that we know of seems geared to satisfy the set of problems we see as most urgent during the next several years, because they do not relate to large-scale production-mode operations. There is a very real need for a practical, production- and service-oriented data management system to be developed for utilization during the immediate future.

Such a system is needed to carry library operations during the immediate or near future, a period, we hope, of research and development on extremely large file utilization (*i.e.*, over 1,000,000 record files) and a period in which there is certain to be further development of high capacity, lower cost, storage hardware. Further, the need is dual: first, to satisfy operational requirements of libraries in order to continue with immediate library system development (*e.g.*, responsive circulation systems), and second, to provide a real operational environment in which to identify needs and develop, implement, and study large data base systems for the future.

Two advantages of systems development in an operational environment which offset some of the obvious difficulties are: first, the system development must deal with the whole range of real problems, including many not visible beforehand; and second, the system must be developed at production, not pilot size, and therefore system development can and should result in an operational production system.

The Chicago experience in complex system development, implementation, and operation has provided the background necessary to help us delineate the problems facing further library systems development. We feel that if our system development is to continue along the logical path toward large data base utilization, large-scale computer software development must be undertaken.

A generalized data management system, in part because of its generalities, is extremely expensive to develop. The more general, the more versatile, and the wider the range of applications it is designed to handle, the more expensive it is to develop. The more general the system, also, the more inefficient it tends to be in operation for a specific application. Generality is not indefinitely extendable either, and all systems have limitations. These limitations determine the most practical and useful applications for the system.

Bibliographic data processing requirements are complex and specialized enough to cause stress to any known generalized system design. It is probable that a specialized library system is required for efficient operation on a larger scale. Specializing design for library and bibliographic data handling undoubtedly produce a system both more responsive to long-range library needs and more efficient to operate.

There are some unique qualities of bibliographic data and files, and their processing, which both operate against efficient, satisfactory use of highly generalized systems and provide the key attributes for design consideration in the development of a library data management system.

1. Machine processing of bibliographic data requires a very large character set. I won't enlarge upon that except to say that the character set requirements for data input and storage are now limited to a large degree by the output printing capability. As the latter capability changes with the technology, so will the requirements for the former.

2. Bibliographic data include a large number of defined data elements. Most of these are variable length and are stored as tagged strings of unformatted data. Records contain varying numbers and combinations of data elements and are necessarily of variable length.

3. Records are large, most of them being several hundred characters in length

4. Major files consist of large collections of records. File sizes for our library data base are potentially over one million records. Record input to the data base file is not in any order by attribute. Growth is essentially open-ended with very little turnover. The average retrieval rate for any specific records from the library data base is very low.

5. Our processing files tend to be more or less stable in size, in the 10,000 to 100,000 record range. These are primarily turnover files with only a small growth rate but with larger seasonal fluctuations. The daily turnover in these files is usually less than one percent. Input to these files is not dependably in order by any attribute. Retrieval of all records in these files is certain within some determinable turnover time.

6. Library files tend to be permanant files. File redefinitions, the installation of new files, or removal of existing files would all constitute major system changes. The library data management system design need not include the capability for handling file definition with each new input.

7. File indexing requirements are likely to be fixed and relatively stable through time. Almost any substantive changes would cause reprocessing of the complete data base and would not therefore need to be a variable specification of data input.

8. Record and data element definitions are fixed and stable through time and need not be treated as variable specifications for data input.

The degree to which these and other qualities of bibliographic data and data processing affect the system design would, of course, need to be determined during the design stage. The more specifically the needs can be determined, the less general does the software need to be, and, therefore, the less costly to develop and operate. The goal is to develop a practical, satisfactory library data management system. The long-range library capability of providing access to discipline-oriented bibliographic and information data bases, both nationally and locally generated, will depend to a large degree upon ease of access to large-file systems. Ultimate solutions to library circulation and serial handling problems will depend on such access also.

A data management system design can be generalized by making the system applicable to more than one machine system and configuration. Even for identical computers the possible peripheral equipment configurations (including tape drives, disk storage drives, input and output equipment, etc.) can vary widely. To encompass a family, or manufacturer's series, of computers requires consideration of the added differences due to operating system software, core storage size, and other configuration variations. Generalization to cover entirely different, non-compatible computer systems would require capability to cover differences in such basic elements as data character representation, methods of data packing, and other implicit (from the programming view) data handling features of the various machines.

Another way data management system design can be generalized is by making the system applicable to multiple types of data and a variety of uses (and users) of data. This requires being able to handle various types, sizes, and numbers of files; fixed and variable length record structures; varying numbers and combinations of hierarchical levels of data; varying combinations of fixed and variable length data elements; tag, positional, or content indicators for data; varying relationships between physical and logical records; and other variations. The complexities of large, highly generalized data management systems are the inevitable result of attempts to accommodate both of these types of generality.

The library data management system, as we see it, would represent, in many aspects, a compromise between the highly generalized system and the custombuilt, limited-use system. We have proposed to design, build, and implement a system aimed primarily at handling bibliographic and similar rypes of data (*i.e.*, tagged strings of variable length alphanumeric data). There is potentially a wide range of uses for bibliographic data processing, storage, and retrieval within the University, in addition to the Library's needs.

Specifically, our approach to a library data management system would probably include some of the following design parameters.

1. Terminal and teleprocessing costs, at least for initial library implementation, would be concentrated on relatively few terminals with relatively heavy use. This initial development is aimed at library processing use rather than direct student or public access to files.

2. System development, to stay within the bounds of possibility, would be aimed at large file sizes in the 100,000 to 1,000,000 record range. While this is smaller by perhaps an order of magnitude than a total library system, it is nevertheless of a range to handle the data base expected during the next several years as well as routine technical and public service processing files. This file size could handle the in-process file, recent receipts for a number of years, the serial record, and the circulation files. It will be a number of years before machine-readable records of our holdings will approach the one million mark.

3. The system direct-access retrieval capability would be limited to a relatively

few access keys, *i.e.,* only those shown to have the greatest utility in general library processing operations. These would need to be determined by studies during the early stages of the project. It is believed to be well beyond the economic possibilities, at the present time, for any very large file system that must justify its existence to retrieve on all data elements and all key words and titles. The proposed system would evaluate in a practical sense the utility of any retrieval key against the cost of indexing and the overhead costs of the whole system as its size is increased. We believe a well chosen, but limited, number of access keys could satisfy a high percentage of the library's and readers' searching activities. As this system is not initially designed to replace but rather to supplement and extend the existing bibliographic apparatus, the more complex searching requirements could for at least a substantial interim period best be handled in the traditional ways

4. System retrieval routines would be designed for the most paractical and economic use within library operations. Interaction with the computer would not be utilized when it need not be, simply because it is there. Most interactive communication between user and computer to date tends to be awkward, expensive, and appears designed more for demonstration than utility. A library searcher with several hundred items to search does not have time for a dialog with the computer about each item.

5. The system design would be limited to the handling of the types and uses of data required for bibliographic purposes. This capability, although less than a generalized data system, would be responsive to the urgent needs of the library and similar information handling systems today. The system would thus avoid attempting to be everything for everybody for all time, and would be limited in scope to providing a defined set of essential capabilities to be specifically determined during early stages of project development. The developmental effort could therefore take best advantage for savings of the inherent characteristics of bibliographic data for specificity rather than generality.

The software system described for development does not provide in itself a product for the library. It provides a capability. This capability is a prerequisite to further library systems development beyond the present level of accomplishment.

At least three levels of utilization of the system can be foreseen. The first level of utilization would be in applications to existing processing files and could be undertaken as soon as the system capabilities were demonstrated to be reliable. Clearly, one of the first major applications of multi-key access capability would be to the existing In-process File. This level of application would benefit library technical processing operations immediately and would satisfy certain reference and circulation query requirements in regard to status or location of in-process material. Utilization of the system at this level would also make the creation of new processing files, such as for reserve book processing, highly probable.

The second level of system utilization would be to incorporate the date management system as a central utility in the design and development of other large, complex library systems, such as circulation. Having a data management utility available would also make practical development of a serials system much more feasible. If these various library systems (or sub-systems) require a data management capability, then the logical plan of development is to provide a general library data management utility first and postpone serious library sub-system development work until it is available.

The third level of data management utilization would involve its application to large data base systems, *e.g.*, over 100,000 records, which is equivalent to the holdings of a major disciplinary area of the library. The limitations of successful utilization of this level may be as much, or more, economic as developmenta. A tangential problem at this level could involve the utilization of externally generated data bases such as MEDLARS or other discipline-based systems.

These three levels of utilization of a library data management system can be seen rather clearly. It is also safe to say, however, that the potential for change in library system operation and capabilities implied by this development are enormous. It is improbable that the ultimate results of the utilization of this capability can be fully predicted.

We have had assurances of at least partial funding for this developmental program, in addition to the substantive support of the University of Chicago. The library data management system is a central utility for the work we want to do during the foreseeable future. Project development will get under way after the first of the year with the investigations, analyses, and feasibility studies that constitute the first phase of that effort.

References

1. See Section I, *The Chicago Experience* by C. Payne.

The Library of Congress and Library Automation

John Lorenz   Library of Congress

As with so many things that we do at the Library of Congress, this paper is a joint product; in this case specifically Fred Croxton, Bill Welsh, and John Rather, with a review by Henriette Avram between field trips. We have tried here to say something significant both in general and specific terms.

The overall objectives of the Library of Congress automation program are: to improve our services as a research library; to improve the Library's services to other libraries; and to facilitate development of new bibliographic services in the national interests.

The foundation of these services is a comprehensive program for acquiring and organizing for prompt use the full range of library materials produced in all parts of the world. Such a library program must like the famous recipe for rabbit stew begin by "catching the rabbit," but, since the proof of the stew is in the eating, the prime requisite is being able to achieve bibliographic control over the materials. As we all know, in libraries of any size, there can be no physical access to materials unless there is bibliographic access.

The criteria of a national program for bibliographic control must be accuracy, comprehensiveness, flexibility, and speed. From the standpoint of long-range research library requirements, accuracy is mandatory because faulty preparation of the catalog record may result in the physical item being beyond any reasonable expectation of retrieval. Comprehensive is basic because there is no sure-fire way to predict what will be needed for research library purposes in the long run.

Flexibility is necessary so that the record can be of the greatest use to the greatest number of libraries. One cannot get out of a record more than is put in it. Thus, to serve a broad spectrum of national needs, the bibliographic record emanating from a central source probably must be complex. In a machine system it is possible, however, to simplify the record for local storage and use.

Speed is important so that, insofar as is practical, the services of a central agency for bibliographic control are available when needed. Unwarranted delays in the production and dissemination of catalog records create difficulties for users of the service.

In selecting bibliographic control functions and activities for automation, the following criteria are considered at the Library of Congress:

1. Automation of the function must be technically feasible within the state of the art today.

2. It must be possible to automate the function in a reasonable period of time (roughly 24 to 36 months).

3. The function must be of such scope that its automation will have a significant impact on the operations of the Library as a research library and national bibliographic center.

4. Projects and the development work to accomplish them should be related to one another so that their effect will be cumulative with each project laying the foundation for other more complex undertakings.

Automation projects must be developed with an eye to the future, but just imagining the benefits of full automation of bibliographic control does little to overcome the formidable obstacles to reaching that goal. Automation must be the art of the practical. To proceed otherwise would be like relying on science fiction instead of applied science.

Turning now to the automation of LC's bibliographic operations, let me review ongoing and proposed projects to indicate how they may pave the way for things to come.

The Order Division project involves the design and implementation of a machine-assisted system to control acquisition of individually purchased titles. The system will provide benefits in two major areas: assistance in routine clerical work; and increase in control over orders. In the new system, a master record of each order will be maintained in a machine file where it will be continually monitored and updated through its lifetime. The system will produce a variety of reports covering everything from the original order to final payment.

It is expected that the first phase of this project may be completed by the middle of 1971. Present plans call for extension of the system to handle blanket orders, standing orders, and subscriptions. The question of whether acquisitions records produced by this system may be useful for later cataloging operations also will be explored, but the disparity between acquisitions data and cataloging data may be too great to make this use practical in the Library of Congress.

This project has a high priority because its successful completion will enhance the efficiency of a basic component of the LC acquisitions activity thus promoting the comprehensiveness and speed with which the Library collects material for the ultimate benefit of the users of its bibliographic records.

The scope and benefit of the MARC Distribution Service are too well known to require description before this audience. Less publicized are the problems encountered in converting catalog records to machine-readable form at the rate of more than one thousand per week. Despite automation, the present procedures involve a heavy volume of manual paper handling. In addition, the corrections of errors in MARC records during the input stage involves time-consuming procedures and delays, occasioned by batch processing turnaround time. To reduce the cost of input, and thereby to facilitate expansion of the service to other materials, it is imperative to redesign the basic MARC input system so that corrections can be made on-line. This will entail a major design in reprogramming effort which has a high priority among the tasks relating to building the machine-readable data base. In terms of expanding the data base beyond all English language monographs, based on availability of resources, we plan to include audio-visual materials in the next fiscal year. Beyond that, based on evidence of utility to a significant number of research libraries, and availability of resources, we plan to include French, German, Spanish and Portuguese monographs in the following fiscal year.

The RECON Pilot Project, funded largely by grants from the Council on Library Resources and the Office of Education, is engaged in actual conversion of 1968 and 1969 English-language catalog records as well as about five thousand randomly selected catalog records of various ages and languages. The purpose of the project is to test assumptions and procedures outlined in the RECON study under practical conditions. The inestigations include determination of the best means of obtaining the basic documents for conversion; use of various input devices; assessment of the effect of foreign languages and older cataloging styles on the speed and accuracy of conversion; and format recognition.

One of the high costs of input is the editing of the records; that is, supplying the tags, indicators and sub-field codes specified by the MARC format. To reduce the human effort required for this process, the Library is working on a program to recognize data elements by punctuation, spacing, and keywords and to assign the appropriate tags. This program, called format recognition, would enable the computer to take over part of the initial editing. Humans would still have to proofread and correct but a significant portion of what is now done manually would be done by machine.

Format recognition for English-monographic records has been under development since the Spring of 1969. The programs are now being coded and it is hoped that they will be operating early in 1971. The most recent tests and simulations suggest that about fifty percent of the records processed by the program would be done correctly. One can only guess at the running time for the programs, but if computer costs continue to decline while labor costs rise, format recognition seems likely to offer significant cost benefits. If this proves to be the case, the programs will be modified to handle foreign language records, older styles of cataloging, and records for other forms of material. Format recognition will be used also in the conversion of current catalog records by making relatively minor modifications in the input worksheet and input typing procedures.

The development of formats for machine-readable records has been a concern of the Library since 1966 when the original MARC format for monographs was introduced. Since that time, the improved structure of the MARC format has provided the basis for an American National Standards Institute (ANSI) standard. It has been adopted, as many of you know, by ALA, ARL, and COSATI. The structure is also gaining acceptance abroad as is evidenced by its use in the British MARC System and in the International Nuclear Information System (INIS) and its adoption as a proposed standard by the British Standards Institute and the International Standards Organization. And at a UNESCO meeting, an *ad hoc* working group on communications formats, including a USSR representative, accepted the draft ISO proposal.

Content designators (that is, tags, indicators, sub-field codes) originally developed for monographs have been extended to other types of materials in a systematic way to create a family of related formats that can be handled basically by the same system of computer probrams. Formats for monographs, serials, and maps have been published. Formats for other types of material are being developed either at the Library or with the Library of Congress's cooperation. A format for motion pictures and film strips is being developed with the cooperation of groups representing librarians, teachers, and media specialists. A format for manuscript collections is being developed for eventual use in producing the National Union Catalog of Manuscript Collections. A format for music and sound recordings is being worked on at Harvard University with the cooperation of the Library of Congress. In time, it is expected that a format will be developed for pictorial materials.

A high-priority project designed to improve the Library's services as a source of bibliographic information involves the automation of procedures for handling card orders and for producing cards on demand. In Phase I of the project, a system was developed to use optical character recognition devices to read card orders, to sort them by card number, and, after the orders have been filled by a manual search, to re-sort them by the ordering library. This has been a highly successful development, incidentally. Phase II of the card system will make use of a machine store of catalog records to print specific records on demand using an RCA Videocomp. This phase will be operational in 1971.

The success of Phase II naturally depends in part on having a store of records large enough to handle a substantial portion of the card orders. At present there are about one hundred thousand English titles in the MARC data base. Since the majority of orders are for recent English-language titles, it seems likely that by the time Phase II becomes operational, the machine data base should be able to satisfy a large volume of the requests.

Automation of the production of book catalogs of the Library is another high-priority task. To accomplish this requires solving many problems in arranging and formatting the output. In an effort to minimize the problems of computer sorting, a set of rules for file arrangement is being developed to reduce sharply the number of cases in which the filing form of an entry differs from the bibliographic form. By keeping exceptions to a minimum, it should be possible to write programs that will make use of MARC content designators to arrange entries in sophisticated ways.

While details of the rules are being worked out, progress is being made on the logical design of the programs to implement the rules. Modifications are being made to the generalized sort-key building program, known as SKED, so that it can be used as a framework for special-purpose algorithms. A way is also being developed to provide a sort-key field in the MARC record whenever the content designators will not suffice to generate a proper sort-key on demand (for example, if an initial article is to be ignored).

The requirements for formatting entries in book catalogs and the use of photocomposition devices also are being investigated. In the near future, the Library expects to produce a book catalog of the Main Reading Room reference collection and an annual catalog of motion pictures and filmstrips. These projects will provide a testing ground for programs that may be used eventually to produce the entire National Union Catalog by machine methods.

Authority files are essential tools for the building of records that meet the criteria of accuracy and consistency necessary for a national program of bibliographic control. Work is in progress on a system to control the file of LC subject headings. Here, we regret to report, the machine techniques used to produce the seventh edition of LC subject headings and its supplements have not proved adequate for updating this large highly volatile file. The programming difficulties of converting the existing machine records to a form suitable for easy maintenance have proven to be formidable. This experience provides a prime example of the need for flexibility in creating machine-readable records. A machine file designed for a single purpose (which in the case of the present subject heading file is printing) often cannot be adapted for any other purpose without great effort. Resolution of this problem also has a high priority in the Library's program for automating bibliographic control.

Investigation of the requirements for a machine file of name-authority records has also been underway for some time and it is expected that the broad outlines of the requirements of such a system will be drawn within the coming year.

A critical area for investigation concerns the reference structure of authority files and their links with the bibliographic data base. Establishment of these links is essential in an automated environment for several reasons. First, automatic production of book catalogs require some means of calling forth on-demand references related to access points that will appear in the catalog. Second, machine searches of the data base will hardly be effective unless there is a way to enter the data base using various forms of name for the same entity. Third, convenient updating of name and subject headings and the records on which they are used depends on the existence of links between the authority files and the data bases. For efficiency, it should be possible to make a change only in an authority file, leaving to the computer the task of making this change whenever necessary in the bibliographic data base. The development and implementation of a reference structure system is, therefore, a fundamental requirement for machine-assisted bibliographic control.

Another imminent project involves the consolidation of the indexes to the LC classification schedules. The initial conversion and merging will be done on contract by the Columbia University School of Library Service. With this foundation, the Library will develop a system for updating the index on a continuous basis. Other related projects that merit early consideration are the development of a MARC format for the schedules themselves, and investigation of the requirements for adding shelflist information to the MARC data base to control the LC collections.

The most important new project related to bibliographic control involves the cataloging-in-publication pilot project that may begin early in 1971. Many of you remember it as cataloging-in-source; it is now CIP. CIP data will be put in machine-readable form so as to generate reports to the publisher and control records within LC, as well as to supply another product for the MARC distribution service. Libraries that receive the CIP MARC tapes will be able to use them as a prime source of acquisitions information which can be used to produce order forms and in-process records and to provide the nucleus of locally produced catalog records.

To accelerate completion of cataloging, when the published book is received, LC plans to develop a system for updating CIP records on-line in the Descriptive Cataloging Division. This sytem may serve also as a prototype for an eventual on-line input system.

At the same time, this project will explore the feasibility of developing a machine-readable Process Information File. This basic LC file contains records for materials from the time they reach the preliminary cataloging stage until a printed card is available. It is used to prevent unintentional duplication of titles, duplicate cataloging and to locate materials in process. In its present manual form, the Process Information File rarely provides more than a single access point (usually main entry) to the record. By automating the file, it should be possible to provide multiple access and to maintain the file more efficiently. In addition, the close correspondence between preliminary cataloging information and the final catalog record, makes it worthwhile to explore the possibility of taking advantage of these interim records in producing the final MARC record.

The existence of the process information file in machine-readable form would also permit analysis of work in process to identify critical backlogs and to analyze the work-flow in other ways. Although many categories of searches in this file could be batched, its successful use would require on-line searching capability. Development and implementation of this project depends on the development of on-line, disk-oriented systems at LC which still require development.

In the difficult field of serials, as many of you know, a pilot project in the area of science and technology serials is now under way at ARL under the monitorship of the National Libraries Task Force. This jointly supported project is now expected to continue development at the Library of Congress after July 1971. The assignment of standard serial numbers for a core collection of serials may also become part of this effort. It is hoped that the Library of Congress can also initiate such a project with outside funding in 1971.

The foregoing review of projects involving automation of bibliographic control shows their close relationship to each other and indicates how they will contribute to the eventual development of an integrated system for this purpose. But before this long-range goal is achieved, however, many technical and administrative problems must be resolved. Some of the difficulties of automating on-going operations are: (These will sound familiar to some of you as you have heard them before at this meeting, but this is the LC version.)

1. The need to continue manual operations until automated operations have demonstrated their practicality is costly.

2. Building a data base to the level necessary to sustain meaningful operation is also expensive.

3. The magnitude of hardware costs must also be fully appreciated. The cost of storage can be very high for a large data base. Talking about on-line systems and real-time access in a document retrieval system is cheap; the cost of maintaining such a system is expensive.

4. The realities of software costs also must be recognized. Programming for sophisticated processing requires many man-years of high priced staff time. Even when basic programs have been developed, they require continuous maintenance to enable them to cope with unforeseen conditions and to adapt them to new conditions.

5. It is vital to keep in mind that automation cannot by itself resolve the

technical problems of bibliographic control. Automation of catalog records does little to minimize the problems of uniquely identifying bibliographic entities and of relating them to one another. There is no immediate prospect that the computer can exercise the judgment necessary to make many of the distinctions necessary for bibliographic control. For the foreseeable future, it seems this task will have to be performed by humans

Beyond our bibliographic efforts, which are probably of most interest to you, we are also pleased to report that Congress, which appropriates most of the funds for these efforts, is becoming increasingly interested and knowledgeable about the application of automation in getting the information it needs for its own work. We are doing as much as we can to build on and meet this interest not only to improve our services to Congress but with the expectation that their appreciation of the benefits of automation will have a positive effect on their support of the total library automation effort across the country.

One important application here which is already well underway is the use of the Administrative Terminal System as an input device to build a bibliographic data base dealing with materials on current subjects of interest to Congress—often periodical articles—which are used to answer frequent inquiries from Congressional offices. This mechanized data base is being used for current awareness Service on a pilot basis. The Selective Dissemination of Information (SDI) system developed at IBM has been applied to this data base using profiles for various research staff members in the Legislative Reference Service and a limited number of others. It is our plan to assist the Legislative Reference Service in making a Current Awareness Service available from this data base to a broad group of users, most likely key Members of Congress and Committee staffs, early in 1971. From a computer programmer's point of view, most of this work is completed. From a reference point of view, many profiles remain to be written, and considerable work still remains to be done on the vocabulary to be used in indexing incoming items and writing profiles.

Perhaps the area of greatest day-to-day importance to Members of Congress and their senior assistants is information on the status of bills, hearings and other legislative actions. Thus, automation of the calendars of Congressional Committees and of the publication of the Legislative Reference Service called *Digest of Public Bills* constitutes an exceedingly important area for our attention.

For the past two years the calendars of the House Banking and Currency and the Judiciary Committees have been produced using ATS and the computer at the Library of Congress. This is one project in which we have already been able to show a cost saving over the traditional preparation and printing. We expect it will soon be possible to write a general manual on the automated preparation of legislative calendars. Each Committee will then have the opportunity of deciding for itself whether or not it wishes to make this particular application of automation, and the Library of Congress will be ready to assist those who develop this service.

Current status of bills is maintained on the ATS and published in the *Digest of Public Bills*. Until now we have applied ATS only to improvements in the input and turn-around for the *Digest*, but we are looking forward to producing the entire document with the aid of the computer and the Linatron at GPO. The system which is needed can be viewed by the systems analyst as a general purpose program for producing an abstract journal using a computer. Each bill has a descriptive heading, a text summary, and index headings. Our objective is to produce the *Digest* using a program sufficiently general that it can be applied to other abstract-type publications.

The Copyright Office is another important area of LC responsibility and operation in which we believe there will be benefits from computer applications. A major systems analysis of the Copyright Office was conducted by Library personnel about 18 months ago, and steps began soon thereafter to automate some of the service procedures. We began with programs to control the accounts of copyright registrants, which also constitute a general control of the work flow. Needs have already been identified for the control of correspondence related to pending registrations and to the status of original registration actions. Input and other summaries are needed for managerial control of the Office itself. One of the goals of the Copyright Office is to complete registrations within three to four weeks from the date of their receipt. While this is not always possible, the volume of registrations—now over three hundred thousand a year—is such that it can be materially assisted by early identification of bottlenecks and work buildup in the registration process. We believe the computer can be of good advantage here.

We are also planning for all of the Library an improved management information system through computer applications. We hope to have an automated manpower roster and summary of employee qualifications in the near future. These can provide us, when used with the payroll files, with an improved labor distribution and cost collection technique by which we can better evaluate the application of our manpower and our fiscal resources. Similary, the computer can be used to help us control our inventory of equipment and supplies, the status of our contracts, and the maintenance of our current statistical records of our work output—all important tools for sound management.

We are also developing general purpose applications which will be very important. One of them will be a teleprocessing system more or less independent of data and terminal equipment being used. This will enable application programmers to make use of our computer environment to solve specific on-line problems without doing and redoing such laborious jobs as developing checking procedures and interface routines for every application and every terminal. The Library already has developed some general purpose programs to select from files, to order records, and to produce reports. The SKED program, for example, is already available through the IBM Program Library. Another will enable us to process selected data from our files and forward it to photo-composition devices such as the Linatron at GPO.

Supporting the Library's automation activities is a Computer Service Center. The objectives of this Center are to give efficient service based on firm standards and dependable procedures, give fast turnaround to jobs both large and small, and have the capability of furnishing its customers data which will indicate the quantity of work they generate and the cost of performing such work.

The Center now has two 360/40's, each with a 256-K core. They share three 2314 direct access storage devices, eleven tape drives, three printers, and two card reader-punches. External storage, that is disk drives and tape drives, can be switched from one main-frame to the other by the operator. The second piece of equipment was selected to be an exact duplicate of the first to give us back-up capability. This was necessary because we now have 32 remote terminals operating into the Center. We are now in the midst of converting programs to OS/360 in order to use the increase throughput and increased flexibility which this equipment gives us.

The work described so far is aimed at one goal—the development of an effective environment for all the specific computer applications which are to come. We recognize the importance of carefully developed procedures and standards if we are to make efficient use of our equipment. It is essential that there be firm technical standards, effective documentation, and sound standardization software available to all applications on our computers if we are to be efficient.

More work needs to go into forward planning if we are to be prepared for change. On the one hand, we can anticipate increasing workloads and new demands. On the other, we can look forward to improvements in hardware and software and lower costs for computer power and storage as compared to manpower costs.

Our analysis of the studies of the predicted use of the massive files projected for the central bibliographic apparatus of the Library of Congress indicated that two abilities are critical: first is the ability to have a high density of access to large files in real-time, and second is the ability of the Library, both in processing and reference, to interact efficiently with these files. As a part of our forward planning, two studies of the state-of-the-art now being completed in these critical areas: one on terminals and a second on file organization.

The terminal study defines functional modules or smallest pieces which can be built into work stations to perform essential functions. It then assesses the current and developing state-of-the-art against these modules. Areas for improvement are pointed out. The final printed report of this study should be available before the first of the year.

The file organization study looks at the various uses which must be made of massive data base-type files with special attention to the use of individual elements within records. It does not presuppose as has usually been the case in earlier file structures that unique physical or logical files will exist for each function. Using a series of mathematical models, file usage is simulated, bottlenecks are predicted and automation technology is considered both at the logical and physical file level.

The Library is not supporting the development of special hardware. The industry is moving in our direction, perhaps not as fast as we could wish, but it is moving far more rapidly than a few years ago. Plans for the new data base integrated management information systems needed by almost all large complex business organizations—industrial and government—will require almost the same high densities of access and almost the same file structures that we require. We have tried by our studies to develop benchmarks by which we can evaluate the developments of others and spot industry trends.

As we look forward to the equipment which will be available five or ten years from now, we shall be considering whether hundreds of user terminals will actually be available to library patrons or whether patrons will furnish their requests to intermediaries, much as was done in the days of the telephone subscribers and manual switchboards.

We must look into the changes in our approaches which may be necessary to enable greater numbers of inquiries and file-use actions to occur in a very short time with relatively small amounts of file scanning and printing being done.

We also plan to stay abreast of the development of specialized peripheral equipment. Paul Reimers (whom many of you know), Coordinator of our Information Systems Office, has frequently spoken about the Piece Identification Number, or PIN. If appropriately tied into the mechanized acquisitions and processing operations, and if the piece identification data were affixed to the spine of the book, PIN could provide not only for automatic charging and discharging, but also for automatic shelfreading and inventorying. In a sense we are seeking for library material the address reader that the Post Office Department is seeking for its applications. The same kind of device is now becoming available to department stores for inventory control.

We are also looking forward to equipment to store and manipulate text as such rather than as alphabetic and numeric characters. We have long had microforms and digital computers available, but the two are as yet ineffectively married, and some form of automatically manipulated graphic storage can be anticipated for the future.

In planning for the future of our library automation program at LC, we believe that most of the projects mentioned must go forward simultaneously. We are, in effect, expressing our priorities in terms of the proportion of our resources placed on each project and the speed and depth of implementation instead of sequence of implementation.

We can assure you that in everything we do, we are keeping very much in the front of our minds, not only the implications for the Library of Congress, but for the total national and, in some respects, international library automation effort. With our emphasis on procedures, standards, and the other aspects of our computer environment, we should be able to improve the documentation of our computer programs which would permit us to make our programming results generally available through existing program libraries.

When resources become available, we also plan to document older programs so that they too can be distributed.

It is obvious that to move all of us forward to our goal of the best and most efficient library and information service for all users, large amounts of money will be needed. We believe these amounts will be somewhat less depending on the development and application of national and international standards and the transferability of software and hardware developments. One of the most significant activities on the horizon may be the progress being made by a high-level international committee in developing an international standard bibliographic description which would lend itself well to format recognition.

As a closing and perhaps a provocative thought, what might the benefit and costs savings be if, say, by January 1, 1975, all of the major libraries of this nation or the world could agree to close their present catalogs and move forward on to a single bibliographic standard which would make possible a truly efficient interchange and transmission of bibliographic information?

Discussion

Questions from the floor were answered by members of the entire panel, which included John Lorenz, William Welsh, and Fred Croston, all of the Library of Congress.

Question: Could you repeat that schedule of CIP, audio-visual and foreign language materials?

Mr. Lorenz: CIP we hope to begin January 1971. Extending the MARC data base to audio-visual, we hope July 1971. Going beyond to French, German, Spanish, and Portuguese monographs, we would hope July 1972 or sometime thereafter.

Question: Will MARC tapes have a mixture of both MARC records and CIP records?

Mr. Welsh: No. CIP will probably be a separate tape service. When the book is received in bound form and fully cataloged it will of course go into the regular MARC data base. That may be true of audio-visual materials as well.

Question: What would it take to raise the priority of expanding MARC to other foreign languages sooner?

Mr. Lorenz: We don't have a feeling that there is enough good use of MARC as yet. I think if we felt that we had thirty to fifty users or potential users of MARC we would have little trepidation about moving ahead faster, but we don't really see that on the horizon as yet. We feel that before we go to Congress for the substantial increase in funding which this would require, that we must be able to illustrate that there is the demand, the need for this service across the country. Our hope is that this will have shown itself by the time we prepare our budget request for fiscal 1973. I believe our estimate of the cost of expanding MARC to the four other languages is about as great as it is to do the English monographs.

Mr. Welsh: As a matter of fact it's higher. We are now cataloging at the rate of about 240 thousand titles a year. English language materials account for about 80 thousand; French, German, Spanish, and Portuguese for about 80 thousand. The cost would be greater for those four languages than for English language materials.

Question: I would like to ask Mr. Lorenz to speculate on something. I commented earlier about the number of data bases that are being made available such as NASA, Chem abstracts, and so on. There are probably fifty I would guess right now, and in two years we will have about two hundred. It's clear that there are already a number of organizations that every week take the MARC tape, send it through their file management system, load it onto some disks, and hang it there for on-line searching.

The question I would like you to speculate about is, how many places in the United States should there be a complete searchable MARC file. Every one says obviously it's not 24 thousand, or 15 thousand, or ten thousand, or five hundred. As you look five years ahead, do you envision five hundred, two hundred, ten, five, one, or none and why?

Mr. Welsh: I believe in our report to the National Commission we addressed ourselves to this question. I don't now recall why I come up with a specific figure, but I think the figure was eleven. We were conceiving of eleven regional libraries which would be adequate to service the need.

Question: Are you still projecting operating economies for the new mechanized ordering system? If so, what are the magnitudes?

Mr. Welsh: We don't know as yet what the order of magnitude is. I should correct one thing here, we have had a mechanized order system for many many years. This is in essence a redesign. We are introducing the MARC format into the order division with the hope that subsequently we can enrich that record and use it in the Process Information File so that we eliminate the MARC production as we now know it. Many of the features we built into the system for the order division are based on the assumption we can use that record in subsequent processing steps.

Question: Are tapes coming from BNB in the MARC format being processed at LC?

Mr. Welsh: We are doing this experimentally but without any significant results as yet, because we can't establish that the use of BNB tapes can beat the existing manual system. This is probably because we haven't explored the proglem in depth. BNB produces a card record for our blanket order dealer, Stevens and Brown, and selects from that record. Unselected items are then sent in card form to the Library of Congress, where they are distributed by class number to the reference department and recommending officers. We can't find a way to beat that in the MARC system. We do expect, however, that once we have recognized the need for an item on the BNB tape, we will use the keypunching that has been done by BNB.

Directions for the Future: A Panel Discussion

Moderator: Herman Fussler
                 Director of Libraries
                 The University of Chicago Library

Panelists: Carl F. J. Overhage
                 Director, Project Intrex
                 Massachussetts Institute of Technology
                 Director, New University Information Technology Corporation
                 Cambridge, Mass.

                 Robert Blackburn
                 Director of Libraries
                 University of Toronto

                 Rutherford Rogers
                 Director of Libraries
                 Yale University

Herman Fussler The University of Chicago Libraries

Introduction

The broad class of problems that we have been discussing are basically concerned with cost and effectiveness in the quality and extent of access to recorded
knowledge and information in our society. Perhaps part of the confusion in some
of our discussions has to do with different approaches to that basic problem, *i.e.*,
whether we are trying to improve the absolute quality of access without regard
to cost, whether we are trying to maintain existing levels of access and reduce
cost, or whether we may be forced to diminish the quality, character and extent
of access in order to reduce costs, or some combination of the above. It is evident that we are very clearly handicapped by extraordinary difficulties in the
determination of costs and values of access to knowledge and information, and
this difficulty affects our ability to make reliable and accurate judgments with
respect to our priorities or alternatives. We are dealing with intellectual and design problems at both a local and a national level. We are also dealing with economic problems of extraordinary difficulty, with technical issues and related
problems of unusual complexity, and a variety of organizational and administrative issues.

We are really talking, though people tend not to say it very often, about
whether we are designing essentially local, regional, or national systems; whether
these systems are discipline-oriented, material-oriented, institutionally-oriented,
regionally-oriented, or oriented in some other manner. We are also talking about
how these systems, whatever their patterns may be, can be linked together.

I think I should also say, in response to a previous comment that the user
had not been mentioned very often, that it seems to me absolutely explicit as
well as implicit that we are talking about users and their needs as we talk about
the efforts to improve libraries and information access. If we are not doing so,
then indeed we are in serious difficulty. I would argue that there are many deficiencies in the current patterns of institutional, regional, and national access.
Some of these deficiencies are very severe and the solutions to them are not altogether obvious.

I think that we should also emphasize that while today and yesterday we
have been talking during the conference primarily about computer-related systems, this is really only one class of problems relating to the basic improvement

146

in the access of our society to information and knowledge. The panel will, I hope, stress this somewhat broader emphasis.

The subject for this panel is stated in the program as "Directions for the Future—Observations Concerning Realistic Possibilities and Appropriate Action." It is evident that the conference has already had a good deal of information and discussion with respect to potential directions for the future and some pertinent observations with respect to realistic possibilities. The members of the panel are anxious to avoid unnecessary redundancy this late in the program. We will therefore try to be terse, and we have agreed to divide our presentations into essentially three interrelated areas, recognizing that there are some overlaps. I propose to state these three areas and introduce all three speakers.

First, Carl Overhage will talk briefly about the issues relating to technical problems, levels of application, and economic restraints. Secondly, Robert Blackburn will address himself to problems relating to national coordination, planning, standards, common systems, utilization, and related issues. The third speaker is Rutherford Rogers, who will speak on the problems as they relate to a single institution.

Technical Problems

Carl F. J. Overhage Massachusetts Institute of Technology

In countless discussions of the future of libraries, one of the dominant themes has been the impact of new technology. The question that has generally emerged from such discussions has been this: How can new technology be intelligently exploited to provide better access to information resources?

I should like to outline some of the directions in which answers to that question may be found. My projections will be based on experimentation that has been successfully carried out over the past five years in a number of places, notably the three universities whose programs have been reviewed at this meeting. Following that brief exercise in technological forecasting, I shall express some doubt whether the question we asked in the first place is still the right one, and I shall end up by suggesting that, temporarily, we may have to redirect our attention toward other goals.

It is abundantly clear now that digital data processing techniques—computers for short—will be extensively used in the bibliographic control of our growing collections of recorded knowledge. The great power of these techniques will be exploited by librarians in technical services and by users as well as librarians in bibliographic searching.

In performing these functions, we shall progress beyond the batch processing techniques of our early experiments. Direct interaction with the computer in a dialog is the wave of the future that will ultimately advance to the procognitive systems envisioned by Licklider.

The creation and maintenance of the data banks required for these bibliographic systems is an intellectual task of such large magnitude that it will be undertaken only one in each field of knowledge by some appropriate central agency. Whether that will be the Library of Congress, or the indexing and abstracting service of a professional society, or a great public or private research center is an important question of national policy, but the answer is not essential to a technical forecast. The important point, in the present context, is that the computer techniques under discussion permit a user to interact with a data bank from a remote terminal. Thus, users and bibliographic resources will be interconnected in networks that will gradually expand from local clusters into world-wide systems.

What about the full text of the documents to which the computer-managed bibliographic service will guide the user? Computer storage of massive amounts of full text will remain prohibitively expensive for some time to come. Rapid facsimile transmission of printed pages or their microfilm equivalents is technically quite feasible but so expensive that it will be used only for work of exceptional urgency. The early solutions for full-text access will be based on machine copying and on microfilm and microfiche techniques which at long last seem to have reached the threshold of wider acceptance. On-demand duplication onto paper or microfiche will replace circulation for many library users, especially users at a distance. A particularly exciting prospect is the use of high reduction ratios to reproduce an entire book of several hundred pages onto a single microfiche or microcassette.

I must now turn to the painful matter of reconciling all this glittering technology to the economic realities of library budgets. In the past, my stance on this issue has been like this: We are talking about a new mode of access to information resources which may be sufficiently powerful to constitute an entirely new way of doing intellectual work. Its course of development may be comparable to the progress of high-speed computing in tasks formerly done with tables, slide rules, and desk calculators. Computers are expensive, but they have enabled men to extend their intellectual reach and to deal successfully with problems that had previously defeated them by their complexity. If it becomes clear that a similar extension of intellectual power can be provided by future library technology, then—I used to say—the necessary budgets will be forthcoming.

Well, I still think that eventually the money will be found. But, ladies and gentlemen, this is November 1970. Most of our great libraries are in deep budgetary trouble, our universities are struggling with unprecedented deficits, and our national priorities are directed away from intellectual goals. In such a situation, experimentation can and should continue; at least one node of the future network should be established at a major library and its operation studied; but I can no longer escape the conclusion that the large-scale introduction of new technology into our libraries will have to wait, no matter how powerful a mode of access it can provide.

It seems to me, in fact, that at this time the issue is survival. For the next few years, the right question to ask about new technology in libraries is not how it can improve access, but how it can reduce costs. That, at any rate, is the view of the university administrators from whom my signals come.

How can essential services be maintained with reduced budgets? The only answer to which most librarians will agree is to develop cooperative schemes with other libraries so that each can reduce its local holdings and subscriptions. Nobody expects that library users will love such a regime, but let us keep in mind that the issue is survival. Only librarians can decide whether the most effective form of cooperation can be built around a single lending and backstopping mechanism, or whether a less centralized network is indicated, in which each major library constitutes a resource for the others.

The contribution of technology will be to lift the operation of such a scheme to much higher levels of effectiveness than the traditional inter-library loan procedures. The indispensable first step must be the creation of a sensible structure of fees for interlibrary services, so that the library that contributes most of the materials is not also the one that pays most of the bill. Once this is done, the introduction of technology can be planned with a proper regard for economc realities.

The initial apparatus will not be spectacular. Teletype circuits will handle the essential communications. Existing facilities for machine copying and microphotography will be improved and expanded so as to minimize the physical transfer of materials by parcel service. Computers will be used sparingly, where economies can be achieved in technical service operations, or where the cost of doing searches on bibliographic data tapes can be justified. John Macdonald and David Kaser[1] have described two outstanding cooperative systems of this type.

You will recognize, of course, that this modest instrumentation is a possible first stage in a transition to the information transfer network of the future. But, for the near term, the initial scheme must be judged on its own merits. Once it has come into successful operation, the participating libraries will work toward some form of computer-stored union catalog which can be interrogated from each teletype terminal in the system.

I am at the end of my remarks. After describing a vision of the enormous power of future information networks, I have presented a scheme for the near term that appears bleak and pedestrian by comparison. But if you share my belief that libraries are in great peril at this time, you may agree that this is the sensible path into the future.

References

1. See Section I, *Administrative Commitment and a Course of Action.*

National Coordination

Robert Blackburn University of Toronto

My assignment is to say a few words about problems of national coordination in planning for automated systems, and in particular about a proposal that has been made by the Association of Research Libraries. The use of the word "national" in this connection calls up international consideration, but I shall not complicate the matter by pressing that point here. After what we have heard about the uniqueness of hardware configurations and the uniqueness of libraries, and the practical problems of transferrability, one may wonder whether there is anything useful to be said at all about national coordination. As I understand it, application programs are not transferrable unless the environments are identical, but there can be useful exchange among libraries at the level of systems logic and general design, and so my topic is valid.

It is clear that all developments, collaborative and otherwise, are subject to money being available. The severe financial constraints which Carl Overhage referred to are very real and they worry me greatly because they could change our programs not only in rate of progress. I can't help wondering what would have happed to Columbus if Queen Isabella had said, "Sorry old boy, I really can't spare anything but a few earrings and I suggest that for the foreseeable future, you confine your explorations to the Mediterranean." Obviously, the New World would have been discovered by somebody else. And if librarians are too quick to accept financial barriers, even ones which look to be insurmountable, no doubt other people will find the money and will develop regional and national networks in their own way. I'm glad that Carl wants at least one future node to be kept alive in one major library, and it would of course be desirable to have at least three or four for the sake of variety.

I have no answer to the economic problem, but the shortage of money makes it more important than ever for us to have clear goals and priorities. These are necessary to optimize the effect of limited energies, and to keep us from economizing ourselves into a blind alley.

Many of you know about the effort being made in the direction of planning by the Association of Research Libraries. Last Spring, ARL appointed a small *ad hoc* committee to specify procedures and requirements for a review of automation in research libraries. The committee's report was adopted in June and published in the ARL proceedings, I think the quickest way to summarize it for you is to read a part of the preamble. "For several years the members of ARL, collectively and individually, have been more and more concerned about the orderly development of computer applications to bibliography and to the operation of research libraries. From the national point of view, ARL and other agencies have sought ways to arrive at a general pattern within which orderly development could take place, but have not been successful. It becomes increasingly clear that the library community needs a rational definition of objectives and a national strategy for attaining them. We think the review of automation for which we are to prepare specifications should be a position paper concerned with future course of computer-based data-processing in large research libraries. While it must take current operations and problems into account, it should not ignore the more distant future. It should not be a projection of current efforts or a forecast of technical capabilities. It should define goals in terms of library functions, examine the practical constraints, and propose priorities for the next five years. We suggest five years as a planning period for which developments can be imagined if not foreseen, and within which practical progress may be made.

"We do not suppose that such a position paper would be taken as the ultimate word on its subject, or that it should have any prescriptive or prospective authority, but we do think it could be extremely useful as a statement of informed opinion, a thoughtful and consistent approach to some confused and difficult matters. It could provide guidelines for institutions and for granting agencies, and a rational strategy for the attacks that have to be made on major problems. It could be a means of enlightening legislators and university boards concerning the reality of these problems. It should help to increase the overall rate of progress, reduce the amount of wasteful duplication in local efforts, and help to avoid a variety of local divergencies which could otherwise grow into long-term incompatibilities.

"Obviously, the position paper cannot be written by a volunteer committee. Ideally it should be done by a seasoned philosopher thoroughly versed in the needs of scholars, a theory and practice of bibliography, the design and application of computers, and the management of research libraries. Since the only people we know with all these qualifications are otherwise engaged, and since there is a real urgency for the job to be done, we suggest that it should be done by a team of two or three wise people with the best possible combination of these qualifications, each devoting perhaps two or ten months of time to it. We think the matter is so important that ARL should spare no effort in enlisting the best people for it. They should of course receive appropriate compensation and the means to do whatever travelling and consulting they deem necessary. In the course of their work, they may have to call on ARL institutions to provide data and staff consultation time.

"The position paper, when completed, should be reviewed by a small ARL committee which would recommend to the Board concerning its publication or other use. The paper should not be shaped or limited by the following outline but should deal in some way with each of the matters indicated."[1] In the outline which follows, the main headings are, A, Objectives; B, Constraints; C, Priorities.

There may be some among you who feel that this kind of approach is very dangerous, that it would tend to limit the free and unfettered invention implied in a multitude of local experiments. The alternative, in terms of what we know, may be free and unfettered stagnation. This is the kind of choice we have to make and it seems clear to me that American research libraries should at least try for an orderly national plan.

References

1. Association of Research Libraries, Minutes of the 76th meeting, June 27, 1970, held at Detroit, Michigan.

Problems for the Single Library

Rutherford Rogers   Yale University Libraries

Everything has been said; all I can do is underline what is perhaps obvious, but maybe this is worth doing. As a migrant worker, I am interested in money and I seem to have been talking to the same people that Carl Overhage has because I think we must, as I have felt for quite a long time, be much more conscious of cost than we have been. In the last two days, we have heard a fair amount about this and I think today more than yesterday. But in the immediate future, we must pin down with much greater precision the economics of automation or, as Jim Haas said this morning, the entry into a new kind of reality.[1]

In this connection, looking to the immediate future of a single library, I think the divergent opinions expressed here on the validity of time-sharing and of on-line operation will be paramount concerns. We must determine to what extent we can afford on-line operation. As Paul Fasana and others have said, we must also begin to worry about the impact of automation on users, and what users really want. The grand conception of a fully on-line system with implications for a revolution in information handling and retrieval can only be justified if indeed we produce the revolution and it proves to be what is wanted.

In more prosaic and specific respects we will need in the early future to develop a viable circulation system. We seem to know what the parameters are, we seem to know what the necessary hardware is, and yet we don't seem to be able to produce this animal. We also have to solve the immensely complex problems of serials control.

It must also be apparent that no one library can store the totality of MARC data year after year and yet we must have access to it. Therefore, individual libraries must begin to demonstrate the feasibility of tapping either regional or national MARC data stores, and it is probably not too soon to start worrying about the cost of individual machine readable catalogs for libraries that have miltimillion volume collections.

To achieve these objectives in a period when technology is changing rapidly, and when we must attain a much higher reliability in software as we have heard repeatedly in the last two days, will be no mean task. And I would be less than realistic if I did not emphasize the difficulty of finding funds for further experimental work. I hope that the fund granting agencies present at this conference, admirable though their support has been thus far, will recognize that we are far from the promised land and that development funds substantial in amount and duration are still needed.

A word of understanding, however, is in order for the fund granting agencies themselves. They obviously cannot fund automation in two thousand libraries. I believe this problem may not be as great as it may seem and that help can be found to assist not only in such decision making, but also in the equally vexatious problem of whether and to what extent emphasis should be placed on regional or networking efforts as opposed to research in a single library.

References

1. See Part I, Section III, *Administrative Commitment and a Course of Action.*

Discussion

Question from the floor: Over the past day and a half I have a metamessage that has leaked into my head. Money is getting very tight and one must be more careful about how it's used and must worry about cost effectiveness. Mr. Blackburn made the point that in periods of tight money one has to be particularly concerned with careful definition of goals and priorities. I think that one should always be careful about those things, but that it's only when money is tight that we do what we should be doing all the time. I'm wondering if tight money, and this is the metamessage, will not be a positive inspiration and aid rather than a deterrent. About a month ago I was in Canada and I heard a number of university libraries talk about some of their work with the MARC tapes. I was impressed with the innovative things that they have done that I hadn't heard about before. I kept saying to myself, "Gee, they have done an awful lot with practically no money." And it suddenly began to dawn on me that maybe one of the reasons they have done so much is that they didn't have the money. So my question is, do you think it will help to have no less money?

Mr. Rogers: I think in all administration we ought to be very cost conscious. I've said this frequently on the space problem in libraries. It's very easy to be aloof in our administration of space while we have it. And I think this too is a mistake. Nonetheless, having said that, I do think that it is obvious in what has been said in the last two days that a lot of experimentation still needs doing, and I know from having been inside a library that was carrying on a very ambitious automation effort, that you simply can't do these things without some supplementary money. I don't think it's within the power of the individual institutions at this particular time to make the progress we want. In that respect I certainly agree with Carl. I hope that outside money will not dry up; if it does, I do think that we are in real trouble.

Mr. Overhage: I think the problem is that we are redirecting our effort as a result of budgetary restrictions. We are now beginning to address another problem. The problem on which we were engaged before this era of austerity came upon us was in many respects a more challenging problem because it was really directed toward an extension of what man can do. I think there was something very exciting about it. We will go on with that problem but I'm distressed by the fact that the effort is being slowed down and that we must now turn our attention to what technology can do to reduce costs. This is good; this is desirable. Maybe it's good for our souls but I think the other problem is a more fascinating one.

Mr. Fussler: I would like to add a small footnote to that. I'm not sure that money has been all that pervasive throughout the land. A good deal of the developmental work has been done on very very tight and stringent budgets and staff support. Perhaps we should ask now if there are other questions?

Mr. Haas: What structure is required to promote the development of a rational national system for library automation?

Mr. Blackburn: It would be tempting to throw this question back to Jim Haas who is Chairman of the ARL committee which adopted this report, but I was responsible as Chairman of the *ad hoc* committee. The *ad hoc* committee was only a way of getting a recipe written that might begin to answer this question. There are two requirements which so far have not been found. One is money and the second is a small team of people who could and would be able to find the time to work out the kind of recipe or plan that is really needed.

Having chaired this committee and written the report, I feel a bit like a person who says, "Well, the cat should obviously have a bell on it." The question remains, who is going to bell the cat and how is it going to be done. I don't know. This was the problem that ARL was trying to get to. The recipe that has been proposed is that somebody or some small group of people who really know a great deal about the problem should be provided with enough time to think the matter through, travel across the country, gather ideas, and make a comprehensive proposal of some kind. I don't know what that proposal would be.

Mr. Fussler: May I add to that very briefly? I think this focuses on a very fundamental problem relating to the design of the information structure of the country. It has been evident in the past five or ten years that a large number of organizations, some of great influence, power, ability, and others of lesser influence, have commissioned or undertaken a wide variety of fairly basic national or other kinds of planning studies, either for single disciplines, a group of disciplines, all of "science or technology," for libraries, or of some other kind. Appropriate agencies to implement such plans in a complex society, where information is structured, generated, and used in a very complex manner, are not altogether visible. I am sure there are hopes that the proposed National Commission on Libraries and Information Science could accept a major role in this area, but it seems unlikely that even such a group as this will have the funding, the staff, or the resources to carry through the planning and determination of the national priorities for a comprehensive set of systems. Such a Commission would surely help to provide an umbrella under which more forward-looking and constructive planning could be done, but there is no single agency that can embrace all aspects of this problem. If there were, I am sure that there would be serious objections to its trying to exercize such a role. Yet it is evident that we are trying to plan a complex transportation or delivery system with all kinds of multi-gauge tracks, different kinds of engines and cars, a ticketing system that is anything but universal, and countless other problems. Some improvements would have enormous advantages. The problem is how to achieve reasonable standards, avoid unnecessary redundancy, remain fiscally solvent, maintain intellectual and other kinds of freedom, provide for rational diversity, for flexibility, for sound design, and at the same time avoid a monolithic monster.

This is not a very good answer to a very relevant question, but maybe there is not one, except as we try to reach an understanding and a consensus of probable ways, means, and priorities.

Part II

THE STANFORD COLLABORATIVE LIBRARY SYSTEMS
DEVELOPMENT CONFERENCE: SELECTED PAPERS

The following section contains a selection of the papers presented at the First Collaborative Library Systems Development Conference held at Stanford University, October 4–5, 1968. The complete proceedings of the Stanford conference were edited by Allen Veaner and Paul Fasana and published by the Stanford University Libraries in 1969. The versions printed here have been slightly revised and edited.

National Collaboration and the National Libraries Task Force: A Course Toward Compatibility

Samuel Lazerow   Chairman, National Libraries Task Force on Automation
Library of Congress

Cooperation among the national libraries is not a new or recent concept although it has never been pitched at as high a level as at present. Earlier examples include the following: As early as 1901, the Librarian of Congress, in reporting to the Congress on the state of the Library's collections, commented that few books had been purchased in recent years for Agriculture "because the well organized library of the Department of Agriculture is adequate to the demands," and, with reference to materials in Medicine and Surgery, he explained that "Owing to the accessibility of the library of the Surgeon General's Office and its liberal administration, there has been little expenditure by the Library of Congress in these lines."[1]

In 1944 the Army Medical Library (now the National Library of Medicine) joined with the Library of Congress in a "systematic review of the classification schedule for medicine."[2]

Since 1945 the Library of Congress has recognized NAL's responsibility to collect comprehensively in agriculture and its allied fields and NLM's similar responsibility for broad coverage in medicine and its allied fields.[3]

The largest single contributor of cooperative cataloging copy to the Library of Congress in 1948 was the Army Medical Library "in accordance with an agreement reached the previous year, according to which this library took principal responsibility for the cataloging of medical books. . ."[4]

And so it has gone, as the three national institutions have endeavored to advance their services by combining and sharing resources and skills whenever possible and appropriate.

As we all know, the reasons behind these collaborative efforts are even more compelling today—the great quantities of material being generated in every field of knowledge; the accelerating costs of acquiring, accessioning, cataloging, and servicing these expanding collections; the mounting pressure from scientists, other scholars and users to have quick access to information; the increasingly difficult task of providing interdisciplinary linkages.

It is the increasing urgency of these problems that has led today's librarians to recognize that some traditional library methods are inadequate and that they must look to the new technology for some positive remedies.

In June 1967 the directors of the three national libraries announced in San Francisco during ALA's annual conference, their institution of a coordinated national library effort "to speed the flow of research information to the Nation's libraries and to the scholars and researchers who use them.[5]

At a press conference at that time, these directors announced their agreement on adoption of "common goals as each proceeds to automate."

They pointed out on that occasion that "this effort to achieve systems compatibility at the national level has far-reaching implications for library automation and library systems of the future."[6]

The *broad purpose* of the program, as defined by the directors, is to improve access to the world's literature in all areas of human concern and scholarship, so that comprehensive access to the materials of learning can be afforded to all citizens of the United States."

Specific goals indicated in the joint announcement were "the development of a national data bank of machine-readable cataloging information" and a "national data bank of machine-readable information relating to the location of hundreds of thousands of serial titles held by American research libraries," along with the essential objective of achieving compatibility in as many areas of the three libraries" operations as possible.

Our Task Force was announced at that time as the vehicle for guiding this cooperative effort.

The Task Force (composed of one member and one alternative from each of the three national libraries)[7] has identified specific problem areas requiring detailed study and has named working groups to go into these problems in depth.

Currently ten working groups are active in the following areas:

1. Acquisitions
2. Bibliographic Codes
3. Character Sets
4. Descriptive Cataloging
5. Generalized Output
6. Machine-Readable Format
7. Name Entry and Authority File
8. Serials
9. Subject Headings
10. Systems.

All groups have made important progress, as will be evident from the accomplishments to be outlined here.

Each group is chaired by a national library staff member knowledgeable in the problem area concerned, and the memberships are composed of staff having responsibilities in the pertinent areas in their respective national libraries.

Determination of mission statements for each group was a first order of business.

Meetings are held weekly or at the call of the group chairmen who report frequently to the Task Force in brief written reports or in oral presentations.

Last June an all-day session with all group chairmen, at which we were privileged to have Mr. Fasana present, brought the Task Force up-to-date on the progress of each group and provided an opportunity for a profitable exchange among the groups themselves.

You can well understand that a number of the difficult problems cut across several areas and it is important for groups to be aware of developments in areas other than those of immediate concern.

The automation of serial controls, for example, while the major concern of the Serials Group, involves the groups on Character Sets, Generalized Output, and Machine-Readable Format as well.

We have not yet worked out an entirely satisfactory mechanism for assuring referral of related problems from group to group, but we have found frequent joint discussion and reporting is one useful approach.

The Task Force itself meets weekly for two or more hours of discussion on a variety of topics ranging from compatibility in filing rules to procedures and steps leading toward conceptualization of a hypothetical working system.

An *Advisory Committee*, composed of representatives from major professional societies, has met once with the Task Force and once in executive session. Jim Skipper is Chairman of the Committee. Its primary purpose is to assist in communications to and from the library community and to give the Task Force the benefit of other librarians' thinking with respect to coordinated national library automation programs.

I might add at this point that we hope for a close liaison also with the Collaborative Library Systems Development project.

The libraries in the Collaborative Systems Project have a higher degree of similarity to each other than do the three national libraries. Our task is complicated by important differences in size and subject specializations. Early in my work as Chairman it became evident that we must examine the present resources and responsibilities of each of the three institutions and the policies and constraints under which each operates in order to search for optimum relationships.

Our study confirmed the conclusion that the three libraries have unique responsibilities involving the collection and dissemination of materials in all languages, in all forms, and from all parts of the world.

The National Agricultural Library has this responsibility for Agriculture and its allied fields, and the National Library of Medicine for the preclinical sciences and for medicine and related fields. The Library of Congress' responsibilities extend to all fields of knowledge, but its cooperative acquisitions arrangements with NAL and NLM, to which I have alluded earlier, defer to those libraries in their special areas of responsibility.

The clientele served by each of the three libraries is similar, with LC having special responsibilities to the Congress, NLM to the medical community, and NAL to the agricultural community.

All serve the general public, although other users may have higher priorities. Each serves other Federal agencies, and each has responsibilities and cooperative arrangements with other libraries, Federal and non-Federal. All have international as well as national service responsibilties.

Services provided by each institution include use of the collections on the premises, interlibrary loan, reference, bibliographic services, publications, photocopying. Each library has varied specialized services related to various user groups.

The common purposes and services indicate that there is sound basis for pressing the quest for a national library system and emphasize the fact that *the national libraries of the United States are necessarily the pivot of any true national information system.*

A basic ingredient to all systems planning on a network level is, of course, the search for standardization in as many areas of an operation as possible.

Because standardization is such an essential ingredient of any plan to avoid duplication of modules and is an absolute prerequisite for any cooperative system, the Task Force has concentrated attention on the development of standards for the inputting, transmission, and dissemination of information in machine-readable form.

I do not need to talk to this audience on the importance of standards in the new technology or the fact that the usefulness of any standard is proportionate to the extent of its acceptance and use.

All of you know that in any given field the acceptance and use of a national standard is complex and difficult to achieve. The Task Force's experience bears this out. We have reviewed and discussed many drafts, debated many issues, and considered a variety of alternatives before reaching the point where a recommendation for the adoption of the standard is submitted to the three directors.

Thus a great deal of expertise goes into the making of a standard—every concerned person or group must have a voice in the work and every effort must be made to eliminate bias if the result is to be eventual adoption as a national standard.

Despite this lengthy process and the unavoidable backward steps that accompany it, I report with considerable satisfaction some substantial progress.

Of unrivaled importance in standardization and systems development—not only for the three national libraries but for research institutions everywhere—has been the announcement by the directors of the three national libraries of their joint adoption of the *Machine-Readable Cataloging* format (*MARC II*) for the communication of bibliographic information in machine-readable form and the set of data elements defined for monographs within the MARC structure.

You have heard on other occasions the history of the development of the MARC format at the Library of Congress in cooperation with other research libraries, so I shall not repeat the account here. MARC reflects the requirements of many institutions, including the three national libraries. It was reviewed by the Task Force and its MARC group in terms of each national library's individual needs.

Adoption has not committed the institution to use all the data elements described; each will determine individual implementation procedures.

Agreement on this communications format is a positive demonstration of the three libraries' firm intention to extend the usefulness of their collections and services through the application of new technological capabilities wherever economically and technically feasible, and it will facilitate further extensions throughout the library and research communities.

A second major agreement on standards concerns descriptive cataloging practices and here is where I believe we accomplished what many thought was impossible. We got catalogers together.

In announcing their joint decision to adopt standard practices in descriptive cataloging, the directors emphasized that these standards are of major importance to other libraries, whether manual or computer methods are in use.

Of the common elements identified in descriptive cataloging practices at the three national libraries, six created compatibility problems. To achieve standardization each of the three libraries has agreed to change some practices, and the American Library Association has been asked to make changes in several rules.

I should emphasize at this point that a significant factor in our ability to get at the heart of compatibility problems quickly and to find practical ways of resolving differences in view has been the *involvement in the actual work of operating* staff from each institution.

The Descriptive Cataloging Group is chaired by NLM's principal cataloging officer; its other members are top cataloging adminstrators in the other two libraries. Together they were able to come to common agreement on the stumbling blocks to compatibility in their area and on the remedies.

Acceptance of a standard is made appreciably easier if one can assure each director that his principal adminstrator in that area of specialization has agreed to the proposed practice or change in practice.

A recent further accomplishment has been the adoption by the three national libraries of a *standard calendar date code*, which is designed to provide a standard way of representing calendar dates in the data processing systems of the national libraries and may be particularly useful for application in data interchange among Federal agencies and among other libraries.

Date in this code will allow for representation of century, year, month, or day in the Gregorian calendar. Four digits are provided for use in the computer field to represent pre-twentieth century dates; a six-digit code, based on USASI's proposed code and the Bureau of the Budget standards will represent dates in a field limited exclusively to twentieth century dates.

General use of this standard code will eliminate the confusion caused by a variety of date representations.

I have just received from our Working Groups in Bibliographic Codes a draft standard language code, which I will take up shortly with the Task Force. This code will include languages representing the major body of published literature and has been developed in consideration with language specialists in the three institutions.

A *standard character set* for use in describing information on magnetic tape is now under final consideration by the Task Force.

The design of this standard has involved consideration of all the characters any of the three national libraries might wish to use to represent bibliographic data in machine-readable form, consideration of the characters that can actually be put into digital form, and the ways in which they can be pulled out once they are in digital form.

The standard set will include some 170 characters, including diacritical marks and scientific characters.

The Task Force is looking into the need for standards that can assure more adequate control over *technical report literature*. Our Descriptive Cataloging Group is aware of the inadequacy of bibliographical controls over this rising quantity of material and is taking a look at the most feasible avenue for improvement of the situation.

On the basis of a pilot study of the structure of name authority files in each of the three libraries, it has been determined that a mechanized central authority file would be useful. The difference in size of the present files is an important consideration, however, and we await the findings of a larger scale study to provide for solid decisions here.

One of the most critical and difficult areas from the point of view of achieving compatibility concerns subject headings, where expressions of both optimism and pessimism have been voiced from time to time. Anyone who has worked in a medical library, as I have, knows what great problems arise in trying to coordinate MESH and the LC subject heading list; right now, of course, this cannot be done. However, we do have a working group looking into this, and there are indications that with some compromises we may be able to achieve some success here.

The study group in this area has tackled the issues in a most constructive way. Sub-headings in use in each institution are being explored, charts showing the interrelationships of the headings in use have been drawn, and the possiblity of establishing a common list has at least been aired.

Computer output programs useful to the three institutions are being examined, including collective publications, on-line and off-line printing, and console output.

Inasmuch as initial objectives set by the directors included the creation of a national data base for serial publications, the progress of the National Serials Data Program has had a high priority. I am assuming that all of you are well acquainted with this ambitious undertaking, supported jointly by the three national libraries together with funding from the National Science Foundation and the Council on Library Resources, Inc. I will therefore omit the details of the work that has occupied a sizeable amount of the time of our technical people the past year, resulting in the compilation of data elements required for the control of serials, now under consideraton by the three libraries.

Although much more work and many more resources will have to be poured into the program, the ultimate product will be a matchless tool for the bibliographic control of the millions of pieces of serial literature coming into this country from all parts of the world.

We have learned some interesting facts from the serials work to date: first, a machine-based national data bank should be designed to take maximum advantage of computer systems and should not be constrained by the limitations of manual systems. Second, a universal numbering scheme for serials is a basic requirement—the Task Force has been cooperating with USASI's Z-39 Committee in an effort to get a proposed scheme underway here—and third, users' attitudes on implementation are so in variance that it is not likely that the final recommendations will satisfy everyone. But since they seldom do, we are determined not to retreat from our original ultimate purpose of developing a communications format for serials comparable to the MARC format for monographs.

I do not need to elaborate on the reasons why this assignment is far more difficult than the development of MARC I and II. All of you recognize that in

MARC we had the standard printed card as a beginning; with serials we have lacked this standardization, and it is this initial task that has taken the concentrated attention of the staff in the first phase of this vital program.

This compatibility and standardization are absolutely essential to any kind of systems approach. Since last December the Task Force and its Systems Group have been agonizing over the matter of alternate systems and design possibilities. There has been progress in analysis of present methods of each library, and this is continuing.

Our systems work has been handicapped by the lack of a sufficient number of trained people who can devote full-time to the necessary detailed studies for an extended period. The Council on Library Resources has generously assigned a systems analyst to the Task Force, but other Working Group members are carrying additional responsibilities. While the Task Force has made a number of attempts to solve this problem, the difficulty of finding staff with the necessary and unusual combination of computer orientation and librarianship is well known.

There is the further complication that at least for the next few years there will necessarily have to be three discrete systems; our interim objective, therefore, must be to find appropriate ways to build bridges between these systems and to continue to plan ahead for a later time when a more ideal system can be visualized, with a central switching mechanism that will provide access to the total knowledge contained in the three libraries.

Each of the three national libraries is presently committed to automation programs that make it necessary for our systems specialists to plan for appropriate interchange and linking of these systems.

Our Systems Working Group is now attacking this "short-range" planning which involves the coordination of the present systems design work at the three institutions, the identification and planning for the actual interchange of system modules if and where appropriate, and the interconnecting of the three discrete systems.

The NLM and NAL systems are planned to become operational in the early 1970's and to continue probably through much of that decade. LC's approach probably will call for certain segments to become operational in the early 1970's and to continue at least into the 1980's. Selected segments of each system may be available prior to these periods and may be in use beyond these general time frames.

We do know that because of size, the NLM and NAL systems can be expected to become operational at an earlier date than that at LC, although, through the modular approach, LC will have sub-systems being phased into operation ahead of the total capability. It is with these advanced sub-systems at LC that the NAL and NLM systems will be interlinked in the short-range plan. The planning for the interlinking of these systems is necessarily constrained by existing organizational structures of the three libraries, by normal technical constraints, and by their respective assigned missions.

Thus, considerations to date appear to point toward the concept of three data stores mutually capable of receiving and transmitting information. This would mean that each library would create its own store of machine-readable information, with each store having the capability of receiving data from the other two libraries and of transmitting data to them.

Because of the overlap in many fields of knowledge today, because modern science and modern scholarship are so interdisciplinary, it will be necessary to create a situation that can provide for the economical dissemination of information to any community needing it from any repository holding it. We can suppose that the information will come in raw form to the three national libraries, where it will be digested by each library and made available in different forms for different clientele. If the methods by which we digest and store the information are compatible, then we will be able to make it easily accessible from any store in which it is located.

Beyond this we are also faced with the need for long-range in-depth planning for the period beyond the 1970's when there might be more freedom to search for optimum interactions. Such long-range planning must include reexamination of the three national libraries' goals and objectives for the long-term system and consideration of the possibilities for combining functions and integrating certain operations as appropriate. We recognize that it is impossible to continue "as is."

It is essential to pursue the planning for both the short- and long-range time periods simultaneously. Because the possibilities are so far-reaching, this long-range study should begin as soon as possible, and I have been pressing for the search for funds and personnel to make some substantial progress here. The ultimate decisions will remain with the three directors, of course.

Among the Task Force's targets for the months ahead, in addition to acceleration of the National Serials Data Program, cooperation with the Z-39 Committee on the universal numbering scheme for serials, and continued work on standards and compatibility problems, are considerations on the assignment of responsibilities in a national network. This is an essential ingredient of the long-range planning.

It is my firm conviction that any effective system must be based on the principle of elimination of duplication of effort. There is too much to be done in this total area and too many demands on limited resources of talent and money to allow duplication of each other's work. Ideally it would seem logical to allocate sole responsibility for specific functions in specific subject fields to one institution, and the Task Force has had some illuminating discussions of alternative possibilities along these lines, particularly in connection with acquisitions and processing functions.

Again, these are questions that do not lend themselves to easy resolution of the specific responsibilities assigned by statute to a particular library, because of the historical development of individual policies and special relationships, and because of the special competences within the individual libraries for particular functions.

Nevertheless, the Task Force intends to continue its look at possible new patterns that in time might prove useful, economical, and acceptable to all concerned. We are convinced that the time is long overdue when the three national libraries, with their combined holdings representing almost the total of recorded knowledge, can lead the way to a new and exciting era of interlibrary cooperation, both national and international. The directors, in launching this program, have recognized that if we can unite in working out new and more effective and rapid ways of operating our complex apparatus then we will all respond with more awareness and efficiency to the needs of the total research community.

It is too early yet to foresee all the implications this effort can have upon the library community at large. Certainly the adoption of MARC II as a standard for providing catalog information in machine-readable form increases substantially the versatility of its use in libraries because the computer, as we all know, permits a greater variety of approaches to the information than card or book catalogs and because libraries with computer facilities can print out more easily and quickly a greater variety of research tools.

All of the standards we have developed thus far will benefit other libraries desiring to automate, and there is promise that through increased collaboration and sharing of knowledge and resources our common problems can be alleviated more quickly and, hopefully, more economically.

It will all take time. There are no easy paths, and much of the work must be a pioneer effort. The Collaborative Library Systems Development program and the U.S. National Libraries Task Force can cooperate through the sharing of information and specific results of their respective studies. There are a number of ways in which our cooperation can be augmented. Joint meetings at appropriate times could provide valuable give-and-take at the working level. A collective "Skills Bank" might widen the use that we could all make of the scarce and absolutely essential talents of trained systems staff. Directors of all the libraries involved in the two programs might profit from a creative colloquium on a collaborative systems network.

Before closing I want to stress the remarkable achievement that has been realized by the commitment of the Library of Congress, the National Agricultural Library, and the National Library of Medicine to work together in a cooperative enterprise of this magnitude. It is without doubt the largest effort, in terms of talent and man-hours expended, toward national library cooperation that these libraries have ever undertaken. The decision to join together in this effort will have far-reaching results in the long run for librarians and scholars in future generations.

The excellence of American libraries over the years has rested in large measure upon the extent to which cooperative enterprises have been successfully undertaken. We believe that the Task Force's program gives conspicuous evidence of the fact that collaborative effort at the real working level offers the best chance of finding durable settlements to crucial library questions. We hope that our effort will be contagious, and we invite all interested librarians to give us their help and their support.

References

1. Report of the Librarian of Congress, 1901, Washington, D.C., p. 319-320.
2. Report of the Librarian of Congress, 1944, Washington, D.C., p. 79.
3. Letters from Librarian of Congress to Army Medical Library and Department of Agriculture Library, February 23, 1945 and October 24, 1945, respectively.
4. Report of the Librarian of Congress, 1948, Washington, D. C., pp. 92-93.
5. Library of Congress Press Release 67-33, Washington, D.C., June 26, 1967.
6. Ibid.
7. Task Force members, in addition to Mr. Lazerow, are Bella E. Shachtman, National Agricultural Library, and Samuel Waters, National Library of Medicine, who has just succeeded James P. Riley. Alternates are Mrs. Henriette D. Avram, Library of Congress, Abraham Lebowitz, National Agricultural Library, Stanley Smith, National Library of Medicine. Mr. Irvin J. Weiss, Library of Congress, assists the Task Force. Mrs. Marlene D. Morrisey, Executive Assistant to the Librarian of Congress, is serving as staff assistant to the chairman.

Management of the Design and Development of the Biomedical Communications Network

Ralph A. Simmons Head, Information and Computer Sciences, National Library of Medicine, Bethesda

On August the 3rd, 1968 the 90th Congress passed a joint resolution authorizing the establishment of a National Center for Biomedical Communications and designating it as the *Lister Hill National Center for Biomedical Communications* (Public Law 90-456; 90th Congress, S. J. Res. 193). The Center has been endorsed by the Scientific Community as an urgently required facility for the improvement of communications so necessary to health education, research and practice and established as a part of the National Library of Medicine. Its designation as the Lister Hill Center was as a tribute to the career of Senator Hill of Alabama, who has accomplished so much for the health of the American people.

There have been many significant activities and trends in the past few years that have led to the need for this National Center. The Federal Government has played an ever increasing role in the provision of health services and in the development and conduct of medical research and educational programs. The establishment of the Regional Medical Program under Federal sponsorhip and direction through the National Institutes of Health represents a milestone in the organization of national resources toward the improvement of the nation's health. The Veteran's Administration is assuming an expanding role through a variety of programs for the improvement of health and health care. All of this concentrated effort is in response to the demands of society for ever-improving health care and prevention of sickness. It also represents a principle of decentralization of operations of the responsive programs and a centralization of supporting resource allocation. Further impetus to the establishment of the Center has come from the national attention to networks and communications as the way to the improvement of the necessary transfer of knowledge to support the variety of expanding medical programs. It also represents a response to the need for the improvement in the coordination of technology development and application in the areas of information and computer sciences.

The principal responsibilities of the Lister Hill Center for Biomedical Communications can be described by the following four major functions: 1. the design, development, implementation and management of the Biomedical Communications Network; 2. the application of existing and advanced technology to the improvement of biomedical communications; 3. to serve as the focal point in the Department of Health, Education and Welfare for the technological aspects of biomedical communcations, information systems, and network projects; and 4. to represent the Department in the activities of the President's Office of Science and Technology, other Federal agencies and interagency committees in areas related to information and communications. It is the first of these functions—the establishment and operation of the Biomedical Communications Network—that is the principal concern of my following comments.

Why a network at all? What are the advantages for biomedical information services to be gained through networking? These can best be expressed by the five conditions that represent needs for such a network: 1. the existence of a unique collection in a single location that is useful to a dispersed audience; 2. the inadequacy of local collections and the need for complementary support from other sources; 3. the centralization of particular capabilities or unusual resources with a dispersed need; 4. the need for interpersonnel, direct communication; and 5. the justification for the distribution of certain responsibilities among organizations or regions based upon economic or professional capabilities. The linking of libraries, information centers, medical schools, hospitals, and research centers through communications arranged so as to constitute a network can best meet those needs and conditions as described.

The selection of a network for improving the information and educational services within the medical community was also based upon the present state-of-the-art in information and computer sciences. The network when looked upon as a complex process including communications, controls, and feedback and consisting of a variety of components is at the proper step in a "complexity" ladder of technological advancement. We have passed through the stages of the use of the individual computer and then computer systems and now see extensive efforts in the linking of the computer systems into networks. Major research and development is now underway on the next step on the ladder—automatons and the mechanization of intelligent behavior. When you have R & D at the next stage, you know that you are in the right stage on the ladder of technical complexity for the development of an operating activity.

The specific objectives of the Biomedical Communications Network (BCN) against which we can test each stage of our development effort are five in number: 1. to improve research; 2. to provide better professional services; 3. to make conscious and planned decisions on the applications of technologies to biomedical communication; 4. to provide for a more uniform, highly-qualified professional; and 5. to provide for a larger, well-informed citizen audience. A fundamental concept that information systems in themselves are a completely sterile and artificial resource and that they must be coupled with some process forms an additional guide to the establishment of the BCN. In this case, the process with which we must couple the network is that of medical education. This is not surprising if we consider that an important purpose of medical education is the *transfer* of skills, knowledge, and information from a variety of sources through a variety of media to the student and practitioner.

The characteristics of our network can be expressed as determined by the customer requirements. The various services of the network will be available on a decentralized basis and accessible through local hospitals, medical societies, clinics, medical schools, medical libraries, and private offices. These services will be organized along the lines of topical specialties and against the major medical advances accomplished in the latest five years.

The planning to date for the BCN has included the division of the Network into five major component parts, *i.e.*, the Library Component, the Specialized Information Services Component, the Specialized Educational Services Component, the Audio and Audiovisual Services Component, and the supporting Data Processing and Data Transmission Facilities. Our major concern today is the Library Component but, before examining it in some detail, I would like to define the scope of the other elements. The purpose of the Specialized Information Services Component is to communicate information related to specific subject areas to customers in the bio-medical and health-related fields using communications, computer, and other relevant technologies. Its principal constituents are planned to be a referral center, a distinct toxicological information system and a system of information analysis centers.

The Specialized Educational Services Component has as its goal the support of three distinct areas of education: 1. continuing medical education for the medical professional; 2. education of the medically uninformed; and 3. education in related relevant technology for the medical professional such as new devices, new communication media, or new procedures. As the names imply, the Audio and Audiovisual Services Component provides identification of available materials and access to those materials and the Data Processing and Data Transmission Facilities provide the support in the identified areas as required.

The Library Component of the BCN is intended to provide bibliographic citations to biomedical literature, access to the literature itself, and support to the required library operations in such areas as acquisitions, cataloging, indexing, and announcement and reference services. I realize that networks to librarians are really nothing new. The interlibrary loan activities among libraries have demonstrated networking on a regional and national scale. The complex systems of national and regional bibliographic control in the form of union lists and catalogs and the systems of interim source referral services clearly complete the identifi-

cation of the library system as a viable *de facto* network. But with the newer
tools provided by our advancing technology, the network takes on a completely
new dimension. It is the planning for the development and management of this
more advance network that I now wish to discuss in some detail.

Actions on the part of the staff of NLM and others in the medical library
profession over the past few years, supported by specific legislation, have resulted in the establishment of the nucleus of a biomedical library network including Regional Medical Libraries, decentralized MEDLARS Centers, and affiliates
in England and Sweden. Under the Medical Library Assistance Act of 1965 regional medical libraries have been established through Federal funding at Harvard,
the University of Washington, the College of Physicians in Philadelphia, the John
Crerar Library in Chicago and, soon to be added, Wayne State University and the
New York Academy of Medicine. These institutions, as you know, have received
grants from the National Library of Medicine to provide specific services to their
respective regions. In addition, NLM has contracted with a series of institutions
to provide specialized MEDLARS services for customers located in their respective areas. These activities, known as decentralized MEDLARS centers, are at
Harvard, Colorado, UCLA, Alabama, Ohio State, and Michigan. The services include the formulation of literature citation searches on local computers or the
transmittal of the searches to NLM to be run there. Affiliated MEDLARS Centers
are also in operation at the National Lending Library in England and at the Karo-
linska Institute in Sweden.

The future Library Services Component of the BCN is to be built upon this
beginning. It is expected to add to the numbers of regional medical libraries and
to the decentralized MEDLARS Centers, to include the various systems of Federal medical libraries, to extend to all university medical libraries and networks,
and to reach the individual hospital and other health science libraries. These organizations will be grouped under the Library Component in four basic levels of
network participation and the levels will be principally determined by the access
provided at each to the various data bases to be included. These levels are as follows:

Level 1—The Lister Hill National Center for Biomedical Communications.

The National Library of Medicine is to serve as the hub of the BCN and of
its Library Services Component. It will include the major input processing for
the construction of the bibliographic data bases, *i.e.*, MEDLARS and *Current
Catalog* files, with input support from other levels as appropriate. The network
control and management will be exercised from the Center and the major data
bases will be accessible from on-line machine storage. Major computer and communications facilities will support this Center.

Level 2–Decentralized MEDLARS Centers/Regional Medical Libraries.

This second level of the network will be characterized by major computer facilities providing on-line access to the majority of the data bases located at the Lister Hill Center. This access is to be through communications links to the central files at NLM or by the placement of these files in on-line computer storage at the secondary centers themselves. There will also exist communications links among the Level 2 nodes in what can be termed a horizontal pattern.

Level 3–Regional BCN Access Centers.

The third level nodes are to be terminal access centers with input/output devices and communications equipment permitting the transmission of alpha numeric data between these centers and the Lister Hill Center and/or the Level 2 centers. The communications with the two higher levels of the network will be with the computer files at those levels and with communications terminal devices for simple message transmission. Links will also be provided among the fifty to seventy-five access centers comprising this level.

Level 4–Local BCN Terminals.

The fourth, and last, level in the network will include 150 to 200 local terminals consisting of input/output equipment for the exchange of alpha numeric data with any of the nodes in the other three levels and among those in the fourth level itself. This exchange will be only data transmission from communications terminal to communications terminal and will not permit linking directly to a computer file.

An essential part of the network planning effort is to identify other related activities and to build the proper interactions with these activities. The four major communities are shown in Figure 2 and there are also listed a sampling of specific activities that will have an impact on, or will be affected by, the Library Services Component.

Our program at NLM for the development of the Biomedical Communications Network is under the direction of Dr. Ruth Davis who is the Associate Director for Research and Development and who also has been named as the Director of the newly-created Lister Hill National Center. It is her belief, and that of those of us on her staff, that the development of the BCN as a service-oriented mechanism demands effective and formalized management policy and procedures which we have chosen to call *The BCN Management Process.* Such management processes have been shown to be critical to successful network, or system, implementation during the ten to fifteen year history of system design work. There is a rather extensive body of documentation—principally report literature— that has grown up around the subject of system design. An over-simplified and yet very useful review of the element of system design can be gained from their arrange-

Figure 1. The Lister Hill National Center for Biomedical Communications.
Library Component of the BCN

LEVELS OF NET-
  WORK NODES

                                        LHNCBC
1 — — — — — — —   NETWORK
                                          HUB

                          REGIONAL   REGIONAL
2 — — — — — — —   MEDLARS   MEDICAL
                          CENTERS   LIBRARIES

                                                       MAJOR
                            BCN   ACADEMIC &
3 — — — — — — —   ACCESS   HOSPITAL
                          CENTERS   LIBRARIES

                           LOCAL   LOCAL
4 — — — — — — —   BCN   MEDICAL
                         TERMINALS   LIBRARIES

Figure 2. Relationships with Other Activities

—Identifiable "communities" of activity
  • Education
  • Health Services
  • Library Services
  • Communications

—Specific related activities
  • Regional Medical Program
  • Medical Library Assistance Act of 1965
  • Library Programs within Office of Education (ERIC)
  • EDUCOM
  • SUNY
  • National Libraries' Task Force

ment in Figure 3. Formalized management procedures must be followed to ensure attention to these elements and to provide adequate control and direction

Figure 3. Elements of System Design

—Action Environment
  • Where
  • When
  • With What
  • With Whom

—Design and Description of Action

—Target Environment
  • For Whom
  • Where

during the entire network design and implementation cycle. There is no question but that effective management has become a pacing element in all applications of technology. In addition, management provides the means of accommodating to the rapid pace of technological development, the complexity of networks, the diversity of organizations involved and the frequent and unavoidable changes in requirements. Effective management is in essence equivalent to an orderly approach to a problem. The steps to be followed in the solution of the problem can be listed in many ways. Those shown in Figure 4 can be recognized as most fre-

Figure 4. Scientific Method of Problem Solution

  • Recognize Indeterminate Situation
  • State Problem in Specific Terms
  • Formulate Working Hypothesis
  • Devise Controlled Method of Investigation
  • Gather and Record Data
  • Transform Data into Meaningful Statement
  • Arrive at Assertion
  • Relate to Body of Established Knowledge

quently used in relationship to the solution of a scientific problem such as in biology or chemistry. They can also be used, however, as the outline to be followed for the solution of management problems and form the basis for the approach known as scientific management. It is this approach to management which provides the necessary stability and continuity to maximize the performance of individuals involved in the system process.

The purposes of the BCN Management Process are: 1. to delineate the requirements, policies and procedures for the conceptual, definition, design, development, acquisition and initial operational phases of the program and 2. to prescribe the significant management actions for integrating and fulfilling the responsibilities of the organizational elements involved.

The objectives of this Management Process can be clearly identified. They are:

1. *To ensure effective management throughout the network cycle.* For the BCN, the cycle is comprised of the conceptual, definitive, design, development, acquisition, and initial operational phases.

2. *To balance the factors of performance, time, cost, and other resources to obtain the BCN.* This objective involves the preparation of the necessary budget submissions, related programming and planning data, funding documents, and resource allocation schedules. It permits the assignment of priorities and either precludes schedule slippages or prevents surprises in such slippages.

3. *To minimize technical, economic, and schedule risks.*

4. *To control changes to requirements* so as to minimize slippages and ensure maximum utilization of work completed or underway.

5. *To provide documentation supporting decisions made and actions taken.*

6. *To establish a discipline, or blueprint, for the Lister Hill Center Staff to follow* so that the coordination of planning and action is maintained between the management officials responsible for the various phases of the network cycle.

7. *To manage and control contractor efforts.*

8. *To identify and schedule significant actions to be accomplished and to effect their accomplishment.*

9. *To establish requirements for the flow of information between the responsible managers and organizational elements.*

10. *To undertake the research and development efforts necessary for the BCN.*

The customers or the user communities associated with each of the BCN components can be separately treated during the early stages of the BCN development cycle. This is not due to their disparate composition but rather to the disparate nature of the services or products offered by the various BCN components. Although one of the distinguishing characteristics of the BCN is its unification of education and information resources for maximum benefit to individual customers, the nature of this unification does not derive primarily from the customer. Rather, the BCN management staff must generate feasible and alternative means of effecting unification of product so that selection of the appropriate means can be consciously made by responsible authorities and users. This separation of customer group and services by BCN component should be recognized as an essential feature which has permitted parallel but separate efforts to be undertaken for each component. The unifying effort is the responsibility of the Lister Hill Center staff.

The management process for the network program is dependent upon adequate documentation which defines both the BCN and the management process itself. The generation of this documentation is an essential element of the management process. A review of the "system" literature has allowed the staff to select a minimum but critical set of documents which will be necessary for the BCN implementation.

Management must be presented with a logical and complete array of information if the required decisions are to be made, from that to undertake the design in the first place to the more specific directions as to the specifications for operation and the acceptability of the design itself. The planning must be laid out in an orderly fashion to provide this required information to managers, to the designers, and to those who are to implement the system after acceptance. The environment within which the system must operate and the expression of need for the operation being developed must be clearly outlined and, with management endorsement, constitute the justification and statement of objectives for the entire project. From this point, the planning descends through a chain of increasing detail in the expression of objectives, performance requirements, description of system to meet the needs, engineering design of the system, and provision for test and evaluation of the resulting system. Accompnaying this design planning must be the management plan that describes the responsibilities for developing, testing, evaluating and operating actions and assigns these responsibilities. It also includes resource and work schedules to be used as controls for the entire project.

The documentation set selected to meet these demands includes four distinct elements: 1. the Statement of Requirements; 2. the Technical Development Plan; 3. the Network Engineering Plan; and 4. the Network Management Plan.

The *Statement of Requirements* includes both a description of the general requirements for the network, or its components, and the specific operational requirements. It discusses the needs of society for improved communication of biomedical knowledge and defines these needs against the total background of all possible customers in our society. It also presents the basic philosophy and concepts for the BCN as dictated by the expressed needs. This first major segment of the document series must set the stage for all later efforts by placing those efforts in the context of the total community and providing the expression of the basic mission and/or objectives of the total project.

Within this first document of the series there must also be included the next level of planning—the specific operational requirements. These must be established from the general objectives previously defined and must delineate and/or define the following series of activities or facts:

1. The services and products to be provided by the BCN to meet the needs of the users;

2. The functions and operations to be peformed in order to produce these services and products; and

3. The characteristics of the customers in order to ascertain the match of users against the designated services and products.

The general services and products must be further defined in terms of such parameters as quality, quantity, timeliness, reliability, accessibility, and format. The orderly and systematic presentation of the general and specific operational requirements as outlined permits one to proceed to the development of the technical specifications and constraints for the Network and its components.

The *Technical Development Plan (TDP)* translates the statement of requirements into a coherent description of a network which, when operational, will satisfy the users' needs. The TDP is the bridge between the intended users of the network and the engineers and technicians who will direct the design and development of the network; it defines the operating environment and prescribes the general parameters of the network. It provides the foundation on which system engineers can postulate detailed network designs, formulate operating specifications, identify specific development tasks, set schedules, and estimate detailed resource requirements. The outline for the Technical Development Plan for the BCN is as shown in Figure 5.

The next, and third, document in the set is the *Network Engineering Plan.* It covers the system efforts which normally begin after the network requirements have been established and continue until an operating system is accepted by management. The Engineering Plan covers system definition and system design. It builds upon and refines system requirements previously defined so that they can be translated into design requirements. A series of iterations is oulined which being with gross trade-offs among cost, performance, and schedules and proceed toward final system definition and implementation. Previous studies which affect system design are reviewed and documented as part of the Engineering Plan. Several design approaches are examined and evaluated, based upon proper considerations of variables such as services to be performed, facilities, communication, computer programs, procedural data, training, testing and evaluation, logistics, and intrasystem and intersystem interfaces. In this process, major technological problems which would cause unacceptable delays are eliminated. As the process continues, performance requirements and constraints are documented. The objective of the Network Engineering Plan is to make possible the selection of the best design approach from the alternatives examined and then ensure that the desired system is designed at the least possible cost. The presentation of a formalized structure of management efforts to establish and maintain positive management control of the progress of the BCN development is contained in the Network Management Plan. The basic ingredients of

Figure 5. Technical Development Plan

Defines operating environment
Prescribes general parameters of network
Identifies resources
Outline of content

* Concept
  —General description of operations
  —Recapitulation of requirements

* Components
  —Network organization
  —Major characteristics
  —Operating parameters

* Network Integration
  —Engineering description of components and communications
  —Related networks

* Users
  —Refinement of user characteristics
  —Impact on network re
  • • Location and type of facilities
  • • Information to be communicated

* Resources
  —Estimates by component and by FY
  • Procurement
  • Construction
  • Contracts
  • Equipment rent
  • Communications
  • Salaries

this Plan is a road map defining the major management actions to be accomplished during each phase of the Network development. It is to provide all levels of the participating management with a common understanding of the administrative, financial, logistical, and other supporting factors what are essential to the implementation of the BCN project. The Plan shows the interrelationships of the Network Components and outlines the Network interface with other systems. It identifies and contains information on: a program summary, schedules, program management, operations, manpower, organization, finance, and work authorizations. The Network Managment Plan is a tool for project control and direction. It provides a systematic way for the Project Director to make intelligent judgments on resource allocation and phasing of project activities.

Figure 6 presents the entire BCN Management Process on a single chart. It is divided into the four major phases identified as conceptual; definition; design,

Figure 6. The BCN Management Process

Objectives

- Ensure effective management through network cycle
- Balance factors of performance, time, cost, and other resources to obtain BCN
- Minimize technical, economic, and schedule risks
- Control changes to requirements
- Provide documentation supporting decisions made and actions taken
- Establish a blueprint for staff guidance
- Manage and control contractor efforts
- Identify and schedule significant actions and effect accomplishment
- Establish requirements for flow of information between managers and organizational elements
- Undertake necessary R & D for BCN

development and acquisition; and operational. Work is currently taking place simultaneously in all four phases as dictated by the conditions in the real world situation demanding service now. It is not possible to proceed as would be theoretically desirable completing each phase before moving on to the next.

As with any activity, the success of this BCN Management Process depends upon clearly defined lines of responsibility for the accomplishment of each phase of the Process and for each element within a phase. The staff of the Lister Hill National Center for Biomedical Communication has the responsibility for the overall process and is supported by other elements of the National Library of Medicine who have been given roles of responsibility, approval or coordination in specific functional areas of the process.

The University of Chicago's Book Processing System

Charles Payne System Develeopment Librarian

and

Kenney Hecht Programmer, the University of Chicago Library

This paper will go into detail about Chicago's automation approach: why we have proceeded the way we have; our results so far; and, also, what we have yet to do to complete our first phase development. The Library of the University of Chicago is now into the third year of its project to mechanize bibliographic data processing. This project has been funded, in part, by the National Science Foundation.

The current project staff is as follows: the Library systems staff consists of 3 full-time persons, in addition to myself, and, of these, one works full-time on operational and cost studies and one started to work this week; the computer system and programming staff is approximately 2.5 F.T.E., which is down from a high of 5; the data input clerical staff varies from 5 to 6 F.T.E.

One of the goals of project development has been to eliminate or decrease much of the manual record generation, processing and maintenance normally associated with the library technical processing operations—acquisition of materials, fund accounting, payment processing, cataloging, book preparation or finishing (binding and labeling), book distribution, and catalog maintenance—and to reduce this manual paper work by use of computerized data processing. We have felt from the beginning that the handling of bibliographic data was the key factor in library automation. Following logically from this we have worked from the beginning with the concept of the unit record—integrating all of the various processing, bibliographic, and operational data within a single record in the machine file. Our design was to be able to create a record and to update it at any point in the technical processing operations; to enter data, partial or complete, at any time and subsequently be able to use, amend, or correct these data; to signal desired output at any time and get it at the desired time in the proper format, and positioned in an array designed for easiest use. This is what we now have in operation.

This integrated design has been, most certainly, more difficult in the execution than a more standard functionally oriented design would have been. It required initial development of plans including all phases of technical processing; it required a very large effort to define bibliographic and other data elements (at a

183

time before MARC definitions were available); it required, in our earlier phases working with computer operating software that was inadequate and unreliable so that substantial effort went into debugging, modifying, and extending the operating software as well as into development of the library system supervisory and utility software and the applications programs. Further, because of the long-range nature of a complete system development, and because of some intense pressures from both within and without the library to become operational, it was decided to build a full-scale, operational system—full-size, full-rate—from the start and to implement the various capabilities of the system into library operations as soon as they become available. We took this approach rather than to initially build a test or model-sized system. As many of you know, no complex, interrelated set of programs for on-line operation can be completely debugged quickly. It is a matter of testing all possible sets of conditions. We have, on occasion, experienced gross failures of certain programs some months after they were considered operational when a different, untested set of conditions would occur. (This kind of problem, however, would undoubtedly also occur following any system changeover from a model-sized to a production-sized operation.) Add to this the extreme difficulty we had (before we learned how to do it better) in adding new programs and capabilities to a highly interrelated system without fatal upsets to other previously stable parts of the system. You can probably understand why this development has, at times, sorely tried the patience of almost everyone involved—the programmers and computer system people, who were under pressure; the library staff, who had responsibilities for ongoing operations, whether the computer system was up or down; and even I fear, at times, we tested the patience of the library administration.

We attained eventually (this year) a level of development which begins to make the effort seem worthwhile. We have started to reap some of the benefits of this method of development.

I have recounted some of the hazards and now I want to list some of the positive aspects and long-range benefits:

1. The system as developed is not a purely theoretical one nor a simplistic version of library operating requirements. The operations and products have been tested and developed in use. For example, the catalog card format programs have become extremely versatile and can handle any of the wide variations in bibliographic records that we encounter, within the limitations of character set or as long as the record does not overflow to more than 16 cards.

2. We were forced to work with the whole range of bibliographic and processing data elements from the beginning. In effect, we undertook the most complex aspect of development first. This has already paid off in terms of making subsequent development easier.

3. In spite of the fluctuating consistency of operations for an extended period, the system did during this time produce large quantities of usable and useful products to augment ongoing manual operations.

4. Perhaps the most important benefit is that the programs, because of necessary changes, have been honed and sharpened and standardized in ways that make any changes and additions much easier to accomplish.

5. The system as developed is beautiful, in a sense, in its independence of the terminal or printing equipment used for input or output. We have no immediate plans to make use of CRT terminals, but if this utility were to be incorporated, it would be simple to do, in terms of programming changes. It is also relatively independent of how we want to operate—in an on-line or in an off-line, batch mode. We were able (and I could even say forced) to re-evaluate our original ideas concerning on-line operations. This allowed us to utilize on-line operation where it was most beneficial and to go to batch operation where that mode proved to be more efficient. To explain what I mean, I need to mention our experiences with errors and error correction. As it turns out, error correction quickly becomes the key, critical factor in machine processing of bibliographic data. Error rates are atrocious. The use of clerical typists to keyboard data in all the many languages of the world results in high error rates and there is not much that can be done about it. We have, therefore, tried to make error correction as easy as possible. We have at least three levels of error correction. The first level makes the corrections before being read into the machine system. Not counting first level errors, the rate runs to about 25% of the item records processed. We have found that on-line operation is most essential for data read-in (not keyboarding—we keyboard into paper tape) and logical error message response, essential for calling up and receiving item record printouts (this when things are so mangled that the hard-copy worksheet from keyboarding does not help), and also for the error correction read-in and its error message responses. In our system this allows us to make error correction at any time right up to the minute that the catalog cards or other products are produced. Many items go through the error correction cycle more than once. A very high percentage of our 25% error items are corrected in this manner so that their products are produced in the batch with which they started. On the other hand, we did not find that on-line control of routing output production was very useful and we have abandoned it to a large extent. If a change occurs making printout equipment in the library practical, we can resume on-line control very easily.

6. The final benefit that I want to mention is that the system as evolved is ideally suited to the use of externally generated machine-readable data, such as MARC II data, and we intend to take advantage of this as quickly as possible.

We still have a lot of work to do on our system, with a number of applications to incorporate, before we will have completed our basic Phase I development. This Phase I development is our major effort for the first three years of the project. I would like to describe what we have, what we are working on, and what we are planning. Even though this system is called the Book Processing System, that name is not totally accurate. The system is designed to cover not just books or monograph processing, but also serial ordering, fund accounting, payment processing, and cataloging—most of serial processing except for serial issue check-in and serial holdings records.

Data input is, of course, a prerequisite to any machine data processing and this was one of our earlier accomplishments. We initially developed our own tele-processing software and have maintained it, for reasons of efficiency, even though utility software has been available to us for some time. The Library has developed a Data Processing Unit which handles input and output on the machine system. Work is channeled from library operational departments to this group. We do not have input equipment in other locations. Also, keyboarding of data is not directly on-line, but into paper tape. The paper tape is utilized, in effect, as a giant buffer. First level error correction can be added to the tape anytime subsequent to the error or on a second tape to be read after the first. In the latter case, the machine receives both the error and the correction and processes to make the correction.

All data is input in the form of tagged data elements. One type of data element merely contains information to be maintained. A second type of data element not only contains data but initiates action within the machine system depending upon what the data are. A third type can initiate action merely by being present with no regard as to the data content. Data goes in as a string of tagged (and thus defined) information and they are maintained in the machine file in this way. Formatting is strictly an output processing function.

Signals for output are also input as tagged data elements and result in the required output array, or stack building. On a signal to print, either on-line or as a batch processing job, each item in the stack is sequentially formatted and printed out. Catalog cards are printed in arrays for the desired catalogs or other locations receiving cards; the arrays are in filing order whether for main entry catalogs, author-title-subject dictionary catalogs, or shelflist catalogs. These programs are all operational; they are quite sophisticated and extremely versatile. No further changes are currently planned in this area. Catalog card production has been the most affected of our operations by the systems changes we have gone through and this production has suffered considerably through up and down cycles of production. I decline to state that we are finally doing 100%

of the Roman alphabet cataloging on the system, although we have made the push this week to go to 100%. We have recently been processing about 150 cataloged titles per day, producing an average of 11 cards per title, for a total card production of about 1500 to 1700 per day. This rate represents 75 to 80% of the current Roman alphabet cataloging work.

We utilize the same bibliographic data, with different formatting and a different output array directory, for book cards and pocket label production. Catalog card sets are based on title, but book finishing products are required for each physical volume. The programs handle this by an expansion of a relatively simple holdings statement. It is not unusual for this operation to produce 20 or 30 sets of cards and labels for multiple volume and multiple copy materials.

This production operation also covers a wider range of materials than does catalog card production. Cards and labels are being produced for virtually all materials in Roman and non-Roman alphabets. The Romanized, or transliterated, entries and titles are used. This provides us with a machine record that is acceptable for some uses though not for catalog cards.

The system has handled book card and pocket label production for the library for a long time, though not always with the one-day currency desired.

The programs for computer formatting and printing of purchase orders have been completed and tested except for the final full production-run testing. We are planning a coordinated effort to get this implemented into library operations as soon as we all get back to work. Programs are also completed for production of a daily fund commitment list. This would be the first step of a more complete fund accounting system. As this list makes use of order data, its implementation is dependent on that of the order printing operation.

We have proceeded with order printing development even though we are working with the CLSD group in a joint design effort covering all of acquisitions work. There is no great conflict here, however. Any emerging joint design that Chicago could adopt would need to be hung on our existing data processing system. Order printing requires a set of data element definitions and some forms and formats. The set of data elements we use are not in gross conflict with the CLSD list and could be easily modified. Forms and formats will probably, of necessity, be governed by local considerations for some time in any case. We look forward to CLSD efforts that would go beyond purchase order generation, perhaps to include telecommunication with large vendors.

The areas of CLSD effort that are of most immediate interest to the Chicago development are fund accounting, payment processing, and management reporting.

We have substantially altered our thinking, particularly on payment processing, since these discussions have begun. The daily fund commitment list, mentioned earlier, is really an interim, partial fund accounting effort. It is likely that further work in these areas will await results of the joint design effort.

Chicago also has an automatic overdue order claiming operation designed and ready for programming. We will not proceed with this immediately, pending further discussion with the CLSD group. To date, CLSD discussions of claiming have not gone far enough to resolve conflicting ideas, although we all agree to the need and, in some ways, the method of application.

We are both planning for and working toward prompt utilization of the MARC II data in our system. Our programming staff has studied the MARC II format, as released, and have developed plans for conversion of MARC data to meet the requirements of our systems. Program coding will not begin until further and final information is available concerning the MARC II format. We are also developing our plans so that MARC data can be incorporated into our system in the most efficient and utilitarian ways. We have decided that, initially, we will attempt only to convert MARC data to the Chicago format. We will not attempt two-way communication initially simply because our cataloging is not in sufficient depth to meet the MARC requirements and because there has been no clear indication from the MARC staff as to how they intend to cope with this. We have a system well suited to the use of MARC data. Operationally, we intend to process the MARC tapes into the system as they arrive and make use of the bibliographic data elements as early as possible in our processing—even for ordering, if MARC is fast enough.

We, too, are convinced of the necessity of nationally generated bibliographic data. We look forward to the point where MARC data can relieve us of substantial portions of data input and, we fervently hope, error correction.

We have other products and operations in the planning or designing stages, including new book lists to be generated for subject or departmental locations that receive books. These subject book listings would be yet another product use of the bibliographic data used many times before. Because non-Roman alphabet materials have been included for cards and labels, these lists would be comprehensive if not elegant.

Another area of control that we are very interested in is bindery shipment control, with bindery tickets and finished book distribution lists as further products of the system. This development has not proceeded to the programming stage yet and will probably be one of the last efforts of the Phase I development. It has at least one interesting application for catalog card production, book card and label production, and new book listing and this is the timing factor. One may not want to advertise new books or prepare products for their finishing while the books are still at the bindery.

This system, as described, both the completed and the uncompleted applications, comprise the basic Phase I design. We plan to have much of the system in operation by the end of the year. It was intended to stabilize the routine operations of the library and to provide a sound, modern operating base from which to build in the future to the more sophisticated, information-access libraries we all hope for.

The system with which the Chicago Library Automation project is presently running consists of an IBM 360, Model 50 computer with 512 thousand bytes of core storage, 10 2311 disk drives, a 1403 Model 2 high-speed printer, 2 9-track tape drives, and 2 7-track tape drives.

The software system is IBM-OS-MVT. This is multiprogramming with a variable number of tasks. This means that a variable number of programs can be running in the computer at the same time. The library tele-processing programs are in the computer from 6 to 14 hours a day while other programs are being run and other tele-processing operations may also be going on.

We have two print trains for the 1403 printer. A standard one which has only upper case letters, numbers, and very few special characters, and the special library print train which has upper and lower case letters, numbers, and many more special characters. The standard train is kept on most of the time because of the greater speed it permits. The library train is mounted whenever library printing is being done. Almost all of the regular library production printing is presently being done by regular computer operators on the midnight shift.

Eighty-five operational computer programs have been developed thus far. They vary in size from 96 bytes to over 4200 bytes. These programs are stored in two libraries on the 2311 disks. One of these libraries on the disk is a library of programs in which individual programs are stored. The other is a library of phases (a phase is a group of programs linked together and operating as one). In this all the programs for a single function are stored linked together under one name. When the on-line tele-processing receives a command from the remote terminal to do input—it calls in from this library the input phase as a single package. When it is commanded to print a record, it brings into the computer from the disk library the file printing phase, etc.

Those processes that are batched jobs work much the same way. A small deck of cards (usually under a dozen) is read into the computer from the card reader. This small deck brings into the computer from the disk library the phase it needs, and initiates processing.

I would like to give you a brief description of the library system from the programming point of view. The system as seen from this end can be broken down into a number of phases on the basis of function. The phases are as follows:

1. The tele-processing phase: This phase consists of 13 programs which control the passing of data back and forth between the computer and the remote terminals at the library.

2. The command processing phase: These 2 programs accept the commands from the remote terminals at the library and initiate the appropriate action, bringing in from disk storage whatever processing programs are required.

3. The input processing phase: This phase consists of 16 programs. These programs check each incoming record against the library computer file to see if it is a new record or the updating of an existing record; scan the input for invalid data tags; edit out unwanted blanks and control characters. They scan for output requests; create an entry in a list for those records with output requests; perform the necessary changes in the record depending on whether the new data is in addition to the record, a correction, a deletion, or a totally new record; and write the new or updated record on the library's computer file.

4. The utility programs: Two of these programs print out records from the file as they appear in the file (this may be done on the remote terminals or on the high-speed printer); a second set of 5 programs reorganize the file, check for file errors, and provide a backup copy of the data file.

5. The distribution interpretation programs: This consists of two phases. The first phase of 12 programs takes the list of records requiring output, selects those which are for catalog cards, reads the record, checks it for errors, creates a card by card list and sorts this list by location and entry. It saves the list on a disk file, prints the list, prints any error messages, and prints a count of cards by location. The second phase of 10 programs takes the list of records requiring output, selects those for orders, reads the record, checks it for errors, creates an order by order list, sorts it by dealer, saves the list on a disk file, and prints the list, any error messages, and a count of the orders by dealer.

6. The catalog card printing phase: These 18 programs select an entry from the expanded list of catalog cards to be printed, read the selected record, do a quick check of the record for mandatory data and redundancies, format the call number, format the lines, format the cards (main entry, added entry, shelflist— single or multiple, as needed), and either output the formatted card to some printing device or print a message about errors found in the data.

7. The book card and pocket label printing phase: These 19 programs select an entry for cards or labels from the list of records requiring output, read the selected record from the library's computer file, do a quick check of the record for mandatory data and redundancies, format the call number, format the text, and print out the formatted item or error message on some output device.

8. The order printing phase: These 16 programs select an entry from the list

of orders to be printed, read that record in from the library's data file, do a quick check for mandatory data and redundancies, format the text of the order, sum up the fund commitments by fund, and output the formatted order on some printing device.

Looking over these phases again, you will see that no phase consists of a single program. The reasons for writing the phases as sets of small programs, rather than having each phase as one large program, are the result of some planning and much experience. These reasons are 1) to write as many reusable routines and programs as possible, 2) to make the phases as device independent as possible, and 3) to make the phases as easily maintained and changed as possible.

Point one: To write as many reusable programs as possible. When I was describing the phases, you may have noticed that many of them included the same function. For instance, input processing, the utility programs, the distribution interpretation, the catalog card printing, the card and label printing, and the order printing phases all must read records from the library's data file into the computer. So one program is written that reads the record from the data file into the computer. It is written for maximum efficiency and minimum running time cost. All of these phases can then use this one program avoiding any duplication of programming effort and cost. Perhaps the most telling example of the savings in time and effort that are possible, is the difference between the programming necessary to implement catalog card production (the first formatted output phase written) and that necessary to implement order printing (the last formatted output phase written). Implementing the catalog card printing required the writing of 18 programs, an effort that took many, many months. However, these routines were programmed to be usable in more than one phase. So when it came time to implement order printing, a set of 16 programs, only four new programs had to be written. The other twelve were taken exactly as they were from the catalog card phase. The fact that we had to write four new programs illustrates the fact that we have not totally mastered the art. Ideally, we should have a generalized output formatting phase that requires the changing of only one program from one type of output to the next.

Point two: To make all the phases as device independent as possible.

This is one of the lessons we learned the hard way. Computer hardware and software is a rapidly changing field. It is desirable to be able to take advantage of new equipment and system advances as they become available. To do this we have isolated those parts of each phase that require device dependent coding. Then when the equipment changes, only the isolated program need be changed and the basic operation of the phase is not touched. Thus, if it should become advisable for the library to change its input method, or to make it more flexible, only one program need be changed. The library could start inputting directly from the keyboard of a remote terminal in addition to the present paper tape, with only about a week's programming effort. With the inclusion of a conversion program they could input data into their data files from outside sources such as MARC II. This flexibility is necessary in order to have an enduring automated system.

Point three: To make the phases as easily maintained and changed as possible.

The small size of the individual programs is the single greatest aid to maintenance possible. It is by nature easier to understand a small isolated program than a large complex program. Then when there is an error in a phase the programmer can separate the individual program containing the error and work only with it to correct the error. This may mean the difference between having to keep in mind 40 or 50 pages of coding and having to understand a three-page program.

The library system is a developing system. The library's file organization and data record structure permit the addition of new data elements to the data base. To avoid having to change the programs whenever additional data elements are added to the data base, we use tables. The input phase has tables of valid data tags; the output programs have tables of the data elements to be included in the particular output, the sorting programs have tables of articles to be removed for proper sorting, to name a few. If the library wanted to add a new data element to its records, for example, a national book number, and it wanted this number printed on all catalog cards, the designated tag for the book number would need to be added to the table of valid tagging codes in the input phase program and the tag would need to be added to the table of data elements included in the catalog card output. No other programming changes would have to be made.

Needless to say, we have not always succeeded in carrying out these three points in the programming. But the effort to do so is beginning to pay off in the decreasing time and cost needed to implement each succeeding phase of operations.

Economic and Operating Realities of Present-Day Hardware and Software in Library Applications

William F. Miller Professor of Computer Science and Associate Provost for Computing, Stanford University

and

Richard N. Beilsker Programming Manager, SPIRES/BALLOTS, Stanford University

When Allen Veaner asked me to speak he really wanted someone to "tell it as it is." In order to do that, you first have to see it how it is, and then the "telling-seeing" makes for a reasonable aphorism. I admit that I'm not certain whether I see it as it is or not. My colleague, Dick Bielsker, has sold information systems; I have never done so, although I have sold a lot of other hardware/software systems—perhaps as many as thirty of them over the past fifteen years. From that standpoint I suppose I can venture a pretty good approximation of how it is.

One of the things I have encountered time and again is people asking, "Why is it so difficult to engineer hardware/software systems? What really is the difference between engineering the composite system and just a hardware system alone?" It seems to these people that engineering a hardware system (and we have been doing this for some time) is a lot easier than engineering the composite system. In fact, judging from the reports I've gotten about the informal conversations after yesterday's meeting, I conclude that a lot of difficulties are being encountered in engineering library software systems. Well, if I can talk as "Professor Miller" for a few minutes I will try to explain the real problem here.

The reward, and at the same time the retribution of software is self-change. That little fact comes back to haunt us and to help us in many different ways. In one of our introductory computer science courses we are told that a program and a machine are essentially the same. That is a very useful idealization, particularly in regard to the dynamics and logic of programming the machine; but in real implementation the self-change part is delegated to the software. Thus one might say: in the real world, engineering of hardware is different from engineering of software or hardware-software composites, because in engineering the latter kinds of systems one deals with machines that change themselves. And therein lies the heart of the problem.

The side effects of self-change are the things that haunt us. They cause all the little and not-so-little bugs that we encounter in interfacing with the operating systems. I'll elaborate on this situation in several different ways.

One of the first considerations in the development of systems is to take a good look at what we might call the economics and complexities scale. We face this problem from the beginning; that is, it is already a problem when we start the process of selecting equipment. It comes at us also in the management of the project, which includes the software applications programs, that we try to undertake.

In the selection of hardware one of the first problems is whether you are going to choose stand-alone equipment—that is, one for you and you alone—or whether you are going to share equipment with the computation center or some other group. Now, what are the advantages of sharing? It's very clear that you have a large, or comparatively large, operating group available to you. You also have a large array of processors and programming languages available. In addition you have a maintenance group and some kind of operating system. With the shared-equipment approach, then, you have a great deal more flexibility than you would get if you were developing all your own capabilities and interfaces from scratch. On the other hand, interfacing will all these systems comes back to haunt you because of the complexities that are introduced by increasing the number of processers in the system. So right here we see that there is a competition between the economics of scale and the complexities of scale. More on that later when we talk about operations and cost of hardware.

Let me say something about styles of interaction. The style of interaction between programmer and machine has a lot to do with the cost and rate of progress of your project, and with overall scheduling. Let us consider the following styles of interaction: batch processing, remote entry without text-editing, remote entry with test-editing, and interactive processing.

As you might expect, batch-processing will be the cheapest mode of interaction per unit of operation. It has been common experience that a project will move a little faster if you put on remote entry or remote entry with text-editing. The overall programming costs will not increase very much. You will find that as you go to remote entry with text-editing, for example, you will pay more for unit operation, do fewer operations; you will, in fact, be paying about the same for the overall development, but you will cut the development time somewhat. Before continuing, I would like to add that a number of installations are trying to get precise measurements of these programming costs.

I should further like to point out that management of the project is different for a remote entry text-editing development environment particularly with respect to documentation. In the batch-mode, things move slowly enough so that the programmers spend part of the time (between debugging runs) developing flowcharts and other communications aids. There appears to be a tendency for people working in a text-editing environment not to do this; I have observed, particularly when higher-level languages are used, that documentation suffers considerably. Applications programs are less well documented today than they were in the "good old days" when flow charts and program write-ups were supposedly prepared by programmers as a matter of course. I am not putting down higher level languages by any means. The point is this: it is easier for the programmer to understand what he's done when he uses a higher level language to do it; it follows, especially with the relatively rapid response in a text-editing environment, that more time is spent on getting the program written faster, and less is spent on meaningful documentation. The result is, of course, that at or near the end of the project you have to go back and make up for all the documentation that was not prepared on an "as you go" basis. I have put a heavy emphasis on documentation and communication because I am oriented to general systems where you are trying to get this kind of information to a large number of people. If you are working on a little self-contained system, you can probably get away with a lot less documentation, but in the general purpose area, documentation is a most important consideration.

Another problem encountered when deciding on the kind of interaction to use involves how much of the software you will be able to generate. That is, how much of the software will you develop, and how much do you intend to get from the manufacturer? If you choose a batch orientation you can always get a batch processing system from the manufacturer. If you want a remote entry or interactive system, chances are that you will have to do a lot of the development yourself. Now, the prospect of developing your own system is most attractive; if your staff is big enough, you may be able to do this. But even here you can see problems developing down stream. For one thing, the machines themselves are being continually changed. Manufacturers continue their development of a machine after it is installed; these developments might be made for reasons of maintainability or to permit installation of new kinds of equipment. Changes can continue over a period of years. If you develop your own software you will either have to reject any given engineering change or change your software to accommodate it. Suppose you decide to reject the change. That might be an easy solution for the time being; what happens a year later, say when you wish to add a new piece of equipment that is dependent on an earlier engineering change? If you really want or need the equipment you must now make the retroactive hardware change and, in addition, modify your software. This can prove to be very difficult indeed.

Suppose that you go along with the manufacturer's software. Well, it is still not uncomplicated because his operating system is going to change periodically. But he will try to develop an interface so that your applications programs will run from version to version of his system. Let me point out that if you go through a number of operating systems during the developing of a piece of equipment, or rather a system, you might make as many as a hundred different changes; this is going to require a lot of reprogramming and all the rest, so the decision to build your own software or stick with the manufacturer's is complex and important. I'm sorry to say that in the end this decision is not often made on purely rational grounds. Very often you go along with what a colleague is doing or, more often, you go along with what the computation center, with whom you interact, is doing. You seldom have full control over this development yourself. But it is a question you should realize requires study and attention.

The next problem is that of scheduling and operation. My experience shows that an applications group interacts one way with an R & D computation center, and quite another with an administrative data processing center. If, for example, you are interacting with an administrative data processing group, you will find that you are faced with a relatively rigid type of operation. They are not as elastic, say, as a research group or a student group. At the same time, because they are more rigid, you can fix a more definite schedule. On the other hand, they are usually in direct competition with you for that part of their operating day during which your programming group would like to use the machine. By contrast, suppose you are interacting with a research oriented computer center; here you would find that the users—the students and research people—are more flexible in regard to using the machine. You could probably rearrange your computer run-times so that you do not directly compete for the same time-slot.

There are actually three groups that have to get on the machine: the hardware engineers, the software maintenance programmers, and the applications people. As we look at increasingly large systems, we find the hardware and software maintenance tasks taking large chunks out of the operating day. With a small machine, one in the hundred thousand dollar class, you can get by with a few hours a week maintenance; perhaps you can squeeze a lot of that into the weekend. But on very large systems, you will find that hardware maintenance alone can require three hours a day. Software maintenance takes another hour plus and your operating day is really cut into. Let me point out that machines are not yet designed in such a way that the hardware maintenance can be done concurrently with other regular operations. The engineers have to run special diagnostic programs to check out all the processors, for that reason they must take over the machine *in toto*.

As a case in point, the Stanford Computation Center's computer system requires an average of two and one-half hours of preventive maintenance daily. Then there is about an hour and a half's worth of software maintenance in addition to that. Let me point out again that we still lack really adequate models for our software systems, and we rely a great deal on experience to effect the fine-tuning development of our systems. We do not as yet have sufficient conditions to guarantee that our software is "correct." This means that we are frequently turning up bugs, and in this debugging process, which can continue for years, we end up making modifications to our software system. This ties in with what I said earlier: self-change is at once a reward and a retribution.

So we see that very large systems mean large chunks of maintenance time. When we talk about trying to form large public utilities out of one or more large machines, we must realize that the scheduling of these mandatory maintenance functions is going to diminish the economics of scale that we hope to achieve by having the big, powerful machine in the first place.

At this time, let's take a look at some computer hardware prospects. One of the things heard repeatedly from the manufacturers is that computing is going to get cheaper as time goes on; frankly, I do not look for any real economies here within the next ten years. Consider the last generation of computers, characterized by the IBM 7090. This computer showed up around 1960 and was on its way out in 1967. There are still a lot of them around, but as a "generation" they lasted for seven years. When you look at the difficulty experienced by many users who are trying to get into third generation hardware, you can conclude that the current generation will be around ten years or so. Setting 1967 as year one, I figure that it will be 1977 before the next batch comes in. It is my observation that as IBM goes, so goes the industry. You can talk to Control Data or to Burroughs or to any of the rest, and they will be very candid about their position with respect to the "leader." This suggests that we will be stuck with this line of equipment for a few years, although this might be a blessing really. Many of you are probably aware of the trauma involved in getting into the third generation; a lot of managers do not relish going through all this again soon just to get into the fourth. It has been facetiously stated that project managers will not let the fourth generation in the door until they are promoted, leaving the heartaches to the fellows who take over the line responsibility for getting the new generation computers on the air. Well, I don't know about that, but the statement is an indication of the magnitude of the pain. I believe that we will not see too dramatic a change from third to fourth generation machinery and software. IBM is working more in the direction of extending and improving their current line. Other manufacturers have few thoughts beyond their current generation.

What you are probably more interested in, however, are the prospects with regard to large files, mass storage, and terminals. Again we have been told that terminal costs are going to go down dramatically, and that we should all look forward anxiously to this. They will go down, but I do not think dramatically so. The companies that are getting into the computer and terminal business are still young and are trying avidly to develop their talents. Cost of the basic components are not going to diminish dramatically, and many of the small companies are still unsure of their markets. The teletype-writer part of the terminal business looks pretty stable; I don't see any reason for these prices to go down very much. For graphic terminals I think my point about the market being unclear holds, and I don't see any dramatic change downwards here. As a guess, the prices could go down perhaps 50 to 100% over the next few years.

A related consideration is that of communications costs. All that can be said here is that we are going to be faced with communications costs in the development of non-local systems. Currently, communications costs are linear with transmission distance; since this is so there has to be some optimum geographic distance, over which you can operate and beyond which your communications costs will exceed operating and local equipment costs. This would suggest that a number of optimally placed regional centers would be more economical than one very large national center. Of course, communications costs can change, and the linearity argument could be removed if we were using some kind of special orbiting communications satellite. But for now, I feel that the costs, even if they become lower, will be essentially linear with distance, and we are still faced with determining the optimal size of a network of regional information processing centers. One thing is clear, I feel, and that is that we cannot arbitrarily communicate across the entire country without being overwhelmed by the communications cost.

Turning to the mass storage area, I am afraid that the picture is not too good. Experience shows that we can very quickly saturate virtually any storage device you can get. If you really want to have everything available to you, you think in terms of stacks of magnetic tapes and associated drives. This, of course, is the most expensive mass-store, with the cost per bit-to-be-accessed working out to something like five hundredths of a cent. This will be about halved when you go to something like an IBM 2314 disk drive. The cost per bit with a photo-digital store will be about .00015 cents, with a much slower access time, of course. The photo-digital store is the cheapest (per bit) device manufactured, but it is being taken off the market for lack of interest. There are currently only two in operation: one at Lawrence Radiation Laboratory in Berkeley, the other at RadLab, Livermore. The photo-digital store works with film chips. The machinery is designed to do photographic processing, and stores the developed film chips in cannisters. These cannisters are individually accessible and are mechanically transported to reading stations where the chip can be removed, read optically and then replaced in the cannister. If you desire to rewrite information, you go through another photographic development operation.

Thus, the photo-digital store is essentially a slow-writing, slightly-faster-reading device. It has a capacity of 10^{12} bits, roughly equivalent to 20,000 magnetic tapes; so you see, it isn't really all that big. I'm sure that certain of you are already facing storage problems of that size and even greater. In fact already I have the problem at the Stanford Linear Accelerator Center. Out there our experimental physicists can load up to 20,000 tapes in less than three years, so we have a very real interest in mass-storage devices. I might point out that, in additiion to the mechanical-monster aspects of photo-digital storage, we must also consider its price, which is high, and the fact that there is limited experience in its use. These considerations are, however, academic since manufacture is being discontinued.

Let's spend another minute on tapes. You have available about 10^{10} bits of storage per unit; you can see that in order to match the photo-digital storage we just spoke about, you would need a hundred of these tape units—a football field full!

Incidentally, I have a limited, but useful, measure in this area; surely you have more precise calculations than the following, but to make a point to a group of students I once calculated that to punch up every character in a two million volume library would require the services of a Rose Bowl full of key punchers for one year. That works out to one hundred thousand man-years of keypunching. So we could say that the Rose Bowl full of keypunchers constitutes one unit (of information); some of my students promptly named the unit a Miller. Anyway, the point is that I believe that the development of information systems will tend to be more local discipline oriented systems than out-and-out, all-encompassing general, library fact retrieval systems.

That brings us to some remarks about cost and performance of systems. There are five components for developing an information retrieval system: conceptual design, systems design, user program, hardware related matters, and documentation and administration, by which I mean administration of personnel matters, space, general project costs, and so forth.

While we are on the subject of personnel, I point out that in the conceptual design stage you are going to need high-level people; by this I mean people who have four or five years of demonstrated proficiency in software design work, particularly overall systems design. They are not easy to find. In fact I will predict that we will fall short—far short—of all the expectations and ambitions of people in this country regarding the development of information processing systems. It boils down to a people bottle-neck; as simple as that. We are simply not able to produce people of requisite quality and competence quickly enough to fill the stated needs and stated goals of many of our information sciences people. So keep in mind that you might have to modify certain developmental goals for the very real reason of scarcity of qualified systems designers.

In the systems design area the conceptual design is concerned with data management, storage design, and what you are going to do with the project; the systems design is primarily concerned with the processing of algorithms and with the interactions of your system with the operating system in which it is embedded. The designers must understand the operating systems very, very well in order to handle the interaction, or interfacing problems. Of course there are the user programmers; these persons—you can think of them as applications specialists—have to understand what is being developed in enough detail to tailor the applications for its use, and to provide feed-back information to the system designers.

As for the hardware, it seems reasonable to try to develop some degree of machine independence, at least with regard to a line of equipment. I think one very often finds in these kinds of development the kinds we are discussing now—that the developers will switch from one machine to another. If you start with your own stand-alone equipment, you are likely to have a small machine; later on, you might have to move up a size or so. On the other hand, if you start working with the central computer, you might find out that in the course of development you have an opportunity to continue your work on a different machine, perhaps a stand-alone of your very own.

My model for the development of such projects around a large laboratory—such as we have at the University—goes something like this: I think one should develop a rather complete, general purpose software-hardware system . . . a centralized complex of computer power. As you begin to define special functions of stand-alone size, you pull these out of the central complex: you start to specialize. You now have few of the complexities of scale; true, you lose some of the economies of scale, but only initially. As you develop within your specialization, you start picking upon efficiencies attendant thereto, and there comes a time when the operation should be transferred to separate equipment. Knowing just when to do this is the trick. Anyway, throughout these developments you will usually find that people change hardware at least once, going either from a general purpose to a small special purpose computer, or building from a small stand-alone system to a larger one. The big point is that it is most desirable to design in as much machine independence as you can.

Documentation is necessary at every level and in all phases of design and development. You can have the best ideas and what-not around, but if it isn't nicely arranged and intelligibly written down and communicated, you really have nothing at all. I suggest a technical writer from the beginning; he should report to the project manager.

The administration of the project should not and cannot be neglected. People, even many gifted and experienced ones, do not as a rule administer or coordinate themselves, as many of you have doubtless learned. You need a project leader and he needs some staff asssitance. The leader, or manager, must interface the project with the computation facility, purchasing personnel, publications, perhaps even plant people. In the instance at hand, there are the formidable tasks of technical and higher-level administrative coordination, both of which require considerable effort and attention in a project like yours. Systems design will be coordinated by the administrative or executive assistant; technical coordination is the responsibility of the project manager. Of course, there is also the very real need for timely coordination of persons working on the applications and of things.

Now a word or two about environment. This is something over which one does not always have a lot of control. For one thing, people in the university have a tendency to use what equipment is available to them. As you have probably observed, it is important for your designers to understand as accurately as possible what the application is all about. Among other things, this means that the designer has to get out and talk to the user. He has to interact with him directly. This seems to be a "resource" that is not so readily sought out and used. The graveyard of many a system has been a design that is not in the context of the user's environment.

Remember also that in systems design you must consider the differences between stand-alone or general purpose interface. In the former, people must know the hardware cold; in the latter they have to know the operating system cold. The user programs depend upon people who know *both* systems and applications, with the emphasis going to applications knowledge. I reiterate my preference for the hardware environment: I like to see the development start and take shape under the general system, followed by a pulling out of the special functions as you develop a fuller use and need in that area.

As for elapsed time, I can cite an actual real-time development project, one that was about eighteen months long overall. Conceptual design ran about a third of the time: five to six months. Now you must recognize that there is always feedback in an effort like this; this shows up during implementation and the reason is the one I spoke of earlier: the lack of complete models that describe systems that change themselves. The self-change of a program means that you do not—you can not—see all the side effects of various perturbations in design here and there. You simply do not have adequate models to define the side-effects of self-change. So during the implementation you are always running into the need for little practical things that have to be incorporated. Okay, a third of the time in conceptual design, and then the rest of the period, twelve months, was the completion of the systems design. The user's programs are developed on the way; their development runs parallel to the rest of the design effort. Documentation is continuous; it should span the width and breadth of the project.

The costs: Most of you know what it costs to hire people. The total for the project I have been talking about ran to about $200,000 over the eighteen months. About two-thirds of that was salary; the other third covered hardware: machine use, storage use, terminal use, and so on. That's rough, but it should give you a picture of the major breakdown.

Computer Operating Systems and Programming Languages: A Critical Review of Their Features and Limitations for Processing Bibliographic Text

Thomas K. Burgess Manager, Systems Development, Washington State University, Pullman, Washington

For the benefit of those of you who are not technically familiar with computing, it might be well if we view the operating systems again from the standpoint of the user and not from the standpoint of the computer scientist or the computer center director. Prof. Miller viewed the operating system from inside itself; that is, a view of the operating system as the operating system sees itself. My view, I think, will be more turned toward the way the user sees it, and the way the user sees the obstacles that are caused by the operating system when he is trying to get his particular task accomplished.

First, we need to define an operating system: it is a collection of programs which provide for servicing of what is loosely called jobs or tasks, the things that you and I submit as programs to the computing center. We have operating systems because computing facilities are rather expensive and an institution must try to get the greatest amount of efficiency out of a system. The basic idea is to provide a job stream which most effectively uses the computing facilities. In the early days of computing one could get "hands on" the machine. One could sit down with his job and the computer and play with it. One could work his job all the way through or just portions of it. But demands on the equipment progressively increased and soon there wasn't enough time to allow everybody to schedule his own time on the system. The institution couldn't afford to buy more equipment and much of the user's time was obviously "sit and scratch your head" time, while the machine sat there and waited. Therefore, system designers began to build ways and methods of reducing idle time by developing executive systems, or, as they were originally called, monitor systems, which allowed a more efficient utilization of the equipment.

Let's take a look at some of the parts which make up this collection of programs. Operating system components consist of many things nowadays. First, there's a job control language translator. This provides a specialized language for you to describe to the machine the job you want to do, and what parts of the equipment you need to use to get your task done. The operating system wants to know your needs because it has another part called the job scheduler, which tries to allocate available resources to those needs at the time most appropriate for that need. Originally, job schedulers ran just against the JCL cards which were removed from the decks. The machine operators obtained a listing of the jobs in the order in which they should be run, and the machine operators then put the decks in this order and then ran them. This didn't work very well because the operator had to stop every once in a while to run through the list and schedule more jobs. This was not a totally efficient use of the system, so designers began to add "spooling systems," which could store all jobs in a queue. This permitted the job scheduler to look at jobs waiting to be executed, jobs that could be deferred, new jobs that should be added, and the jobs that were finished and could be removed. Thus, the job scheduler can at any time assess the total resource requirements and optimally determine which job should be run next, based on the requirements that the user established in specifying what facilities he needed for his job.

This means that the system is not now scheduling the total machine, but is scheduling the components of the machine to do a given task. The system now has to have some way of knowing when specific components have finished their tasks; for this purpose, it needs an interrupt capability. This is a method of handling all of the inner machine communications; that is communications between those parts of the machine that tell each other what they're doing, so the machine knows what is going on. The interrupt system also includes ways of checking for errors and methods for handling program interrupts. It includes a series of programs which looks at what caused the interrupt and on the basis of that, and the current job mix in the system, and the current status of the entire machine, decides what to do next.

Another group of programs in the compiler sections of the operating system is input-output. This makes effective use of the peripheral equipment on the machine. The user no longer has control of the way data pass in and out of the computer.

There are two other parts of the operating system that I think are worth talking about. One is the program library. This is a group of very frequently used programs that are stored in the machine. They may include nothing but small sub-routines or they may be very complex programs. Because this series of programs is used by many people, it's more effective to store them in the machine than to have them read in each time they are needed.

The last part of the operating system is the compilers and assembly languages with which the applications people do their work. They are also in this program library, as are most of the other program groups I have mentioned previously. I want to spend some time on languages, because they have many effects upon how we can do our job.

There are numerous kinds of programming languages around. It would be almost impossible to name all languages that exist. The earliest languages were assembler languages, which by original definition were one for one transformations from some language which was more easily understood by people, to the binary language that the machine understands. These developed into more complex languages that no longer really represent a one for one transformation. What is known as a macro instruction has been added. Macro instructions are small pieces of code that in reality are sub-routines, but which extend and add more cababilities to assembly languages than were available previously.

Another grouping is the so-called higher level languages. These languages allow us to communicate our ideas to each other more easily and allow us to program more easily. These languages represent a "one for many" transformation, *i.e.,* one statement in the higher level language generates many machine code instructions. High level languages have had a diversified development. They tended towards specialization in accordance with activities and interests of their users, because users tend to develop a certain technical language with which they communicate with their peers. We now have a large number of higher level languages, each one devoted to specialized tasks. There are languages for civil engineers, architects, just about any kind of specialty. There is even serious talk about languages for librarians. Many of these languages are not frequently used. Many are not even always available for use on a particular equipment.

There are three major groupings of languages. First there are the algorithmic languages; they are the languages for the mathematician or scientist who wants to do complex calculations. Foremost among them is Fortran, a language primarily designed for those who have very little input data but who require a large amount of calculation with very little data to output. Hence, Fortran's input-output facilities are small, rigid, and not very flexible.

Secondly, there are the business oriented languages, which were more or less thrust upon the industry by the federal government. These languages are designed for handling large amounts of numeric data with very little calculation involved— a little adding, subtracting, keeping track of business accounts, payroll, etc.

The last specialized grouping of languages, and it's difficult to pinpoint the most popular of these, is the list processing languages. These were developed by researchers working in machine translation; they needed capabilities for string manipulation, that is, manipulation of strings of alphabetic characters, which is what they were trying to do in machine translation. It's hard to pick out one of the foremost of these; SNOBOL is probably the most common.

Only very recently has there been any reverse in the trend of specialized languages to bring us back to more generalized languages. In IBM, the thrust towards a language called PL/1 is probably the only really good move in this direction.

PL/1 is a relatively new language, and although its specifications are very clear, its implementation is somewhat limited. There's a big difference between a specification of a language and its implementation. PL/1 is getting better each time we get a new version of the operating system; the language is much improved, better defined, and the compilers are much more efficient at producing smaller amounts of code which run faster on the machine. In PL/1 we have a combination of qualities: the algorithmic capabilities of Fortran, the input-output capabilities of Cobol, and the string manipulation abilities of the list processing languages. In PL/1, it looks like we are getting the type of language which is at last capable of meeting most of the requirements for library applications.

But again I say, there is a significant difference between the implementation and the specification of languages, and it depends upon the particular computer. This is the reason why you'll find that in some cases a program compiled in one language at one location will not run on a machine in another location which has the same kind of compiler. The impact of these languages on program development means that we really have to look at the job we want to accomplish, and once we've figured out what that is, then we need to pick the language in which we should write. This doesn't mean that we can say that for the total library automation task we ought to use PL/1 for everything. This means we need to look at *each* of the individual tasks. There are many things that can and should be done very effectively in assembly language; many can and should be done in Cobol and Fortran as well. We have to look at the task.

Another reason for using these higher level languages is ease in programming maintenance. As the operating systems change and as our requirements in the library change, we find that it's necessary to modify existing programs. If you have a program that's specified in something that looks like English, it's easier for somebody who never saw it before to understand it. And so it's better for us to write in the higher level languages because of this ease in programming maintenance.

Now let's go back to operating systems, and look at the criteria behind development of operating systems. First of all, the main purpose of an operating system is to maximize component utilization, *i.e.*, the CPU, all the input-output devices, all the storage devices, and all other units.

The second major function is to provide better user services. This means that the people who design operating systems look to see if they have a large number of jobs in a queue waiting to be processed. To the designers, each job represents a user. Here we have a "one user, one job" idea on the part of these system people, so that they treat each job with equal priority in terms of trying to meet user requirements. We all know that this is not true; for instance, payroll jobs are not "one user" oriented. There are many other multiple user jobs and certainly the things the library wants to do represent many users, not just a single user. A second bias in user services is the "short job bias." It is a direct consequence of the "one job, one user" bias. In other words, if we can run a whole lot of short jobs through the machine, then we've satisfied more users. We all know that in most cases we don't have short jobs in the library. The last bias is against jobs that require a large amount of input and output. Again, this is based on the requirements of users that have short jobs with little I/O. But library jobs use a large amount of input and output time because they tend to be involved with massive strings of characters.

The third criterion in designing systems is ease of software maintenance. Systems are dynamic and the computing center's requirements are dynamic; system configurations must change, so the system should be designed to make it easy for the system programmer to get in and maintain it. It should also be designed so that he can easily extend the system to cover the new equipment.

I would now like to outline a few of the major operations problems in university computing centers.

The first problem is the wide job mix which the center must perform. It is faced with extremes of complexity that one does not find either in a service bureau or specialized, single purpose facility. The job mix ranges from the kinds of programs that physicists and chemists run for 16 hours, to the student program which takes longer to load in the machine than it does to process. Fundamentally, operating systems were not designed to cover this tremendous job mix; they were designed to cover the job mix that is found in most service bureaus or in a single research or data processing center. To cover this wide mix, users are sometimes forced to make modifications to the operating system.

A second problem, one of a political nature, is scheduling: do we schedule jobs automatically on some equitable scheduling basis, or do we establish a priority system? This can produce quite a severe political hassling between the computer center and their users. The center would prefer to do it on a completely automatic basis, but they haven't been able to achieve this goal. But as soon as you allow any kind of priority, then everybody wants a priority. On college campuses the computing centers are usually tied fairly closely to the Computer Science Department, and this can constitute still another problem. The Computer Science Department treats the computer as its own piece of laboratory equipment; it is theirs and for their use alone. The Computer Science faculty and their students take this possessive attitude which conflicts with the rest of the users and those who are running the system. Computer Science people come in and want to have their job put first in the queue. Well, if the operators are students and are taking courses from the faculty members, they probably will get their job placed first in the queue. So again there is a priority problem.

Lastly, university computing centers face financial constraints, both in terms of support for maintaining the system itself, *i.e.*, in providing in adequate systems staff to meet all of the university's requirements, and in providing adequate equipment itself.

These are some of the problems. How do they affect us in the library? First of all, as most of you know, library jobs are input-output bound, not only from inside the machine, which is moving data from disk storage into the CPU for processing, back out to some other storage device, but also in processing from an input medium into the machine, and then out into some output medium. All of our jobs run up against the short job bias. The bias looks like the super-market express line; if you have less than 10 items, you go to the express counter and get serviced right away. Except that in a computer, you've only got *one* counter and with your big basket or two big baskets, you have all these little people with less than ten items popping in front of you, and if there's enough of them, you're not at the head of the line anymore, you're at the end. With that kind of problem, how do you get to the head of the line? The only way is by some intervention in the operating system that provides you with some internal priority in the machine which says, "No more people are going to be placed in front of this job; it's going to be done." This usually means some manual intervention by the computing center staff. At this time, there isn't any way of automatically looking at a clock and saying, "This job has been in for eighteen hours, we had better get it to the top of the queue."

Spooling has provided a whole series of new problems which we never thought existed before. Many of us have grown up from the punch card era. In punch card jobs, we tended to build little programs and link them together into a stream of programs which we wanted to run sequentially. In those days—and we still design things that way—after successful completion of one job, we wish to run the next job. Now we have spooling, not only on input, but also on output. With spooling, a job is run in the CPU and a data set built in some external file. At some later time, again according to priorities, it is printed or punched to your terminal. With big operating systems being not too stable in operation these days, there can sometimes be troublesome problems between the time the job gets completed and the time you get the data printed out, and sometimes you may never get the data printed out, and it's lost entirely. But as far as the machine is concerned and as far as any of the programs that you wrote are concerned, that job ran to a successful completion. So your next job is going to be run whether or not you've gotten the first job out.

We also found in our computing center that a job was a job, *i.e.*, it was treated completely independent of anything else you might want to do. If a job bombed out in the last five seconds of operating time, for instance, the normal procedure was to put it back in the stream and do it again. If you're talking about overdue notices from your circulation file, and you set a status bit that says, "Yes, I've now printed an overdue notice," and you ran that job again, you're not going to get any notices printed, because they've already been produced according to the file. What we lack here is inner communications from the output spooling queue back into the program, so that you can say, "Yes, indeed, now that I have printed output, I have truly completed the job." Only then can you go on to the next job.

Without this communication, a different kind of program design is required. Now we actually have to provide a physical time lag so that we can get the printout in our hands before we submit the next job into the queue. We can't submit them all together and hope that the system will run. What this has done is lengthen our turnaround time; many jobs that we originally expected would run overnight now take two or three days, because we have to wait to get actual outputs in hand before saying, "Let's go on."

It was a rather rude shock to many of us to learn that you can't go to the computing center and say, "Look, I've now got some money and I want to hang a bunch of devices on the machine to do a new job." With the operating systems that we have today, it just isn't done. Things have to be coordinated. Devices can be physically hung on the machine, but they have to be supported with software packages, and in many cases *we* have to write these software packages, and they are complex and take a long time to write. Also, if we are going to add additional requirements and facilities to computing centers, we've got to give them some lead time.

Earlier we talked about "fail soft" and degradation of systems. The operating systems that we have today provide some of this capability. We need more of these capabilities; we can't, for instance, properly manage our personnel in the library if we can't guarantee that we can get at least some part of our machine processing done each day. It is difficult to find jobs for your marking section when you don't get book labels or pockets from the computing center. If this happens often, pretty soon it's difficult to figure out what you're going to do with all of these people. You can't send them on an eight-hour coffee break! We need to recognize that systems *are* unreliable and go down for many reasons. We must try to build into our system, either in our own application designs or in the basic design, an ability to degrade our activities and still get something done.

And then we must always realize that we are going to have catastrophic failures; power failures are the most notable of this kind. If we're partially through a lengthy job, it's uneconomical to go back and redo the whole job; we should try to pick up from some point and go on forward. This is known as "check point restart," and it means building in certain plateau levels in the processing of the program which —if you fail, you need only fall back to that last plateau, and go on from there. This was brought home to me very strongly when I was building intelligence systems for the Air Force. We were nine hours into a ten-hour sort when the power failed, and we had no check point restart. We had to redo those nine hours.

We've got to insist on better reliability within our total system. We now talk about building systems that are real time, on-line, and yet these systems are of no use unless we can insure that they are working all the time. When you go to a real time system, you can't fall back to a batch system. In many real time systems, it's all or nothing. So you've got to build in reliability. All of these things cost money, and you have to play one side against the other, until you've reached an optimum solution. You must decide how much reliability you can afford or how much you can *not* afford.

Another implication concerns maintenance. On third generation systems, system maintenance is not transparent to the application program. Systems keep changing. Stanford is on version 13 of the operating system; we're on version 14 of the operating system, and we have 15 and 16 on hand, and on and on it goes. In the year 2000 we'll probably have version 979 of the operating system available to us. Because many of these changes are not transparent to applications programs, all of a sudden the programs which worked beautifully for three months are now in terrible shape, and you don't know why. Well, you find out shortly that the trouble is due to changed operating systems. Now you have to perform some maintenance to make them work with the new system.

What are some of the solutions to these problems? One of the first solutions that pops into most people's minds in fighting the scheduling problem is to get his own computer. You can pat it, and if it's working it can run your job when you want. As you can gather from the above discussion of operating systems, if you're going to have your own machine, then you've created for yourself the same basic problems the computing center has. You had better be prepared to face this possibility, and it's expensive to provide adequate expertise in terms of system programmers to maintain the system. It's not the same as installing a 407; it's an entirely different kind of ball game.

What we really need to do is sit down with the people responsible for computing activities on the campus, and with them design a total computer system which is adequate for all campus needs, and buy a system of computers. I don't necessarily mean just a single CPU, but a complex arrangement of computing power on a campus which will meet all of the requirements of reliability, fail safe, fail soft, check point restart, etc. We need these capabilities or we can't live. We can't live in an environment unless we have redundancy or flexibility in the system.

Earlier we talked about system redundancy, *i.e.,* a second unit or copy of the first. But this isn't always necessary. How about flexibility in the system? By building in certain kinds of compatibility between different machines, a job which normally runs on one machine, if that machine is down, can be run on another one. Building in a degree of flexibility allows for degradation of the total system. A smaller machine will take a little longer to get a job done, but at least you're getting something done. We must recognize that there are weaknesses in operating systems, so that you can compensate for the problems.

As we move into the world of on-line, real time operating systems, we must be able to recreate information in case of a catastrophic failure; adequate systems will allow you to recreate this information. This is "backup," and one also needs "backup for the backup," because there are times when you're copying data sets on tape so that you can store them away for just that kind of eventuality, and *that's* the moment when you lose everything, and you've lost both your backup and your original file. Then you know you're in real trouble. So you've got to include in your design some "backup for the backup." I should conclude by emphasizing that this is the most important thing you can do in designing a system.

Developing a Campus Information Retrieval System

Edwin B. Parker   Associate Professor, Department of Communication Research, Stanford University

Introduction

My purpose in the short time available is to attempt a general overview and a brief progress report on the development efforts of Project SPIRES, which is financed primarily by the National Science Foundation. At this stage in our development the name behind the acronym, Stanford Physics Information REtrieval System, is no longer quite appropriate, although we still hope it carries the connotation of high aspiration. Our close collaboration with the Automation Division of the Stanford Library and our commitment to provide the computer software for Stanford Library Automation Project has broadened our perspective and our goals. Funds from the U.S. Office of Education to Project BALLOTS are making it possible to take on that added responsibility. Because of this expansion of both systems and applications programming effort we are proposing a change in the name of our project to Stanford Public Information REtrieval System, as Allen Veaner mentioned yesterday.

Project Goals

SPIRES has two major goals. One is to provide improved information services to members of the Stanford community, beginning with the physicists who are serving as the first test population for our development efforts. The motivation is to take advantage of the new computer technology to extend information services to scientists and other users to a level unthinkable if it had to be provided by current manual systems. In our view, the main advantage of time-shared computing for information services is that, for the first time, we can build systems with two-way communication permitting rapid negotiation between user and system. In technical jargon we call these negotiations 'feedback loops.' It is primarily because of this two-way communication and the facility with which user interactions with the computer system can be recorded and tabulated in the computer that we are optimistic that the developing system will remain responsive to real needs of users. Meanwhile, during the development stage, we need the help of other kinds of feedback, including interviews and user tests of partially developed systems. The first level of new service that SPIRES will provide is what MIT's Project INTREX is calling the augmented catalog. For Stanford physicists this means providing the capability to search several document collections, including the Stanford Linear Accelerator Center preprint collection, Nuclear Science Abstracts, the DESY index of high-energy physics documents, and a collection of physics journal articles. Unlike the current library catalog there is an entry for each abstract in NSA, for example, and indexing under each major word in the title of each article, not just the first. Some collections, including the SLAC preprints, are indexed by footnote citations permitting searches forward in time as well as backward from a given article or bibliography. Since the goal is to meet the information needs of the users, it seems quite likely that there will be motivation to go beyond the provision of augmented catalog services to text retrieval and various forms of data retrieval as rapidly as the technology and available funding permit.

The second major goal of SPIRES is to provide the long-run economic benefits of more efficient internal processing of bibliographic information in the library. In other words, the goal is to meet the computer software needs of Project BALLOTS as they develop their acquisitions, cataloging, and circulation systems. This goal is completely compatible with the first, for both technical and economic reasons. Technically, it doesn't make any difference to the computer programs whether the user is a librarian searching through a Library of Congress document collection, or the library's own In Process collection, or whether the user is a physicist searching Nuclear Science Abstracts, or possibly a small private collection of documents. In both cases the computer system permits the user to perform quickly what might otherwise be a tedious manual search. There are differences in the kind of output formats the different users will require—the physicist may want an alphabetized bibliography while the library clerk may want a purchase order produced. But these differences in output format are small variations in the application of a general system which must be the same for the major function, namely the retrieval process.

Economically, it may be necessary to meet this goal of improved internal library processing in order to be able to afford the improved information services to users that is the first goal of Project SPIRES. As we and our funding agencies have been finding out, development of time-shared computer systems is an expensive proposition. It would be difficult to justify the costs of such development on the basis of the improved service to a small number of users, even such reputedly affluent users as high-energy physicists. My personal suspicion is that once such systems are readily available and have proven themselves valuable, users will be quite willing to spend some of their research funds on the kinds of information service we plan to provide. Meanwhile, few people have budget items for an as yet unproven service. Looked at economically, the library's view that the internal processing service should be provided first, with the user services added as a by-product service, may be the correct one.

Consequently, we are able to collaborate easily with the library in the development of a system that will meet both goals.

Basic Choices

In attempting to provide expanded services to users and improved internal library processing, there are several choices to be made. The first choice is obviously whether or not to go to a computer system, and, if so, whether to go to a batch processing or time-shared system. The decision to go to a computer system does not imply replacing the present manual system. It means adding a searching capability that will permit librarian, library clerks, and scientific users to locate bibliographic information quickly and without drudgery. It will mean that bibliographic information, once typed into computer readable form, either locally or by the Library of Congress, will not have to be typed over and over again. It will mean that more than one person can look at the same part of the same file at the same time without getting in another's way.

This is not a matter of replacing an old manual system with a new automated system—it is a matter of giving the present personnel better bibliographic tools with which to perform their present tasks and freeing them from much drudgery so that they can take on new responsibilities and services. The computer will not be a panacea. It is not likely in the immediate future to provide full text service, for example, because of the high costs of computer storage and the high costs of keyboarding information into machine readable form. Consequently, we have to think in terms of providing visual display terminals that can display information stored on microfiche as well as information stored in digital form for computer processing. In short, the choice of using a computer system is not an either-or choice; rather it is a decision to add one more bibliographic tool to the equipment of librarians.

Stanford's choice of an interactive computer system permitting immediate response to queries rather than a batch processing system providing output at scheduled intervals was a choice that few libraries can take. If both kinds of computer systems were easy to provide, then I'm sure librarians would all opt for the interactive system. Stanford's decision was that a batch processing system, with the slow feedback associated with waiting for the next batch of computer output, would be unacceptable. At least the present manual system is interactive and operates in 'real time.' So Stanford's decision was to wait until interactive processing appeared feasible. However, there are perhaps less than half a dozen universities in the world (Stanford and MIT are the first two that come to mind) where the quality of computing and research in computer science make it possible to make such a choice today.

The problem is that most existing computer time-sharing systems are devoted to applications that do not have the massive storage requirements of large library and information systems. None of the proposed large-scale general-purpose time-sharing systems have yet been successful. For us to tread where IBM and others have so far failed would be foolhardy. We may be foolhardy anyway, but we chose not to wait for someone else to develop a general-purpose time-sharing system. Instead we forged ahead and are attempting a special-purpose super-simplified time-sharing system of our own. If we succeed, we are heroes, and if we fail we are merely visionaries who were ahead of our time. We are convinced that the right way to go for the long run is the interactive system and we are confident enough to think that our chances of producing such a system are good. But we don't recommend it for others unless they are confident they can work at the present frontier of computer systems development. This is not the same thing as writing applications programs for a well-developed stable computer system.

Most of the other major choices are choices of scope. Should we think in terms of a purely local information system or as a component in a developing national or international information system? Should we restrict ourselves to a single discipline, such as physics, or should we expand to include chemistry, medicine, engineering, social sciences, and humanities, etc.? Should we restrict ourselves to bibliographic information or should we expand to include management information such as accounting, inventory, personnel files, etc.? In attempting to meet the information needs of the scientists should we stop at bibliographic information or should we expand to full text retrieval (not necessarily from computer files), and to retrieval from large archives of non-bibliographic data? Will the computer terminals necessary for access to the retrieval system be special for the one application, or should they be the same terminals scientists have in their labs and offices for computer applications other than information retrieval?

I'm not certain that we're making the right choice at all of these choice points, but I can report briefly what choices we have made or are making. One obvious factor in making the decision is economic support. It's one thing to dream grandiose dreams and another thing to propose economically realistic projects during a time of budget cuts and cost-effectiveness evaluation criteria. Another factor is that we must avoid attempting something that is too complex to be successfully brought to fruition given the current state of the computer art. There are obviously economies of scale to be accomplished by making a system general enough to provide more than one kind of service (*e.g.,* both a bibliographic and a management information system). At the same time there are complexities of scale as more general systems are attempted. The lesson of IBM's Time Sharing System (TSS) should warn us away from attempting too much if we hope to complete development within the time and budget planned. We don't want the complexities of scale to overwhelm the economies of scale. The special purpose systems are usually more efficient for the purpose they were intended to serve.

With these considerations in mind we are attempting first a bibliographic information system that is intended to be a local system that can serve as a 'retailer' outlet for the 'wholesale' products of the developing national information systems in the various scientific disciplines. We presume that although batch processing systems (like MEDLARS) may be more efficient as a centralized system, interactive systems will have to be decentralized to avoid the expensive communication costs. This judgment may change, of course, if there is a drastic revision of domestic telephone tariffs after the introduction of domestic communication satellites. Nevertheless, our best guess now is that there will always be need for local or at least regional service, even though there may be network switching to a national information center or centers for infrequently used material. Local systems should be more responsive to local needs than any centralized national system can hope to be.

We are assuming that few users will be able to afford computer terminals solely for the purpose of bibliographic searches, and that we must make our service available from whatever terminals users have. (At Stanford there are already about 100 typewriter terminals in use for remote computation and other computer services.) Expansion beyond physics references and beyond the collections necessary for the library's acquisitions and cataloging functions should be rapid as the appropriate machine-readable data collections become available, provided that there is a user demand and a means of financing the expensive storage costs. Some additional programming is necessary to translate each new data file into our standard internal formats, but that investment is small relative to the programming required for the retrieval system itself. Our prototype system, which we hope to have operational by January 1, was designed entirely as a bibliographic retrieval system, although it doesn't make much difference to the system whether the records being retrieved are records of books or whether they are personnel records. SPIRES was successfully used in a test demonstration of a personnel file earlier this year. The amount of programming necessary to handle additional attributes or output formats is small relative to the rest of the system. The later version of the system, on which we are now beginning some of the design work, will be somewhat more general as we attempt to accommodate other than bibliographic data in a more general data management system. Nevertheless, even that second version of the system may not be general enough to handle all of the complexities of interactive retrieval and editing of scientific data from large archives of physics data or social science archives of public opinion poll and census data.

This plan for successive iterations as we progress to more complex computer systems is desirable for two reasons. One is that there is much that is *ad hoc* in the development of computer systems. We have no theory to permit us to predict with certainty the range of modifications necessary when a new complexity or generalization is introduced in one part of the system. In other words, we can't predict which straw will break the proverbial camel's back. In fact we don't even know the weight of some of the straws we are adding. A more important reason for planning successive iterations is that the major unknown is how users will interact with the system. We need to study how users interact, what frustrations they have, what mistakes they make, what features they find useful or not useful, and so on. We are not trying to develop an optimal computer system. Rather, we are trying to optimize an interaction between humans and a computer system. Consequently, the computer system should not be itself optimized in the usual sense. Instead it has to be adapted to the needs and habits of the users.

Economics

A word about costs of the system may be in order here. It is too early to be able to calculate with much confidence the ultimate operating costs of the kind of system we are developing. It may be that computing costs, particularly the costs of mass storage, will have to come down before such a system as we are developing will be economical to operate. On the other hand, it may be that computer systems, like automobiles, may become an expensive necessity after people learn what difference it makes to have one. I've warned the Provost of this university that our greatest danger to the university budget is not that we might fail, but that we might succeed.

Meanwhile, we are now entering a period of extremely high costs in which we will have the costs of operating an expensive prototype system completely in parallel with existing manual operations at the same time as the costs of continued research and development are expanding. Later, there should be some savings resulting from not having to maintain all of the present manual files in parallel with the computer system and a more efficient computer system than the prototype is likely to be. Also, as the member of users increases the cost per user should come down.

For most users of the system I propose that at least the marginal cost associated with his use of the system be charged directly to the user. This would not be appropriate, of course, for internal use by the library staff itself, or for those early users who are willing to suffer the inconvenience of being guinea pigs for the development group to study. The primary reason for this recommendation that users pay at least marginal costs is not to recover the additional revenue, although that will help. Rather, the reason is to provide the feedback mechanism that will let the operators of the information system know what is most needed by their users. The simple market mechanism of pricing should serve to keep the system in touch with user needs. A secondary benefit would be to avoid frivolous use of a very expensive tool. This proposal, on the surface, appears to run counter to one of the most important educational concepts of the past century, namely, the concept of free information or free library service to all who wish to use it. That important principle can be better maintained, not by putting all the costs of the information systems into overhead charges that the users pay indirectly (out of tuition fees, research overhead funds, etc.), but by making sure that all members of the university community are given funds to pay for their use. We already have such a mechanism in the Provost's computer fund at this university. The same or an analogous mechanism could be used to pay for information services. The same money that the university spends on information services anyway can be distributed to users as tokens that can be spent only at the library or information service. Such an apparently radical proposal is sensible for computer information services because of the capability of the computer system to inexpensively maintain the necessary accounting and billing services.

Implementation Progress and Problems

Our development strategy continues to be one of maintaining responsiveness to user needs. In our initial stages we conducted many interviews with high-energy physicists and with some librarians, and performed a secondary analysis of questionnaires from an American Institute of Physics study.

In our prototype system we have not had internal machine efficiency as one of our major goals. Rather we have attempted to develop as quickly as possible a system that potential users can interact with so we can find from a study of their interaction whether we are really building the kind of system that is meeting their needs. We expect to learn enough from the experience of developing the prototype and from how users interact with it, that a second iteration will be necessary in any case. This goal of optimizing a man-machine interaction is a somewhat frustrating one for many good systems programmers. They would like to get on with the job of developing a full-blown system that has an elegant and efficient internal structure. Interrupting their work for frequent 'demonstrations' of partially developed systems and user tests that always result in suggested changes tends to be an unwelcome frustration that they would rather do without. They often tend to feel that they could finish the entire system sooner if people would only leave them alone to get on with the job. The SPIRES project staff have been extremely patient in the face of such frustrations, primarily because they are able to see the logic of adjusting the computer system to meet the needs of the users, and to live with the frequent user interaction that such a premise entails.

These goals dictated our choice of hardware, operating system, and programming language. We are utilizing a partition in the 360-67 that does not involve the dynamic relocation hardware specific to that machine. The machine itself, since it is the central computer of the Stanford Computation Center, campus facility, was a logical choice for what was at first a research project and later a prototype development. By staying with a standard language, PL/1, and the 360 Operating System (OS), we will remain compatible with most hardware in the IBM 360 series. The overhead costs associated with such a general operating system and programming language may be more than can be carried for long in a system that must be responsive to cost effectiveness criteria. Meanwhile, we economize on our scarce resource, namely skilled systems programmer time, at the expense of computer time. Nevertheless, the moment of truth must come, and we have still to face the hard decisions about which machine, what operating system, and what programming language for the follow-on system.

The most formidable stumbling block in the way of our development was the need for a suitable time-sharing system to permit multiple users to interact with the same system at what appears to the users to be the same time. When we first started this project we had naively hoped that IBM's TSS (Time Sharing System) would provide a general purpose time-sharing system under which we could operate. Rather than give up in frustration when that didn't materialize, our project staff have designed and programmed a special purpose system. Within the last week we have had successful tests with five users interacting simultaneously and have designed the facilities necessary to expand the number of users up to the current physical capacity of the machine, namely, 62 users. There is still more work to be done and undoubtedly there will be more 'bugs' to be tracked down, but we are currently optimistic that the basic system will be up and running by January 1.

File Organization

What is perhaps the key problem in any information retrieval system is the file organization. Given the requirement of rapid retrieval from very large files, a technique of serially searching the file, although useful in batch processing systems, had to be ruled out. Various more or less complicated organizations can be chosen, including threaded lists, directed graphs, balanced tree structures, and others. Some of the considerations to be taken into account include speed of searching, the characteristics of the storage medium or media, ease of making modifications to the file, and the costs of input and file reorganization, if needed. The structure chosen and implemented for SPIRES may not be optimal in some ultimate sense. It does have two important virtues—it is simple, and it does the job. Records are entered into the data collection serially in order of input, with no ordering or organization imposed on them. The costs of periodically reorganizing a Library of Congress file or the holdings file for a large research library would prove too expensive in almost any other organization. The structuring necessary is provided in the index files, which are merely what is called 'inverted files' or inverted lists. We avoid serial searching of index files by using a technique called 'hash coding.'

Associated with each key in each index (*e.g.*, each author name in the author index) there is a list of the locations of all entries containing that key. Serially searching or chaining through a list of keys in a small segment of an index file held in the core memory is not a major task for a computer with the speed of the 360/67. The problem is to minimize the number of accesses to the slower disk storage device (in our case a 2314 disk which has a capacity of approximately 208 million characters of information). This is accomplished approximately as follows: The amount of storage required for the index file is divided by the size of segment (or block) that can conveniently be brought into storage in one access to the disk. The result is the number of different blocks in that index. Some of those blocks are reserved as overflow blocks. The rest are labelled primary blocks. We assign each index term to a particular block by taking some part of each search key, for example, the first three characters of an author's name, pass the internal computer representation of those characters to a computer routine that interprets it as a number, which is divided by the number of primary blocks. The result of the division is discarded and the remainder gives the number of the block into which the key is inserted (during the index building operation) or from which it will be retrieved (during the retrieval operation). If the designated primary block is full, then one of the overflow blocks will be linked to the primary block. Thus the appropriate segment of each index file can be searched with usually only a single access to the disk storage. The index files currently implemented for one or more data collections are Author, Title Word, ID Number, Corporate Author, Conference Author, Keyword, Citation (*i.e.*, journal, volume, and page number of journal articles cited in footnote citations or reference lists). Restricting a search on date (*i.e.*, before 1967, after 1965, etc.) is handled in a slightly different way. Each entry in each of the other indexes included not only the location of the document reference, but the date of the document.

Query Language

From the point of view of the user the window into the system or the handle of the bibliographic tool is the query language. This is a particularly critical area in an interactive system in which the ultimate consumers, students, faculty members, their secretaries, library clerical staff, etc., are directly formulating the query without intervention by trained librarians or programmers. The user shouldn't have to know the internal working of the system any more than a housewife driving a late model car with automatic transmission and all the automatic extras needs to be a trained mechanic or automobile manufacturer. But, like the housewife on her way to the grocery store, the computer user has to smoothly and easily control the powerful machine to get where he or she wants to go. Our concept of a good interactive system is not, repeat not, one in which an intelligent computer system analyzes the user's natural language input and decides what the user really wanted. In short, we are not trying to simulate a good reference librarian. Instead we are trying to provide a simple query language in which users can give simple unambiguous instructions that allow them to get the computer to do what they want it to do. Those instructions should be in a language as close to natural English as possible without introducing ambiguities. The query language we have implemented consists of names of index files that can be searched, followed by the value of what is to be sought in those indexes (*e.g.*, author smith and title library automation). More complex searches can be constructed by combining simple searches with the logical operators "and," "or," and "not." At the end of each input line in the search request, the system replies with the number of documents that have been accumulated using the search specifications. When the number is sufficiently small that the user wishes to see the actual document references, then the command "output" will result in the appropriate information being displayed at the terminal. For those of you who are either computer buffs or linguistics buffs, I can say cryptically that the syntax analyzer we are using employs a simple precedence context-free grammar implemented with a single push-down stack. Allen Veaner said kind things about this language implementation in his talk yesterday, but frankly, we are not satisfied with it. Having implemented a first version with a context-free grammar we are itching to get on to a more sophisticated syntax analyzer which can interpret context. For example, we now have to say "Find author smith or author jones" rather than "find author smith or jones" because our syntax analyzer isn't sophisticated enough to look back at the context of the "or" to see that the index file named author was implied. Instead it expects to find the name of an index file after the logical connector and gives the user a frustrating error message, such as "*or* may not be followed by *jones.*"

Input/update

One important area in any system is how to get the information into the system in the first place, and how to correct it once it gets there incorrectly. We hope that the large majority of our input will come from magnetic tape sources (*e.g.*, LC MARC records) that don't need to be keyboarded locally. If the Library of Congress can't get us bibliographic records fast enough for us to use in our acquisition system and we have to keyboard the information locally in order to produce purchase orders and other output, then the costs of our system will be vastly greater than we would like them to be. I hate to be in the position of being that dependent on other people's efforts, and fervently hope that the Library of Congress will come through with timely data. Delays of merely a few weeks will be very costly to us and, I presume, other users of the MARC tapes. One of our input tapes now is Nuclear Science Abstracts. We hope to expand this kind of service, after we hve digested our present commitments and can find funds for the expensive data storage costs, to include magnetic tape outputs from the American Chemical Society Information system, MEDLARS, and other systems.

Meanwhile some data do have to be keyboarded locally. One such collection is the Stanford Linear Accelerator Center preprint collection. We have considered alternate input devices and have settled on on-line input through a time-shared text editing system as the appropriate way for us. Once the documents are correctly keyboarded they are added to the appropriate data collection and appropriate index entries are constructed in a batch job. But the keyboarding itself is done on-line. This has the advantage of letting clerks use an IBM selectric typewriter instead of a keypunch or paper tape machine. Corrections within a line can be made merely be backspacing and striking over. Striking a single key can delete an entire line. If a word is incorrectly spelled more than once a single change command changes all occurrences. The current charges for use of this on-line text editing system are $4 per terminal hour. We were aware that some suspicious reviewers of future proposals might say that this was an impossibly extravagant way to input data so we conducted a cost effectiveness study. From the point of view of SPIRES/BALLOTS I think this will rank as the most cost-effective cost-effectiveness study on record. We got a third party to conduct the study and a fourth party to pay for it. The ERIC clearinghouse located in our Institute for Communications Research, the clearing house for educational media and technology, has been experimenting with use of SPIRES. They agreed to hire Charlie

Bourne of Programming Services Incorporated to perform a comparative cost analysis of keypunched input and on-line input. We took a 1,000 document collection and divided it into two sub-collections of 500 documents each for purposes of comparing the two input methods. The results were pleasantly surprising from our point of view. The cost per document was 76.6 cents using the on-line input and $1.331 per document using the keypunch. After correcting for some unexpected computer expenses in processing the cards, the projected future expense for keypunched input was 75 cents per document, still within a penny per document of the on-line input. The major differences were in labor costs, particularly for the cost of corrections. These differences helped to offset the 24 cents per document computer cost associated with using an on-line terminal. The results were instructive to us and might even generalize to other places, for example, any other place where you can buy on-line text editing services for $4 per hour or less.

We expect to complete the programming this fall on the generalized update program that will make it easy to make changes in documents already stored in the computer file, with the appropriate changes in the inverted index files being automatically made. That program will still be a batch program. We felt that attempting an on-line file update at this time was more of a problem than we cared to face. A true on-line update is one of the requirements we have for the next iteration of the system after we have more experience with the prototype version we hope to have operational by January 1. Meanwhile, for the next month or two we will continue to use a rather rudimentary update program that allows us to add and delete entire bibliographic entries. This allows us to make any changes we wish and it does make all the appropriate changes in the indexes, but it is a cumbersome temporary expedient.

Terminals

I have been gratified to see how the eyes of librarians, students, and even faculty colleagues sometimes light up when they sit at a typewriter terminal for a demonstration and see the potential of interactive searching. Nevertheless, I don't believe we can provide a satisfactory system with typewriter terminals alone. The problem with typewriter terminals is that the speed of a typewriter is much slower than human reading speed. I suspect that after the novelty wears off, people will find use of the slow typewriter terminals very frustrating, particularly if they hear that there is a better way to do it. Our original plas was to provide service in IBM 2260 CRT display terminals by January of next year. We did in fact successfully demonstrate search capability from 2260s this past summer, as we had earlier on the much more expensive IBM 2250 CRT display. That experience, plus the fact that better display terminals are soon coming onto the market, led us to cancel our order for 2260s. We are now negotiating for the purchase of a CRT display system with much better characteristics. The key feature of the system is that it uses standard television sets as the display device (although we propose to order a version with a different phosphor and a Polaroid face-plate to reduce the flicker problem. Although the television set is a more complicated device than needed for CRT display, it has the advantage of mass production. It will permit us to display a very readable character set including all the characters in the 96 character ASCII character set in lines of 72 characters long. The device also has a hardware capability for full graphic display although the computer costs in providing a full graphic capability may preclude that application for other than experimental purposes. Since it is compatible with video transmission of camera images we think it keeps open the possibility of computer controlled display of remotely stored microfiche collections. That may be a less expensive solution to the full text problem than we are likely to obtain from digital storage for quite some time. Our target date for implementation is April, although next July may be more realistic given the hardware interface and software systems effort that must go on between now and then.

Other Services

As you might gather from the way we have been concentrating on system development, we have so far done very little in the way of providing the applications programming for such services as purchase orders, bibliographies, catalog cards, acquisition lists, and other useful output formats. There will still be a lot of work left after we bring up the nucleus of our prototype system. One feature that we do hope to have ready by January will be a generalized personal file capability that will permit any member of the Stanford community to input his personal files into our format and use our retrieval programs for on-line access to his own records. We also have plans for a selective dissemination of information (SDI) system that will work by having users leave standing search requests with the system to be processed against input files when new collections are added (for example, new preprints or the latest issue of Nuclear Science Abstracts). Instead of mailing the results we'll merely store the results in a file they can query from their terminal (or from one of the public terminals on campus).

If we had more time I'd like to lay out the plans we have for the next five years, or even to give my science fiction talk about what we should expect ten years from now. I think it's obvious that we aren't going to run out of interesting work for quite a long time to come. It's too early to tell whether our efforts will be judged a success or failure, but we are certainly having fun trying.

By way of a closing remark I'd like to share with you my homely management philosophy. I try to hire only people who are smarter than I am and who have all the experience and skills that I don't have, even if I have to pay them more than I make. (And we sometimes have to, given the great demand for first-rate people in a field exploding as rapidly as computing is.) I try to enthuse them with a vision of what can be done and then delegate to them both the responsibility and the authority necessary to produce it. But they get one additional assignment. They have to teach me as they go along, so I can learn how to create a sophisticated computer system in case I ever have to.

Appendix A: The Collaborative Library Systems Development Project (CLSDP): A Mechanism for Inter-University Cooperation*

Paul J. Fasana   Columbia University Libraries

Introduction and Background

The main objective of the collaborative effort, which includes Columbia, Stanford, and Chicago, is to test the feasibility of designing generalized automated library systems. This, we've discovered, is difficult and possibly not technically feasible at this point in time. Traditionally, librarians begin to glow when they contemplate the concept of cooperation. Librarians have cooperated in many areas in the past and have accomplished significant and positive results. There is a danger, though, in assuming that because libraries have been able to cooperate in the past, that they can work cooperatively in the same way in the future. No one would question the desire to cooperate, especially in the complex and costly area of library automation, but one might question the method and feasibility of cooperative work at this time. Research libraries have grown dramatically in size and complexity, and, though there has been a growing semblance of compatibility among libraries of comparable size and scope, the use of computers has tended to emphasize the differences. Admittedly, many, if not most of the differences are small, but they are not trivial and their cumulative effect is telling. My remarks today will be aimed at describing some of the experience gained during the past two years of working the CLSD Project and outlining some of the problems we've encountered.

During the past decade, many have talked about the desirability of initiating cooperative ventures or coordinating development schedules of libraries working on similar automation projects. The benefits that might accrue are easy to envision. Few, though, have attempted to identify the problems that might be encountered or the way in which such ventures might be organized. Ralph Shoffner of the Institute for Library Research, University of California at Berkeley, called a meeting in 1967 to talk about the problems and possibilities of cooperative work. Ten or twelve library automation experts were invited. For two days, we sat around discussing and theorizing. At the end of the meeting a straw vote was

---

*Presented at the "Library Automation Conference" sponsored by the Division of Library Development, New York State Education Department. An excerpt of the presentation was published in the New York State Library *Bookmark*, volume 29, number 10, July 1970.

taken to see which of the people attending would be willing to participate in a cooperative venture. Most of those attending said (I think I was the only exception) that, though they realized that it would be desirable and possibly beneficial, they, personally, would not want to participate or be involved in such a venture.

At about the same time the Association of Research Libraries was interested in promoting the idea of developing generalized and transferable automated systems for libraries of comparable size and scope. At that same time, Columbia, Stanford, and Chicago, libraries of comparable size and scope, were independently about to initiate major design efforts in the area of acquisitions. After discussion, it was decided it would be logical and desirable for the three libraries to attempt to work cooperatively. A proposal was prepared and submitted to the National Science Foundation asking for money which would allow the three libraries to work together to develop an effective mechanism for collaborative work in the area of library automation. The proposal was approved early in 1968 and $60,000 was given to support the project for 18 months.

Objectives

I would like to review briefly several of the major objectives stated in the CLSD proposal. The wording is precise and must be read carefully to understand the original intention of the participants. The objectives reflect a cautious attitude, one that experience during the past two years has tended to reinforce.

A prime objective of the project was to develop and experiment with a mechanism (or framework) that would allow three institutions to work cooperatively. We started with the assumption that we did not know whether cooperative work in this area was possible. Any mechanism developed should consider and experiment with pooling resources, coordinating individual work schedules, and designing generalized systems. I would emphasize that the intent behind this objective was to *experiment* with a mechanism that would provide the means for cooperation, and not to produce, necessarily, a compatible operational system. In order to focus work efforts, it was decided that a particular area, or function, would be selected to experiment with. The area chosen was monograph acquisitions. I would repeat that this decision was made not to see if a compatible acquisitions system could be developed, but to see what types of collaborative work were possible and what problems would be encountered.

A second objective was to develop a painless yet efficient method of disseminating information. The problem of dissemination exists on two levels. First, there are the seemingly endless numbers of people who feel that a personal visit is the only way of finding out what is being done in an automation project. This method may be justified given the uneven (often totally lacking) documentation describing automation efforts, but it is time consuming, disruptive, expensive, and not very efficient. At Columbia, for example, I estimate that 10 to 15% of my time is spent giving critiques to people who have dropped in, often unannounced, to see first-hand what is going on at Columbia. 10 or 15% of a busy schedule is a significant amount of time.

Written documentation is an alternate method of disseminating information and the problems here are many and far reaching. The CLSD objective in this area was to experiment with the prompt exchange of working data among the participating institutions. The problems encountered in attempting to do this are interesting and bear evaluation. Anyone who has worked on an automation project knows that programmers and systems analysts either don't know how to write, or refuse to write. It is far more interesting and challenging, for example, to write programs and run them than to document and flowchart them. As a consequence, program documentation is neglected or hastily prepared and usually not updated with recent changes. Since program development is a dynamic process, there is some justification in postponing documentation as long as possible. In order to facilitate the exchange of data and the preparation of documentation, we decided to develop standards and guidelines for preparing documentation. This has proved to be reasonably successful.

A third objective was to explore the feasibility of creating effective liaison with national agencies such as the Library of Congress, the National Library of Medicine, and the National Agriculture Library. Our intent in this area was to see if we could supplement and enhance their efforts by producing evaluative feedback, such as in the use and development of the MARC service, and in serving as a sounding-board for new projects. Contact with the National Libraries Task Force Project was made and representation at each other's meetings was established. Plans to exchange data were also developed.

Finally, we realized that there was a need to communicate and work with hardware manufacturers. Our intent here was to see if we could identify problems that needed solving, or hardware that should be developed or adapted for library use. A frequent complaint from hardware manufacturers is that they can get no consensus from libraries about what is wanted or needed. Therefore, part of the effort to communicate with manufacturers would involve developing fairly comprehensive specifications which would reflect (hopefully) the needs of the library community.

Structure of the CLSD Effort

A mechanism was established for the collaborative effort which has proved

effective to some degree. Overall planning and control of the project is the responsibility of a "Planning Council" made up of two representatives from each
institution, one being the senior technical person responsible for the institution's
automation program, the second being the director of the library (or his designated alternate). One of the library directors was designated Chairman of the Planning Council. His responsibilities include presiding at Council meetings, reporting
to the funding agency, coordinating (generally) meeting schedules, and formulating (in consultation with the entire Planning Council) general guidelines and
direction for the project. In addition, one technical personnel was appointed Sec-
retary to the Planning Council and was responsible for scheduling meetings, preparing agendas, preparing and distributing documentation, and performing general administrative and technical duties. The intent behind the structure and
composition of the Planning Council was to insure that there would be participation and working involvement of both policy level and technical personnel.
This has not been fully achieved for reasons that I will go into in a moment.

The method of work was considered and it was decided that, initially, we
would experiment with having frequent technical meetings and council meetings
every two to three months. The purpose of the technical meetings was to bring
technical personnel together and allow them to address themselves to the specific
technical problems and design consideration. The purpose of the Council meetings was to review the results of the technical meetings and act upon recommendations made by technical personnel.

Problems

I would like to briefly describe some of the problems that we've encountered
trying to work within this general framework. These can be roughly grouped under four headings: logistical, technical, personnel, and adminstrative.

Logistical Problems

Under logistical problems the most important are scheduling of meetings and
geographic separation. The personnel involved in the project are senior and have
many responsibilities and commitments. The simple task of trying to find a time
suitable to all participants to have a meeting has proved to be extremely difficult
and time consuming. As a consequence, meetings have had to be scheduled
months in advance, and at the last moment often cancelled for some unexpected
reason. This has proved especially critical in scheduling Council meetings with
the result that fewer Council meetings have been held than anticipated, which in
turn created a communications problem between technical personnel and directors.
The several Council meetings that have been held have been devoted more to describing what has happened since the last meeting than to doing substantive work.

Technical meetings have been held far more frequently (almost monthly) but have proved to be less effective and productive than initially anticipated. The most effective meeting pattern is two days. In order to minimize the amount of time spent away from the office, these meetings were held on Friday and Saturday or Sunday and Monday. Needless to say, this creates problems for one's personal life.

The geographic separation of the institutions creates additional problems. If one is traveling from West to East one loses almost an entire day traveling; traveling East to West, the same occurs. Therefore, most of the technical meetings have been held in Chicago, a pleasant enough city in the Spring and Autumn, but brutally hot in the Summer and bitterly cold in the Winter. The preparation required on the part of each person attending the meeting (if properly done) requires at least another full day. This means in essence that every two-day technical meeting actually requires roughly four to five days for at least two of the participants (*i.e.*, the two traveling to the meeting place). Needless to say, this time is taken from other more pressing and immediate responsibilities, which means that if one is terribly pressed for time, these extracurricular responsibilities are usually the ones to be sloughed off. This has a direct and adverse affect on the quality and quantity of work that can be accomplished at a meeting.

Several alternatives to scheduling special meetings, such as conference calls, the U.S. mails, or scheduling meetings during conventions, have been experimented with but have not proved effective. It's virtually impossible, for example, to accomplish any substantive work on a conference call because of the inability to draw diagrams or demonstrate how something works. The mails are in some sense even more frustrating because they are slow and require that all thoughts first be organized and then written down (more about the problem of written documentation in a moment). Scheduling technical meetings to coincide with national conventions has proved impossible because of the hectic pace and tight scheduling characteristic of conventions.

Technical Problems

In the area of technical problems, the most important are terminology, written documentation, systems design considerations, and individual project schedules.

Language generally is richly ambiguous and imprecise. Technical jargon pretends to be more precise but in fact is often more ambiguous and misleading. This at least has been our experience attempting to work together. Part of the problem stems from the fact that the jargon of library automation has not yet been fully developed and is evolving as a blend of library and computer jargon, neither of which is especially noted for its preciseness, stability, and clarity. Early on in the project we found that on a technical level we were spending a great deal of time trying to explain to each other what we meant by, for example, and "encumbrance" versus a "mortgage," or a "dealer's ticket" versus an "invoice." Only after a number of meetings did we begin to understand and appreciate the nuances of meaning on the part of each person. Eventually for technical terms we actually did have to select a single term and establish a common definition. This eventually became the basis of a commonly accepted list of data elements to be used in an acquisitions sytem which has proved to be extremely useful.

Written documentation is an especially vexing problem. We all agree that it is vital to exchange working information but how precisely to do it *effectively* still eludes us. Initially we thought that simply xeroxing working papers would suffice but then found that controlling the paper being generated created a new range of problems. By definition, working papers are not finished documents and are subject to change and revision. After a while, one begins to have suspicions that the version of a paper he is working with is not the latest or most correct. In several instances this was the case and actually caused useless work to be undertaken. The sheer amount of paper in itself can be self-defeating. Technical personnel always have more on their desk to study and read than they can possibly hope to accomplish; increasing this load with working papers of dubious vintage and questionable accuracy often has the effect of causing him to read nothing at all. A solution to these problems is to impose greater control on the writing of working papers which, if carried too far, has the effect of negating the original objective, that of rapid dissemination of working information. The compromise adopted, which is not completely satisfactory, has been to develop a fairly mechanical outline which is used to prepare systems and program specifications. (This offends, often, the more creative literary types on your staff who will almost certainly argue that the outline is more restrictive than helpful. My advice here is to insist that he or she prostitute his or her aesthetic principles and follow the outline as is.)

Systems design problems are of two sorts: procedural systems and hardware systems. The similarity between libraries is often used as the telling argument to support the idea that compatible and/or transferable systems can and should be developed. This concept has, possibly, been over-emphasized and may, in fact, not be true, at least at this stage of library systems development. One is forced at this stage of development to design automated library systems which approximate fairly closely the existing manual system being studied. In a number of areas, not all trivial, there are differences among libraries that either cannot be resolved because of restrictions beyond the libraries' control, such as bookkeeping or fiscal accounting, or because their is a lack of conviction (based on lack of experience) that alternatives are better, equal, or worse. An example of the latter is whether one should include in a systems design a file of orders by dealer because traditionally one has been maintained and, therefore, used; or to discard it because another institution has never had one and, therefore, has no measurable need for one. The question can be argued endlessly with no obvious way of resolving it.

Hardware systems compatibility is another rather dubious truism. Computer manufacturers have tried to convince users that their computer series will offer "upward compatibility" for all programs (*i.e.*, programs written on one model computer can automatically be compiled and run on another computer in the same series), or that applications programs written for one computer environment are easily transferred to another. Both of these statements are, on a working level, not true. Upgrading a computer system from say an IBM 360/30 to a 360/50 requires substantial reprogramming effort. Equally difficult is attempting to transfer a set of programs from one computer environment to another, even within the same series and model; this again requires substantial reprogramming effort. Almost every operating computer system has some unique feature or combination of hardware and software; the result is that each computer environment displays a rather disturbing degree of uniqueness and incompatibility. Since library programs tend to be large and complex, often using the computer to its fullest capacity, subtle, small differences in the hardware configuration or the operating system create formidable programming problems. This problem is so real and immediate that it has caused us to accept and live with the fact that it is technically unfeasible at this point to attempt to develop compatible library programs. At best, what can be achieved is agreement and some degree of compatibility on a systems design level.

Attempting to coordinate individual (or in-house) project schedules with CLSD schedules has proved to be an unsolvable problem. Project development is a complex, volatile activity, requiring that project personnel have almost continual and immediate contact with coworkers. Hundreds of small decisions, each in themselves trivial, have to be made. The cumulative effect of making these decisions in one institution without immediate consultation with project staff in other institutuions is that the resulting product, be it a program, a forms design, or the definition of a data element, displays a high degree of uniqueness. This problem is further aggravated by shifts and changes in areas beyond the control of the library project staff, such as the implementation of successive versions of a computer operating system, changes in hardware, implementation schedules, etc. As an alternative to coordinating overall project development schedules, one which has proved to be somewhat more effective, is the identification of specific areas of work to be done and assigning one of the institution's prime responsibility for doing it.

Personnel Problems

A computer systems design effort requires, especially during its initial phases, the deep involvement of personnel who have broad understanding of library operations and intimate knowledge of computers. Individuals combining these talents are still in short supply and usually hold relatively senior positions within libraries. The nature of collaborative work is such that these are the very same personnel who must participate in the work. I have briefly alluded to the problems of scheduling meetings and being absent from office responsibilities, so I will not repeat myself, except to emphasize that this is a major problem. An alternative that we've considered is to use less senior personnel, but immediately a new set of problems arise. If junior personnel are used, the specific area or problem to be worked on must be clearly and precisely defined, usually by the senior technical personnel. This takes considerable time, and my personal feeling is that, in the final analysis, this probably takes as much if not more time than using senior technical personnel. This is especially true during the initial phases of the design effort. Later in the effort when tasks and problems have been identified and isolated, this alternative should be more productive.

Another personnel problem to be considered is the nature and personality of the participants. (I will contain my remarks here to technical personnel.) Systems work is to a large degree a creative process; the systems designer, as a consequence, is in some way a creative person; the more senior he becomes (it seems) the more creative (and flamboyant) he becomes. When you mix several of these creative types in a work session, one is never quite sure what is going to happen. Add to this the fact that senior technical personnel are accustomed to making decisions and exercising authority which is not usually questioned too closely, you have a working environment which can be rather sticky. Since collaborative work is based on good will and compromise, the work environment is even more strained. In essence, collaborative work requires that technical personnel become conscious of their personal attitudes and work habits and oftentimes modify them. This requires strong motivation, sense of purpose, and dedication to the project on the part of each participant, something that is hard to define, impossible to dictate, and difficult to sustain.

Management Problems

Library automation at this point is still to a large degree an R and D effort.

Successful, large-scale library systems are few. Practical experience in developing, implementing, and running large systems is limited. All of these factors contribute towards creating an ambiguous and continually changing relationship between technical and administrative personnel, and is the source, often of misunderstanding of policy and misinterpretation of objectives. Several of the more important factors contributing to the desire to establish collaborative ventures in the area of library automation is management's very legitimate concern with cost, management's inability to specify precisely what should be done, and management's frustration in being unable to control and understand completely its in-house system effort. This is not because of negligence or lack of interest on the part of the library adminstrator; rather, it's a lack of knowledge, experience, and time. Automation is just one of many problems that a library administrator has to deal with. Administrators, as a consequence, have tended to rely, possibly too heavily, on their chief systems person for evaluation and direction. The objectives of the systems staff are not infrequently at variance with management's objectives; this is not purposeful on the part of the systems person usually, but is a result, often, of his inability to properly understand management priorities and objectives and, in many instances, controlling his own enthusiasm. The solution to this problem, if there is one, is not obvious. Greater management involvement seems to be necessary on a local level, but this in itself is probably not enough. In addition, management must gain perspective by comparing his experience with the experience of his peers in other institutions to see how they are solving similar problems. A collaborative effort ideally would do just this for participating library adminstrators. This is an area where the CLSD Project has had initially at least, the least success. The fault lies, I must admit, to a large degree with the technical personnel. Part of the problem involves the inability of technical personnel to judge how much involvement he should request or attempt on the part of management, how best to select and summarize problems for joint study, how to present recommendations for management's consideration, and how to interpret management's decisions for action. In part, the technical person can be excused because of the daily press of work, his range of responsibility, and the overwhelming amount of detail that he has to deal with. Library administrators, for example, are not interested especially in the virtues of various systems to generate automatically search codes, or what internal coding should be used for character representation. These matters are, though, of vital importance to the technical person. What the library administrator is mainly interested in are the costs of a new system and how they compare with the manual systems being replaced, what chance of success will the automated system have, what immediate and long-range budget implications does automation pose, what policy changes will have to be made, and what are the implications for organization and staff. It is precisely in these areas that systems personnel usually have had the least experience. It is quite obvious that a better and more interactive working relationship is required between library management and technical personnel. How to achieve this is still not completely understood.

Conclusion

My assignment today was to play up the problems and pitfalls of cooperative work, but I would not like to leave you with the impression that the experience during the past two years has been entirely negative. There are many positive results that might be mentioned. I would like, by way of conclusion, to mention just a few.

First and foremost I would mention that in spite of all the problems, frustrations, and aggravations, all of the participants are still on friendly terms. This is probably most significant for the technical personnel involved for the several reasons mentioned above. As recent as two weeks ago when we had our last technical meetings at which some hard-nosed evaluation of MARC usage in each institution was done; we finished the meeting by laying aside differences and having a friendly drink. After an intensive, often abrasive two-day meeting this, in my mind, is an indication of the dedication and good-will that each of us still feels toward the Project.

The most important aspect of the CLSD effort has been the ability to bring together personnel working on a common problem and allowing them to describe their work, theories, plans, and accomplishments to an attentive and knowledgable group of peers, and receiving honest, straightforward evaluation. This interaction has been enormously valuable and influential in the way in which individual projects have developed. The process is subtle and iterative and the tangible results are not easy to identify or measure, but each of us agrees that it has been most useful. A variation of this interactive method of work has been the identification of a problem and the development of a common solution. This brainstorming approach provides each with perspective and dimension which is valuable and usually not possible when working alone.

One of our initial hopes was that there would be some way of pooling and sharing valuable technical resources. Though we have not been able to do this on any dramatic or large scale, we have been able to schedule and organize local work efforts to take advantage of work done in one or another of the other institutions. This has been especially useful in the area of MARC data utilization. Since Chicago was more advanced than Stanford and Columbia in the development of an automated bibliographic handling system, they were able to develop programs and procedures for the use of MARC data relatively rapidly. Their working experience in this area proved valuable to both Stanford and Columbia, saving each of us valuable time and effort.

The possibility of developing generalized computer systems was an ideal that had high priority in our minds when the CLSD Project was initiated. It rapidly became obvious that this was an unattainable ideal for all of the reasons outlined above. Once this was realized, we considered what could be done. Eventually we found that we could work on other levels if the intolerable restrictions and requirements of software and hardware could be circumvented. On one level, that of systems design, significant joint work has been done. The components of a systems design (*i.e.*, scope of functions, approach, data elements, formats, etc.) are relatively independent of a particular programming language or a hardware configuration. These components can be isolated and defined and joint development of specifications for these components is possible. As a consequence, a major portion of our effort has been devoted to working together to develop detailed specifications for data elements, system functions, files (both types of and file structure), input forms, and output products. To date, dissemination of documentation for these components outside of the Project has been done on a very selective basis but has proved useful to those receiving them. We plan to refine these specifications and disseminate them more broadly in the future.

And finally, we've found that working together we've been able to bolster each other's confidence and ego. Developing automated library systems is a long, arduous process, one fraught with frustrations and feelings that often verge on despair. Problems seem to proliferate the deeper one delves into various library operations. Simple or even practical solutions become increasingly difficult to identify as systems are developed and become more sophisticated and complex. The simple fact that one knows that he or she is not the only person struggling with these overwhelming problems is enough to inspire them to continue.

INDEX